BARRON'S

Writing for the TOEFL® iBT

6TH EDITION

Lin Lougheed

Ed.D., Teachers College
Columbia University

BARRON'S

®TOEFL is a registered trademark of Educational Testing Service (ETS). This publication is not endorsed or approved by ETS.

AUDIO AND AUDIOSCRIPTS

The MP3 files and audioscripts for all listening prompts can also be found online at *http://barronsbooks.com/TP/TOEFL/Writing*

Published in 2017, 2014, 2011, 2008, 2004, 2000 by Barron's Educational Series, Inc.
Text © Copyright 2017, 2014, 2011, 2008 by Lin Lougheed.
Text © Copyright 2004, 2000 by Lin Lougheed, under the title *Barron's How to Prepare for the TOEFL Essay.*

All inquiries should be addressed to:
Barron's Educational Series, Inc.
250 Wireless Boulevard
Hauppauge, NY 11788
www.barronseduc.com

Library of Congress Catalog Card No. 2017931010

ISBN: 978-1-4380-7798-7

PRINTED IN THE UNITED STATES OF AMERICA
9 8 7 6 5 4 3 2 1

10%
POST-CONSUMER WASTE
Paper contains a minimum of 10% post-consumer waste (PCW). Paper used in this book was derived from certified, sustainable forestlands.

Contents

APPENDIX

Introduction

The Writing section of the TOEFL® Internet-based Test (iBT) includes two writing tasks: an Integrated Task and an Independent Task.

INTEGRATED TASK

This task consists of a 250–300 word passage on an academic subject followed by a two-minute lecture or discussion on the same topic. The test taker is then given a question about the topic. The test taker must write a 150- to 225-word summary of the important points made in the listening passage and explain how these points relate to those in the reading passage. The test taker may write more than 225 words if time permits.

INDEPENDENT TASK

This task asks for an opinion about a topic. The test taker will use personal knowledge and experience to write an essay of at least 300 words to answer the question. The test taker may write more than 300 words if time permits.

The test taker has a total of 50 minutes to complete these two essays: 20 minutes for the Intergrated Task and 30 minutes for the Independent Task. Both essays must be written on the computer; they cannot be written by hand. The essays are then scored by a human rater and the e-rater, a computer program. In cases where the two scores differ greatly, a second human rater may be consulted. Each essay receives a score of 0–5.

HOW TO USE THIS BOOK

There are three steps in creating an essay: planning, writing, and revising. *Writing for the TOEFL iBT* provides a step-by-step guide for planning, writing, and revising your essays for both the Integrated Task and the Independent Task on the TOEFL iBT. You will learn to follow a simple three-step model and practice applying it to writing both types of essays.

STEP 1 PLAN
STEP 2 WRITE
STEP 3 REVISE

You will have 20 minutes to plan, write, and revise your essay for the Integrated Task, and you will have 30 minutes to plan, write, and revise your essay for the Independent Task. In those limited amounts of time, you must produce writing that is clear, coherent, and correct. This book will help you do that.

Just as you must *plan* your essays, you also need to plan your studying. This book provides you with a plan for studying for the TOEFL iBT essays. By following the chapters in the book in order and doing all the practice exercises, you will learn a three-step method for writing your essays, and you will have many opportunities to practice writing. You will also learn writing skills that you can apply to both tasks and to your writing in general.

The best way to learn to *write* is by writing. You will do a great deal of writing when you do the practice exercises and practice tasks in this book. For additional practice, you can choose topics from the model integrated tasks and model independent essays at the back of the book.

When you are learning to write, you must, at the same time, learn to *revise*. You must make it a habit to revise the essays you write for practice in this book. Revision is as important a part of the writing process as the writing itself.

A good essay takes time—time to *plan*, time to *write*, time to *revise*. When you write your TOEFL iBT essays, you will have a limited amount of time. If you take the time now to learn how to write, you'll easily be able to write your TOEFL iBT essays in the limited time allowed.

QUESTIONS AND ANSWERS

How Much Time Do I Have to Work on Each Writing Task?

For the Integrated Task, after you read the passage for three minutes and listen to the lecture, you have 20 minutes to plan and write your essay. For the Independent Task, you have 30 minutes to plan and write your essay on the given topic.

Do I Have to Use the Computer?

Yes, you do. It is an Internet-based test. Use of the computer is required. You should learn to use the QWERTY keyboard. This keyboard is named for the first six letters on the top row of letters.

Do I Have a Choice of Topic?

No, you don't. For the Integrated Task, you will respond to a question using information from the reading passage and lecture provided. For the Independent Task, you will be given only one topic, and you must write about that topic.

Will All Test Takers Have the Same Topic?

No, not every test taker will have the same topic.

What Will Happen If I Don't Understand the Topic on the Independent Task?

If you study this book, that won't be a problem. You will understand all the possible topics. On the day of the test, you will not receive any help with the topic.

What Will Happen If I Don't Understand How to Work the Computer?

There will be test administrators in the room who can answer your questions about using the computer. They will not answer any questions about the use of English.

What Kind of Pencils Should I Bring?

None. Everything you need to write your essays will be given to you at the testing center. If you need extra pencils or paper, ask your test administrator.

Can I Bring a Clock with Me?

No. Nothing can be brought into the test room. You can wear your watch or look at the clock on the computer screen.

Can I Bring a Dictionary with Me?

No. Nothing can be brought into the test room.

Can I Bring Paper with Me?

No. Nothing can be brought into the test room. Scratch paper will be supplied.

What Happens to the Notes I Take?

You can write your notes in English or your first language. They will be collected and discarded. They will not be seen by the raters.

Is There a Spell Checker or Grammar Checker on the Computer?

No. You will have to do your own proofreading. Don't worry about a few spelling errors or a few mistakes with punctuation or grammar. A few small errors will not count against your score. Hint: If you are unsure how to spell a word, use a word you do know how to spell.

How Long Should the Writing Sample Be?

On the Integrated Task, you should write 150–225 words. You may write more if you have time. On the Independent Task, you should write around 300 words. You may write more if you have time.

What's More Important, Organization or Grammar?

Both are important. A reader judges an essay on its organization, the use of details to support the main points, and your facility with English. See the section, *Scoring the Essay*, for more information on this.

What Happens If I Don't Finish?

You do not need to have an elegantly stated conclusion. What you do write should demonstrate your facility with English. Do not end with an apology. Do not apologize to the reader for what you did not do or for what you think you should have done better.

Is There an Extra Fee for the Writing Section of the Test?

No. The test fee covers all parts of the TOEFL.

Is the Writing Section Required?

Yes. All test takers who take the TOEFL must take the writing section of the test.

How Is My Writing Scored?

Each essay is scored by a human rater and the e-rater, a computer program, on a scale of 0–5. If the two scores differ greatly, a second human rater may be consulted. The score is then converted to a scaled score of 0–30.

Will I See My Scores Immediately?

No. Your scores will be available online and mailed to you approximately two weeks after the test date.

What If I Don't Like My Scores?

Sign up to take the test again after you do all the exercises in this book a few more times. You should see an improvement in your scores.

Where Can I Find Extra Help?

Visit the Learning Center on Dr. Lin Lougheed's website at *www.lougheed.com* to view sample essays.

For test tips and new vocabulary words, follow Dr. Lin Lougheed on Twitter @LinLougheed.

Want your essays posted to Facebook for feedback from others? Post them directly at http://www.facebook.com/EssayTOEFL.IELTS or search on Facebook for "**IELTS and TOEFL Essay Writing.**"

TO THE TEACHER

Writing for the TOEFL iBT presents step-by-step methods for completing the two tasks in the writing section of the TOEFL. By following the steps in order, your students will build new skills on top of previously developed ones. Although the activities in this book are specifically aimed at the two writing tasks in the TOEFL, your students will be learning skills that they can apply to their writing in general. They will learn how to organize their thoughts, develop their essays, and use appropriate sentence structure to express their ideas. The activities in this book are well suited for classroom use. The activities are carefully structured and can easily be completed in class. They can also be done as homework and then corrected in class.

Expanding the Activities

INTEGRATED TASK

(STEP 1) PLAN

This book provides many opportunities for students to plan and practice taking notes on reading passages and lectures. You can provide additional practice by having the students take notes on passages that you or they supply. You can use passages from reading texts, newspapers, magazines, and other sources that are available and are of interest to the students. Encourage the students to read often and to make notes on what they read. Students can bring their notes to class to share with their classmates.

STEP 2) WRITE

This book provides many opportunities for practice writing summaries of reading passages and lectures. Again, you can provide additional practice by having the students write summaries of things they have read or news stories they have listened to. Encourage students to share with the class summaries of interesting articles they have read or movies or TV programs they have seen.

STEP 3) REVISE

While working on Step 3, students can practice revising by checking each other's work, looking at the development, organization, grammar, punctuation, and spelling. The Writing Skills section of the book provides practice with using transition words and variety in sentence structure and can be studied in conjunction with Step 3.

INDEPENDENT TASK

STEP 1) PLAN

In order to plan their responses to the writing topics, students need to be able to formulate opinions on these topics. They must get used to thinking about and describing reasons and advantages or disadvantages. In small groups, students can brainstorm and discuss their ideas on the writing topics presented throughout the book and in the Appendix. Students can then practice writing thesis statements and developing concept maps on the same subjects.

STEP 2) WRITE

When the class is working on Steps 2 and 3, have the students check each other's essays to make sure there is a topic sentence in each paragraph and that both the theme and all the supporting points are mentioned in the introduction. Have the students check the conclusion to make sure the theme is summarized there. The model essays in the Appendix can be used for additional practice. Have the students identify in a model essay the theme and supporting points in the introduction, topic sentences in the body of the essay, and the summarized theme in the conclusion.

STEP 3) REVISE

While working on Step 3, students can practice revising by checking each other's work using the revision checklist. Again, the Writing Skills section of this book can be studied along with these steps.

Writing Skills

While working on this section of the book, you can use the model essays in the Appendix to provide additional practice. You can ask students to look at these essays for examples of transition words, different types of sentences, parallel structure, passive and active voice, or whatever aspect of sentence writing you wish to focus on.

> ### A WORD OF CAUTION
>
> Remind students **NOT** to memorize the essays in this book. An essay will not be rated if the reader suspects it was copied from the model essays.

OVERVIEW—INTEGRATED TASK

Write 150–225 words in 20 minutes.

1. First, you will read a 250–300 word passage on an academic subject. You will have three minutes to read.

2. Then, you will listen to a two-minute lecture or discussion on the same topic. You can take notes while you listen.

3. You will not be able to read the audio lecture during the test. You will only hear it. You will not be able to see the reading passage while you listen to the audio.

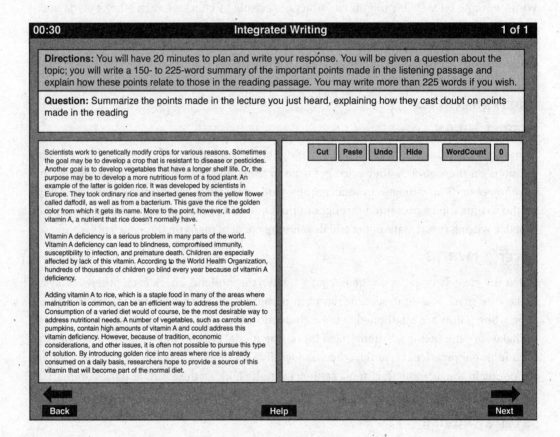

Scoring

The Integrated Task essay is scored on a scale of 0 to 5. The scorers will look at how well you addressed the task of summarizing and comparing the reading selection and the listening selection. They will also look at your use of correct grammatical forms and vocabulary. The chart on page 7 provides some simple descriptions of the characteristics of essays at three levels.

RATING SCALE

4-5 GOOD

An essay at this level

- clearly and concisely summarizes the main points of the reading and the listening selections
- clearly and concisely explains how they support or contradict each other
- uses correct grammatical forms and appropriate word choice
- may have slight inaccuracies in the summary of ideas or occasional grammatical errors

2.5-3.5 FAIR

An essay at this level

- summarizes the main points of the reading and listening selections but may be missing an idea or ideas or may be lacking in clarity
- may not accurately explain the relationship between the reading and listening selections
- may lack clarity because of grammatical errors or inappropriate word choice

1.0-2.0 LIMITED

An essay at this level

- may demonstrate incomplete understanding of the reading or listening selections
- may not explain a clear relationship between the reading and listening selections
- may be difficult to read because of serious grammatical errors

(An essay that receives a score of **0** may be blank, written in another language, or not relate to the topic.)

Sample Scored Essays

The following sample essays were written in response to the sample reading passage and lecture on pages 29–30.

SCORE: 5

The author explains that understanding learning styles can improve learning and training. The speaker, however, suggests that understanding learning styles doesn't always provide a solution.

The author states that understanding learning styles helps individuals learn better and professors and trainers instruct better. The author explains different ways to describe learning styles. Some people learn more easily by listening, others by seeing, and still others by doing. Active learners understand new information by doing something with it. Reflective learners understand information by thinking about it. Sequential learners look at information as a series of steps, but global learners prefer to look at the whole rather than the parts. The author believes that understanding learning styles can improve study skills. Sequential learners, auditory learners, and reflective learners, for example, can each choose the study methods that best suit their individual learning styles. Similarly, instructors and trainers who are aware of the various learning styles can take this into account when planning lessons.

NOTE

The samples in this book include paragraph indents, but you will not be scored down if you do not use them on the test.

The speaker presents a different point of view. First, some subjects have to be taught in certain ways. Math has to be taught sequentially. In addition, the speaker suggests that students "simply aren't interested" in information about learning styles and don't want to spend time thinking about it. Some professors aren't interested in learning styles, either. They just teach using their own style.

REVISION CHECKLIST

- **Content**
  - ☑ Thesis Statement
  - ☑ Topics that support the thesis
  - ☑ Main ideas
  - ☑ Supporting details
- **Fluency and Cohesion**
  - ☑ Transition words
  - ☑ Grammar and Spelling
  - ☑ Sentence variety

Content

This essay addresses the task by giving concise summaries of both the reading passage and the lecture and explaining clearly how the main ideas of both contrast with each other.

The first paragraph states a clear thesis, explaining that the reading and the lecture present contrasting ideas. The second paragraph supports the reading main idea by summarizing the main points of the reading. The third paragraph supports the listening main idea by summarizing the main points of the listening. The paragraphs have topic sentences and supporting details. In the body of the essay, the topic sentences of the paragraphs match the topics introduced in the first paragraph.

Fluency and Cohesion

The essay uses appropriate transition words such as *for example, first,* and *in addition.* There are no grammar or spelling errors. The essay contains a variety of sentence structures such as simple and compound sentences and adjective clauses.

SCORE: 4

The author explains that understanding learning styles can make learning and training better. The speaker says the opposite, that knowing about learning styles doesn't always help teachers and students.

In the reading passage, the author says that understanding learning styles helps students learn better and teachers teach better. The author explains the different kinds learning styles. Some students learn by listening, some by seeing, and some by doing. Also, some students are active learners. They need to do things with new information. Sequential learners see information in sequence. The author says that if you understand learning styles, can improve your study skills. Sequential learners and auditory learners, for instance, they can choose the best study methods for their learning styles.

The speaker has a different opinion. First, some things have to be taught in certain ways. Math is an example. It has to be taught sequentially. Also, the speaker says that students "simply aren't interested" in information about learning styles. Some professors don't interested in learning styles, either.

Content

This essay addresses the task by giving summaries of both the reading passage and the lecture and explaining how the main ideas of each contrast with each other. The writer left out a few supporting details from the summary of the reading. She mentioned active learners but not reflective learners. She mentioned sequential learners but not global learners.

The thesis is clearly stated, explaining that the reading and the lecture present contrasting ideas. The second paragraph and third paragraph support the main ideas of the reading passage and the lecture by summarizing the main points of each. In the body of the essay, the topic sentences of the paragraphs match the topics introduced in the first paragraph.

Fluency and Cohesion

The essay uses appropriate transition words such as *for instance*, *first*, and *in addition*. There are a few grammar errors, but they don't interfere with understanding the essay.

...the different <u>kinds learning</u> styles.
...the different kinds of learning styles.

...if you understand learning styles, <u>can</u> improve your study skills.
...if you understand learning styles, you can improve your study skills.

Sequential learners and auditory learners, for instance, <u>they</u> can choose...
Sequential learners and auditory learners, for instance, can choose...

Some professors <u>don't</u> interested in learning styles, either.
Some professors aren't interested in learning styles, either.

The essay contains a variety of sentence structures such as simple, compound, and complex sentences.

SCORE: 3

The author explains that understanding learning styles can make learning and teaching better, but the speaker says the opposite opinion. Even if teachers and students know about learning styles, doesn't always help them.

In the reading passage, it says that understanding different learning styles help students and teachers better. They can improve learning. There are different kinds of learning styles such as listening, seeing, and doing. In addition, there are active learners and reflective learners. Finally, we have sequential learners and global learners. The author says that learning styles will improve your study skills. You can to choose the best way to study for your learning style.

The speaker says the opposite. First, some things you have to teach them in certain ways. Math is an example. Also, some people don't like learning styles. Some students and some professors don't like different ways of learning. It's too bad because it can help them.

REVISION CHECKLIST

■ **Content**
- ☑ Thesis Statement
- ☑ Topics that support the thesis
- ☑ Main ideas
- ❑ Supporting details

■ **Fluency and Cohesion**
- ☑ Transition words
- ❑ Grammar and Spelling
- ☑ Sentence variety

Content

This essay addresses the task by giving summaries of both the reading passage and the lecture and explaining how the main ideas of each contrast with each other. The writer left out some supporting details from the summary of the reading. She mentioned the names of the different learning styles but did not explain what they are or how they differ from each other. In the last paragraph, she mentioned math as an example of something that has to be taught in a certain way but did not explain how it was an example.

There are some inaccuracies in explaining the supporting details of the lecture. The essay states "Some students and some professors don't like different ways of learning." In the lecture, however, the speaker made the point that some people aren't interested in thinking about learning styles. That is somewhat different than saying that they don't like learning styles.

Fluency and Cohesion

The essay uses appropriate transition words such as *in addition*, *first*, and *also*. There are several grammar errors.

> …<u>doesn't</u> always help them.
> …it doesn't always help them.

> …different learning styles help students and teachers <u>better</u>.
> …different learning styles help students and teachers do their work better.

> You can <u>to</u> choose the best way…
> You can choose the best way…

> First, <u>some things you have to teach them</u> in certain ways.
> First, you have to teach some things in certain ways.

The essay contains a variety of sentence structures such as simple, compound, and complex sentences.

SCORE: 2

In the reading passage it says that it is important to understand different learning style because it can improbe teaching and learning. In the lecture, it also talks about different learning styles.

In the reading passage, it talks about different learning styles that can help students and teachers. They can learn and teach more better if they know this. Some students learn better when they listen, see, or do. Another learning style it is active and reflactiv. And finally there is sequential and global. The author says that learning styles will going to improbe your study skills. If you are an active learner, you can study one way and another way if you are reflactive. This is an example. You have to have a good style.

The speaker talks about learning styles, too. Math is a subject that you can teach sequentially, so it is good for sequential learners. There are some people they aren't interested in learning styles. But some people they are good at learning and their different learning styles can help them.

REVISION CHECKLIST

■ **Content**
- ❑ Thesis Statement
- ❑ Topics that support the thesis
- ☑ Main ideas
- ❑ Supporting details

■ **Fluency and Cohesion**
- ☑ Transition words
- ❑ Grammar and Spelling
- ☑ Sentence variety

Content

This essay attempts to address the task by giving summaries of both the reading passage and the lecture. It fails in both the thesis statement and the summaries to show the relationship between the ideas in the reading passage and the lecture. Both talk about learning styles, but their main points contrast with each other. This essay does not mention the contrast.

The main idea of the reading passage is explained, although the supporting details are somewhat confused. The details, moreover, could be more thoroughly explained. All the learning styles are mentioned, but the differences between them are not explained. The summary of the lecture fails to explain the main idea—that understanding learning styles does not always improve learning.

Fluency and Cohesion

The essay uses some transition words such as *another* and *finally*. There are several grammar errors.

> They can learn and teach <u>more</u> better.
> They can learn and teach better.

> Another learning style <u>it</u> is active...
> Another learning style is active...

> The author says that learning styles <u>will going to</u> improve your study skills.
> The author says that learning styles will improve your study skills.

> There are some people <u>they</u> aren't interested in learning styles.
> There are some people who aren't interested in learning styles.

There are also a few spelling errors.

> ~~improbe~~   improve

> ~~reflactiv~~   reflective

The essay contains a variety of sentence structures such as simple, compound, and complex sentences.

SCORE: 1

In the reading passage it talks about different learning styles, and the lecture too.

In the reading passage, it tells you how you can learn better for what it is your own style. Then it is improve what the teachers and the students do. The different learning styles they are about listening, seeing, and doing. And so too they are actave and reflect. That means if you do something or if you think about it. They are about sequential and globule. That is mean it is step by step or the whole thing.

The speaker is also about learning styles, too. But they are not so good. Some things you need one style. Like for math. Some people aren't interest. Some students, they don't care if it is style. Their teachers, too. They just teach their own style, like the way they do best. If students can do it, good. But if not they can do it, too bad for the students.

REVISION CHECKLIST

■ **Content**
- ❏ Thesis Statement
- ❏ Topics that support the thesis
- ☑ Main ideas
- ❏ Supporting details

■ **Fluency and Cohesion**
- ❏ Transition words
- ❏ Grammar and Spelling
- ❏ Sentence variety

Content

This essay attempts to address the task by giving summaries of both the reading passage and the lecture. The thesis statement does not mention the contrast between the ideas in the reading passage and the lecture. The summaries of the reading and the lecture both mention the main idea and the supporting details, but the details are not clearly explained, and the ideas are often difficult to follow.

Fluency and Cohesion

The essay lacks transition words. There are several grammar errors, for example:

THE STUDENT WROTE: In the reading passage it talks about different learning styles, and the lecture too.

CORRECT: The reading passage talks about different learning styles, and the lecture does, too.

THE STUDENT WROTE: Then it is improve what the teachers and the students do.

CORRECT: This improves what the teachers and the students do.

THE STUDENT WROTE: The different learning styles <u>they</u> are about listening, seeing, and doing.

CORRECT: The different learning styles are about listening, seeing, and doing.

There are also a few spelling errors.

~~actave~~	active
~~globule~~	global

The essay contains a number of awkward sentences, which make it difficult to follow the ideas.

OVERVIEW—INDEPENDENT TASK

Write at least 300 words in 30 minutes.

You will read a question that asks for your opinion on a topic.

Sample Question

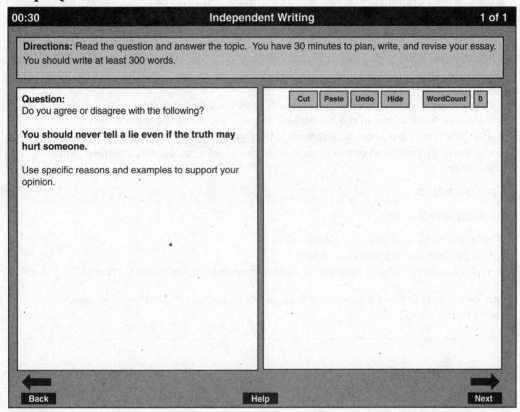

| 00:30 | Independent Writing | 1 of 1 |

Directions: Read the question and answer the topic. You have 30 minutes to plan, write, and revise your essay. You should write at least 300 words.

Question:
Do you agree or disagree with the following?

You should never tell a lie even if the truth may hurt someone.

Use specific reasons and examples to support your opinion.

Cut | Paste | Undo | Hide | WordCount | 0

Back | Help | Next

Scoring

The Independent Task essay is scored on a scale of 0 to 5. The scorers will look at how well you addressed the topic and developed and supported your ideas. They will also look at your use of correct grammatical forms and vocabulary. The chart on page 14 provides some simple descriptions of the characteristics of essays at three levels.

Sample Scored Essays

SCORE: 5

Topic 9

> Some people prefer to eat at food stands or restaurants. Other people prefer to prepare and eat food at home. Which do you prefer? Use specific reasons and examples to support your answers.

Although many people enjoy eating home-cooked meals, my preference is to eat out whenever possible. The main reason is that I know absolutely nothing about cooking. In addition, eating out allows me to spend more time studying and less time in the kichen. And, believe it or not, eating out is often cheaper than eating meals prepared at home.

To begin with, I don't know a thing about cooking. When you don't know how to cook, there is a good chance that what you cook will not be worth eating. In addition to leaving you with an unsatisfied appetite, this also results in a waste of food as well as a waste of money and effort.

In the second place, cooking takes a lot of time. The food you prepare might not actually be on the stove for very long, but you also have to take into account the time needed for the other steps involved in cooking. In order to prepare a meal, you have to spend time shopping for the ingredients, cleaning and chopping them, and then cleaning up the kichen after the meal is over.

Finally, eating out can be surprisingly economicall. Of course it costs a lot to eat at elegant restaurants, but there are other places to enjoy a good meal. Food stands and some small, casual restaurants provides plenty of good food at very reasonable prices. Many places of this type are located near the university and therefore are very convenient for students. It doesn't cost any more to eat this way than it does to cook at home, and it may cost even less.

As my life changes, my preferences about where to eat may change, too. For now, however, while I am still a student, eating out is the most practical choice I can make.

REVISION CHECKLIST

- ■ **Content**
  - ☑ Thesis Statement
  - ☑ Topics that support the thesis
  - ☑ Main ideas
  - ☑ Supporting details
- ■ **Fluency and Cohesion**
  - ☑ Transition words
  - ☑ Grammar and Spelling
  - ☑ Sentence variety

Content

This essay has a clear thesis in the beginning and is also very well organized. The first two of the three body paragraphs give reasons why the writer does not want to cook at home, while the third gives reasons why eating out is better. There are sufficient details to support the main idea in each paragraph. The conclusion paraphrases the main idea rather than simply repeating it.

Fluency and Cohesion

The essay uses appropriate transition words such as *in addition, to begin with, also,* and *finally*. There is one grammar error, and it doesn't interfere with understanding the essay:

> Food stands and some small, casual restaurants <u>provides</u> plenty of good food…
> Food stands and some small, casual restaurants provide plenty of good food…

There are also just two minor spelling errors.

~~kichen~~	kitchen
~~economicall~~	economical

The essay contains a variety of sentence structures such as simple, compound, and complex sentences.

SCORE: 4

Topic 38

> Some people think that the family is the most important influence on young adults. Other people think that friends are the most important influence on young adults. Which view do you agree with? Use examples to support your position.

We are all influence by whomever we meet. We all stand as models to everyone in this world. However, our choice of a model is important especially when choosing a career. I believe that in the case concerning our future and our career, families have more influence on us than friends.

Friends are the ones we spend time having fun, enjoying, playing and so forth. Friends also teach good things and help us. Friends advice good things about life, but not like family. Family always think that their children will become superior ones in the future. They want their children to be smarter than anyone else. However, friends are not such an influential adviser like family. Family feels that time is waste when their adult children have too much fun. However, friends influence us more to play or have fun rather than advising us about our career. Therefore, family puts their substanshil impact on their children in order to shape up their future career.

In the US, most young adults are usually influence by their friends rather than their parents. It depends on what type of influence it is. Usually, people are busier in the US. They don't have time to give important influence to their children. Therefore, the children choose their own way to catch up their careers. Whatever they see around influences them. However, this influence might not be good for their future careers.

Therefore, I'd say family influences their adult children more and better than friends.

REVISION CHECKLIST

■ **Content**
- ☑ Thesis Statement
- ☑ Topics that support the thesis
- ☑ Main ideas
- ☑ Supporting details

■ **Fluency and Cohesion**
- ☑ Transition words
- ☐ Grammar and Spelling
- ☑ Sentence variety

Content

The thesis of this essay is very clear and easy to locate at the end of the introduction. The essay is generally well organized. The writer carefully compares and contrasts the level of influence one receives from one's parents with the influence one receives from one's friends. The thesis is well developed, and there is a conclusion that restates the thesis.

Fluency and Cohesion

The essay uses appropriate transition words such as *however, also,* and *therefore.* There are a few grammar errors, but they don't interfere with understanding the essay.

We are all <u>influence</u> by whomever we meet.
We are all influenced by whomever we meet.

Family feels that time is <u>waste</u>...
Family feels that time is wasted...

Therefore, <u>family puts their substanshil impact</u> on their children...
Therefore, families have a substantial impact on their children...

In the US, most young adults are usually <u>influence</u> by their friends...
In the US, most young adults are usually influenced by their friends...

There is one spelling error.

~~substanshil~~   substantial

The essay contains a variety of sentence structures such as simple, compound, and complex sentences.

SCORE: 3

Topic 46

> **Do you agree or disagree with the following statement? Playing a game is fun only when you win. Use specific reasons and examples to support your answer.**

Some would like to play the game such as, basketball, tennis, swimming, and riding bike for exercises and fun. But some, they play for their achievement. I agree that playing game is fun when we win.

As a matter of fact, when I was in High school, I like to play basketball as my hobby. I was very excited when I won the game. All high schools in Cambodia, they required students to choose one kind of game, such as volleyball, soccer, basketball, tennis and swimming. By that time, I took basketball as my favorite hobby. My school gave me the best basketball coach. He had a lot of experience of training basketball players. My teams and I were trained by him everyday for two months. After two monthes of training, My coach wanted us to compete with other schools.

When the competition day came, our emotion was combined with happy and scare of losing the game. But our coach encourage us. He told us that "don't be afraid of your competitors, they are as same as you, so you have to have a confident in yourself." When time of competition of game started, our coach led us to basketball court to get to know our competitors. The result of competition was my team completely won. My coach and our team were very happy to win that game.

I believe that playing game is very difficult if we don't know a weakness of our competitors. We have to have a confident in ourselves. I agree that playing game is very fun when we win.

REVISION CHECKLIST

■ **Content**
- ☑ Thesis Statement
- ❑ Topics that support the thesis
- ❑ Main ideas
- ❑ Supporting details

■ **Fluency and Cohesion**
- ❑ Transition words
- ❑ Grammar and Spelling
- ☑ Sentence variety

Content

This essay is adequately organized and developed. It shows development of ideas and some facility with English. In the first paragraph and in the conclusion, the writer states the opinion that playing a game is fun when one wins. However, the writer does not directly address the topic, which is more black and white: playing a game is fun ONLY when one wins. It is likely that the writer did not understand the question clearly. The writer uses a personal story to illustrate the thesis. This story seems to indicate that the writer also had a good time playing basketball even when he/she didn't win.

Fluency and Cohesion

The essay does not make use of transition words. There are a number of grammar and vocabulary errors that distract the reader from the meaning.

But <u>some, they play</u> for their achievement.
But some play for their achievement.

When I was...I <u>like</u> to play basketball as my hobby.
When I was...I liked to play basketball as my hobby.

...our emotion <u>was combined with happy and scare</u> of losing the game.
...our emotion was a combination of happiness and fear of losing the game.

We have to have <u>a confident</u> in ourselves.
We have to have confidence in ourselves.

There are some spelling and punctuation errors.

~~monthes~~   months

As a matter of fact, when I was in <u>High</u> school...
As a matter of fact, when I was in high school...

He told <u>us that "don't</u> be afraid of your competitors...
He told us, "Don't be afraid of your competitors...

There is sentence variety but there are also numerous errors in sentence structure.

SCORE: 2

Topic 37

> **Some people prefer to spend time with one or two close friends. Others choose to spend time with a large number of friends. Compare the advantages of each choice. Which of these two ways of spending time do you prefer? Use specific reasons to support your answer.**

People need friends they include in a society. Some people try to find good people but some people just take any person around them. Which means first one is very serious to find friends and second people are not to serious to have friends. Some people prefer to spend time with one or two. Others choose to spend time with a large number of friends.

First of all, some people want to spend time with one or two friends. Those people always take care of their friends very well. For example, when they have a party they can invite everyone to their home even thow it is small. Also, they can talk with each friend before the party is over. Because they don't have many friends so they can be able to talk with everyone. Therefore, all the friends returns home very happy after party.

Secondly, some people want to spend time with a large number of friends. Those people love people also they can get a good advise from friends. For example, when they have a problem they can ask their many friends and then they can collect every answer. Therefore, they are figure it out to fix their problem very easily.

REVISION CHECKLIST

■ Content
- ❑ Thesis Statement
- ❑ Topics that support the thesis
- ☑ Main ideas
- ❑ Supporting details

■ Fluency and Cohesion
- ☑ Transition words
- ❑ Grammar and Spelling
- ☑ Sentence variety

Content

The organization and development of the topic is not adequate. The writer talks about each choice but never accomplishes the task: to express a preference. There is a good attempt at addressing the task, discussing the topic in English, and demonstrating a basic level of competence as a writer in English.

Fluency and Cohesion

The essay uses some transition words, such as *however*, *first of all*, and *secondly*. There are a number of grammar and vocabulary errors that distract the reader from the meaning.

Which means first one is very serious to find friends…
This means the first one is very serious about finding friends…

Because they don't have many friends so they can be able to talk with everyone.
Because they don't have many friends, they can talk with everyone.

Therefore, all the friends returns home very happy…
Therefore, all the friends return home very happy…

There are some punctuation errors.

Those people love people also they can get a good advice from friends.
Those people love people. Also, they can get good advice from friends.

For example, when they have a problem they can ask their many friends…
For example, when they have a problem, they can ask their many friends…

There are several spelling errors.

~~to~~	too
~~thow~~	though
~~advise~~	advice

There is sentence variety but the many grammatical errors make it difficult to follow.

SCORE: 1

Topic 43

> **Some people say that physical exercise should be a required part of every school day. Other people believe that students should spend the whole school day on academic studies. Which opinion do you agree with?**

I agree an opinion that students should spend the hole day on academic studies. Because there are have many opportunites for students to be a very good student, like, they have a lot time to spend studies, also, they will be effected by school when they are stay in school. Because of many people staying in library to spend their study, I think that, It will advise me to follow them. More over, staying in school is good for students to enrolling to university. Because they don't have to think something of outside so they really have to think of their lerning, this is a good idea for students to stay. Besides that, if they go home to study, it is ok. But when you are studying in your home, suddenly your father or someone call you at that time, I think, you are confusing about your study. Anyway, I still like to spend the whole school day on academic studies, Because there are have enough books and have many things to use in my knowledge. So I love staying in school day to increase my knowledge.

> **REVISION CHECKLIST**
>
> ■ **Content**
> ❑ Thesis Statement
> ❑ Topics that support the thesis
> ❑ Main ideas
> ❑ Supporting details
>
> ■ **Fluency and Cohesion**
> ❑ Transition words
> ❑ Grammar and Spelling
> ❑ Sentence variety

Content

This essay is flawed on several levels. It is possible that the writer does not fully understand the task. The writer seems to think that the choice is between staying at home or staying in school. The writer doesn't say why one should spend the whole school day on academics and does not address why some physical education would be bad. The information is not organized into an essay, but is all one paragraph. There are insufficient details to support the author's opinion.

Fluency and Cohesion

The ideas are unclear and there are no clear transitions between them.

There are quite a number of grammar errors. In fact, there are errors in nearly every sentence.

I agree <u>an opinion</u> that students should spend the whole day on academic studies.
I agree with the opinion that students should spend the whole day on academic studies.

Because <u>there are have</u> many opportunities for <u>students to be a very good student</u>...
Because there are many opportunities for them to be very good students...

...they have a <u>lot time</u> to spend <u>studies</u>...
...they have a lot of time to spend on their studies...

There are a number of punctuation errors, mixed in with other errors.

I think <u>that, It</u> will advise me to follow them.
I think that it will be advisable for me to follow them.

There are several spelling errors.

~~hole~~	whole
~~opportunites~~	opportunities
~~effected~~	affected
~~more over~~	moreover
~~lerning~~	learning

There is very little sentence variety.

WRITING STRATEGIES

1. Understand the directions before you begin. Focus on the task not the directions.
2. In the integrated task, take notes as you read. This will help you remember the key words.
3. In the integrated task, as you read, try to guess what the lecture will be about.
4. In the integrated task, take notes as you listen to the lecture. This will help you understand the relation between the reading passage and the lecture.
5. Read the question carefully and understand what you are to do.
6. Make an idea map to help you organize your essay.
7. In the integrated task, write at least one paragraph about the reading passage and at least one paragraph about the lecture.
8. Write in English. You will not have time to translate your essay from your native language into English.
9. Use words and grammar that you are familiar with.
10. Pay attention to the time. Leave a few minutes to go over your writing so you can correct any mistakes.

TIME STRATEGIES

1. The Integrated Task lasts a total of 25 minutes. You will have 3 minutes to read the article and then you will listen to a lecture for 2 minutes. Following that, you will have 20 minutes to write your essay. Divide your writing time as follows:

PLAN	3 minutes
WRITE	14 minutes
REVISE	3 minutes

2. On the Independent Task, you will have 30 minutes to write your essay. Divide your writing time as follows:

PLAN	5 minutes
WRITE	20 minutes
REVISE	5 minutes

3. The time remaining is shown on the title bar of the computer screen. Check the time periodically.

4. Use your planning time to write a good outline or idea map. This will help you focus your writing time.

5. You should write 150–225 words for the Integrated Task and at least 300 words for the Independent Task. Don't try to write a lot more than this. You won't have time.

6. Time yourself when writing essays for practice. This will help you get used to writing a complete essay within the allowed time limit.

Self-Test

2

Try the Self-Test for the Integrated and the Independent Tasks now. Pretend you are taking the actual TOEFL. Later, as you study this book, come back to this Self-Test and take it again. When you finish the book, take the test one last time. See how much easier it is. See how much you have learned about planning, writing, and revising.

INTEGRATED TASK

Give yourself 3 minutes to read the passage. Then listen to the lecture. The lecture will take about 2 minutes. Don't forget to take notes as you listen and read. You should begin thinking about your planning as you do this. Then write an essay in response to the question within 20 minutes. Write between 150 and 225 words.

Divide your writing time like this:

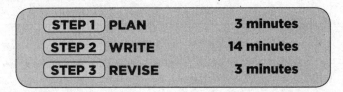

STEP 1 PLAN	**3 minutes**	
STEP 2 WRITE	**14 minutes**	
STEP 3 REVISE	**3 minutes**	

 **READING**

Read this passage within three minutes.

Concern about the phenomenon known as global warming has been growing in recent years. Earth's temperature is rising, largely as a result of human activity. Since the Industrial Revolution, humans have added significantly to the greenhouse gases in the Earth's atmosphere through increases in activities such as cutting down forests and burning fossil fuels like coal and oil. Greenhouse gases hold heat in the atmosphere, and to a certain extent, their presence is natural. An artificial increase in the amount of these gases, however, leads to a rise in temperatures on Earth.

In the middle of the twentieth century, scientists discovered that Earth was getting warmer. Then they discovered that carbon dioxide levels in the atmosphere were increasing. They realized that there was a relationship between rising temperatures and rising levels of carbon dioxide. Most of this carbon dioxide comes from emissions from industrial activity and gasoline-powered motor vehicles.

Earth's average temperature increased almost 1.5°F during the twentieth century. Scientists predict that during the twenty-first century, temperatures will continue to increase. What changes could this bring about on our planet? We have already begun to see changes in weather patterns, snow and ice cover, and sea level.

Changes in weather patterns may lead to increased flooding and drought worldwide, as well as more frequent extreme weather conditions such as powerful hurricanes. Rising global temperatures may also result in increasing water scarcity and in extinction of numerous plant and animal species. But not just the weather will be affected. Changes in climate can lead to economic losses, particularly in the agricultural and transportation sectors. One report predicts a possible 1% drop in gross domestic product and a 20% decrease in per capita consumption worldwide.

 **LECTURE**

Track 1

Listen to the lecture.

Summarize the main points in the reading passage and explain how they are strengthened by the information presented in the lecture. Write on the lines provided, your computer, or a separate piece of paper.

_____

_____

_____

_____

_____

_____

_____

_____

_____

_____

Revise

Use the following checklist as a guide in revising your essay. You may not be familiar with some of these items now. You will learn about them all as you study this book.

> ## REVISION CHECKLIST
>
> ■ **Content**
> - ❑ Thesis Statement
> - ❑ Topics that support the thesis
> - ❑ Main ideas
> - ❑ Supporting details
>
> ■ **Fluency and Cohesion**
> - ❑ Transition words
> - ❑ Grammar and Spelling
> - ❑ Sentence variety

A model essay is on page 177. Your essay does not have to match this model. It is only one of many possible responses.

INDEPENDENT TASK

Read the topic and plan your essay. Write an essay on this topic within 30 minutes. Write at least 300 words.

Divide your writing time like this:

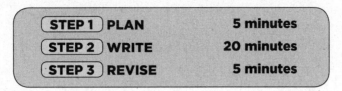

Essay Topic 1

People attend college or university for many different reasons. Why do you think people attend college or university? Use specific reasons and details to support your answer.

 Write on your computer or on a separate piece of paper.

TIP

Remember to time yourself when writing the essays throughout this book. Follow the suggested time management plan on page 21.

Revise

Use the following checklist as a guide in revising your essay. You may not be familiar with some of these items now. You will learn about them all as you study this book.

REVISION CHECKLIST

■ **Content**
- ❑ Thesis Statement
- ❑ Topics that support the thesis
- ❑ Main ideas
- ❑ Supporting details

■ **Fluency and Cohesion**
- ❑ Transition words
- ❑ Grammar and Spelling
- ❑ Sentence variety

A model essay is on page 182. Your essay does not have to match this model. It is only one of many possible responses.

Writing Skills: Integrated Task

3

STEP 1: PLAN

HOW TO TAKE NOTES

Taking good notes is an important part of planning your essay. In this section, you will learn how to take notes on the reading passage and on the lecture and you will learn different ways of organizing your notes.

Reading

When you read, it is important to recognize the topic, the main ideas, and the supporting details. These will help you understand and remember what you read. Identifying these elements will also help you respond on the integrated task.

On the TOEFL iBT, the reading passage is on the computer screen. You cannot mark or highlight it as you could if you were reading a book. You must take notes on a piece of paper. You will need to summarize or paraphrase the main ideas and the supporting details. You will need to compare them to the lecture.

Look at the example below of a reading passage. The first highlighted sentence is the topic or main idea of the whole passage. The other highlighted words or phrases are the main ideas of the paragraphs. Notice that these come at or near the beginning of each paragraph.

 **SAMPLE READING PASSAGE**

Much research has been done into learning styles. Many educators believe that understanding learning styles can greatly improve what goes on in a classroom or training session. Individuals who are aware of their own learning styles can better focus their learning. Professors and trainers who understand different learning styles are better able to design instruction so as to reach all their students or trainees.

Learning styles have been described in different ways. People may be described as auditory learners, who learn best by listening; visual learners, who learn best by seeing; or kinesthetic learners, who learn best by doing. Another system sees some people as active learners who process new information by doing something with it or using it in some way. Other learners are seen as reflective, preferring to process new information by thinking about it rather than by using it. Similarly, learners might be described as either sequential or global. Sequential learners see new information in logically connected steps, whereas global learners understand things better by looking at the whole picture rather than focusing on the parts.

TIP

Every passage has a *main idea*. Every paragraph should also have a main idea. *Topic* is another way of referring to the main idea of the whole passage. A *thesis statement* is what you plan to write about—it is your main idea statement for the whole essay.

Understanding learning styles can improve study skills. Sequential learners, for example, can make a habit of outlining new information. Auditory learners can form study groups so that they can talk with others about the topics they are learning. Reflective learners can find ways to reflect on what they have learned, by asking themselves questions about the material, for example, or by writing summaries.

Professors and trainers who understand the different types of learning styles can take them into account when designing their courses. By incorporating a variety of types of activities into their teaching, professors and trainers have a better chance of reaching all their students and improving the learning experience for everyone.

Listening

When you listen to a lecture or discussion in an academic setting, you listen for the same information that you do when you read for the topic, main ideas, and supporting details. To help you remember what you hear, you can take notes just as you do when you read.

Usually a speaker will give the main idea or his/her opinion in the first few sentences. The supporting details usually follow. You must listen for the main ideas and the supporting details. These will help you understand and remember what you hear. They will also help you when you write your response. You will need to summarize or paraphrase the main ideas and the supporting details.

Look at the example below of part of a lecture. The first highlighted phrase is the topic or main idea of the lecture. The other highlighted phrases are supporting details.

 **SAMPLE LECTURE**

There has been a lot of interest in learning styles over the years, but despite all the research that has been done on the topic, it doesn't present a magic solution. For one thing, there are topics that have to be presented in certain ways, no matter what the learning styles of the students may be. Mathematics, for example, needs to be taught in a logical, patterned way. It is also true that many students simply aren't interested in finding out about their learning style. They don't want to spend time reflecting on how they learn and then applying this to their study habits. They don't see a value in it. Instructors, too, aren't necessarily interested. In fact, many instructors tend to teach the way they themselves were taught. Or they present information in the way they understand it, according to their own style, with the assumption that everyone learns the way they do. So, while the research may provide us with some interesting information and food for thought, applying the results to real-life situations can be problematic.

Outlines and Idea Maps

There are two ways you can organize your notes for both the reading passage and the lecture. You can use either an outline or a graphic organizer, such as an idea map. Use whatever works best for you to organize what you read and listen to. Your notes will not be collected or graded. They are for your use only. It is important to practice taking notes so that you can learn to take them quickly. The time you have for planning and writing your essays is limited.

Good notes will make planning your essay much easier. When you take your notes, you write down the topic or main idea for the entire passage or lecture. When you plan your writing, you also write your main idea for the whole essay, and this now becomes your thesis statement.

OUTLINES

An **outline** can look like this.

INTRODUCTION	IDEA 3
TOPIC/MAIN IDEA	Detail 1
BODY	Detail 2
IDEA 1	Detail 3
Detail 1	CONCLUSION
Detail 2	IDEA 1, 2, and 3
Detail 3	
IDEA 2	
Detail 1	
Detail 2	
Detail 3	

An outline can also look like a simple chart. Look at these outlines and notes for the sample reading passage and the sample lecture.

Outline for Reading

Topic/Main idea	Understanding learning styles can improve learning and training.	
Paragraph 1	Main idea	Improve classrooms and training sessions
	Supporting details	(1) Individuals can study better.
		(2) Professors and trainers can instruct better.
Paragraph 2	Main idea	Different ways to describe learning styles
	Supporting details	(1) Auditory, visual, kinesthetic
		(2) Doing, reflecting
		(3) Sequential, global
Paragraph 3	Main idea	Improve study skills
	Supporting details	(1) Sequential—make outlines
		(2) Auditory—talk in study groups
		(3) Reflective—questions, summaries

Outline for Lecture

Topic/Main idea	Understanding learning styles does not always provide a solution.	
Supporting details	Idea 1	Some things have to be taught in certain ways.
		(1) math—sequential
	Idea 2	Some students are not interested in learning styles.
		(1) don't want to spend time on this
	Idea 3	Some instructors are not interested in learning styles.
		(1) teach in their own style
		(2) teach how they were taught

IDEA MAPS

You can also organize your notes on idea maps. An **idea map** can look like this.

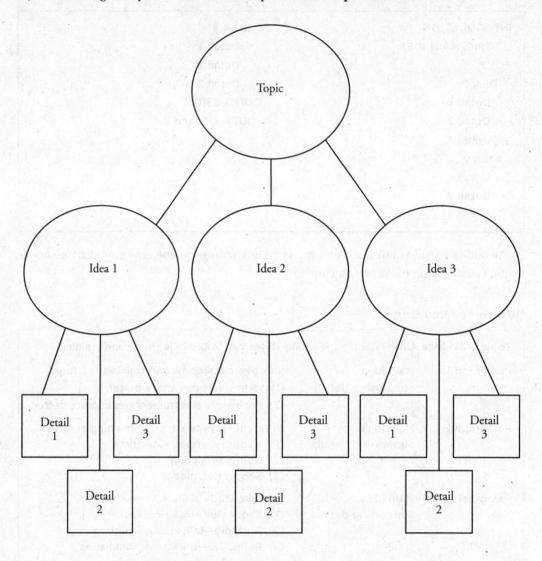

Look at these idea maps for the sample reading passage and sample lecture on pages 29–30.

Idea Map for Reading

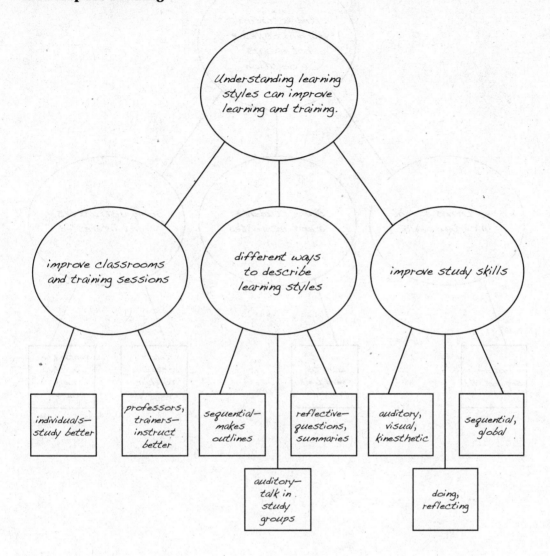

Idea Map for Lecture

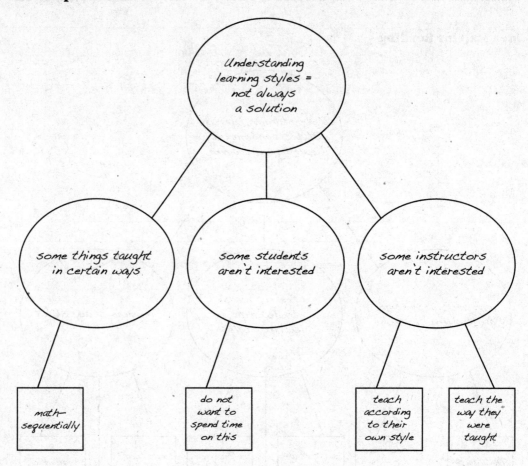

PRACTICE 1

Allow yourself three minutes to read each passage and take notes in outline form. Then listen to the corresponding lecture and take notes in outline form. In your notes, write the main idea and the supporting details. You may have two or more supporting details for each main idea. Photocopy the blank outline on this page as many times as you need and use the copies for taking your notes.

TIP

For extra practice, do these outlines twice: once using just phrases, the second time using complete sentences.

OUTLINE

Main idea

_____

Supporting details   (1) _____

(2) _____

(3) _____

 **READING 1**

Read the paragraph and take notes in outline form.

Invasive plants are a growing problem. In the United States, there are over one thousand species of nonnative plants that have been identified as a threat to native plants and animals. One way nonnative plants are introduced into an area is through gardening. In the past, gardeners cultivated nonnative species for food or medicine. Gardeners still bring in plants from other parts of the world, sometimes because they want hardy or drought-resistant plants, in other cases because of the particular beauty of some species. If the conditions are right in their new environment, these nonnative plants can escape the garden and grow wild. Many of them are very aggressive. Then we call them invasive. They take over an area, pushing out the native species. They may shade out the local plants, strangle them with vines, or deplete the soil of nutrients. The effects on the local ecology can be devastating. Native plants are reduced in number, and animals suffer loss of habitat and reduction of food supplies.

 **LECTURE 1**

Track 2

Listen to the lecture and take notes in outline form.

 **READING 2**

Read the paragraph and take notes in outline form.

Does television affect school performance? Many researchers have found that there are strong links between television viewing habits and children's performance in school. Studies have shown that children who spend a lot of time in front of the TV get lower grades than their peers who watch little or no TV. It has also been shown that children who have television sets in their bedrooms earn lower test scores than children with no television sets in their bedrooms. There are those who see TV as a potential educational tool. However, there are actually very few programs on TV that teach children important academic or thinking skills. Most programs aimed at children, such as cartoons, for example, contain little valuable content. Children who spend more time watching TV, spend less time doing homework or interacting with other people. They learn to be passive rather than active. Research supports the view that parents interested in supporting their children's success in school should keep the television turned off.

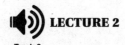 **LECTURE 2**

Track 3

Listen to the lecture and take notes in outline form.

 **READING 3**

Read the paragraph and take notes in outline form.

Smoking prevention campaigns, particularly those aimed at young people, have met with significant success all around the country. The current campaign to prevent tobacco use among teens in our own state, for example, has had a measurable positive impact. This program includes an advertising campaign, the implementation of no-smoking policies for places frequented by teens, and various community antismoking events. Close to 25% of teens surveyed said that they had participated in one of these events during the past year. More significantly, over 50% reported having seen the antismoking ads. The survey also found that those who had seen the ads were much less likely to start smoking than those who had not seen any of the antismoking ads. The public health department plans to continue and expand the campaign so as to reach more young people throughout the state. Clearly, such campaigns can go a long way toward addressing public health issues.

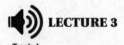 **LECTURE 3**

Track 4

Listen to the lecture and take notes in outline form.

READING 4

Read the paragraph and take notes in outline form.

Many researchers have looked into the effect of mood on consumer behavior. It has been shown that mood affects the shopper's perception of the store, the amount of time spent shopping, and the number of items purchased. A shopper's mood, of course, may be influenced by many things. Something as uncontrollable as the weather can have a great effect on what and how much a person buys on any particular day. A person's work or personal life also influences the mood that he or she brings into the store, and, of course, retailers have no control over this, either. But retailers do have control over their store environment, and this has been shown to have a great impact on shoppers' moods and therefore on their behavior as consumers. Retailers spend a great deal of effort with such things as lighting, colors, music, and product displays in an effort to create an environment that will have a positive impact on shopper mood and thereby increase sales.

LECTURE 4

Track 5

Listen to the lecture and take notes in outline form.

PRACTICE 2

Allow yourself three minutes to read each passage and take notes on an idea map. Then listen to the corresponding lecture and take notes on an idea map. In your notes, write the main idea and the supporting details. You may have two or more main ideas for each topic and two or more supporting details for each main idea. Photocopy the blank idea map on the next page as many times as you need and use the copies for taking your notes.

READING 5

Read the passage and take notes on an idea map.

Advances in technology are usually assumed to increase worker productivity, but that is not always the case. Technology has made it possible for office workers to never leave their desks, and the physical consequences of this can actually lead to lower productivity.

Remaining seated at a desk all day guarantees a level of physical discomfort that negatively impacts a worker's ability to achieve peak performance. Numerous studies have shown that sitting in one position all day leads to back and neck pain. Moreover, constant use of a computer often leads to eyestrain. A recent survey found that many office workers even remain at their desks while eating lunch so that they can answer their email or continue working on a project. This only exacerbates the situation. Even though workers may spend the entire work day at their desks, the resulting physical discomfort has been shown to lead to decreased, not increased, productivity.

What can be done about this? First, office workers need to be more aware of the need for breaks. Getting up and walking around for five minutes every hour or so will give their bodies a rest. Eating lunch away from the office and arranging face-to-face meetings rather than always relying on email both encourage time away from the desk. Second, arranging the desk space is crucial. Use of ergonomic equipment such as chairs and keyboards can greatly relieve strain on the back and neck, reducing discomfort and increasing productivity.

TIP

The reading passage on the Integrated Task is 250–300 words long. Time yourself as you practice reading passages of a similar length while taking notes. Give yourself 3 minutes per article.

Here are some websites where you can find short articles on a variety of topics for reading practice.

http://www.popsci.com/tags/short-science-articles

http://www.medicalnewstoday.com/popular

http://tetw.org/Greats

https://www.sciencenews.org

Reading Idea Map

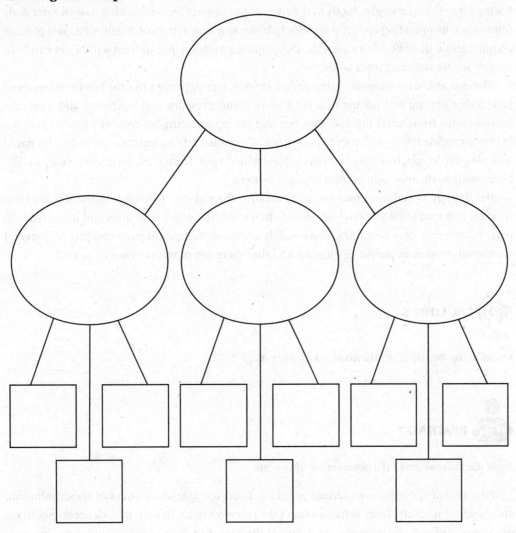

LECTURE 5

Track 6

Listen to the lecture and take notes on an idea map.

READING 6

Read the passage and take notes on an idea map.

Animal-assisted therapy, or AAT, is the use of companion animals to help people improve their emotional and physical health. It is common for psychiatrists, psychologists, and physicians to recommend pets to patients struggling with emotional difficulties. Caring for pets appears to have benefits for physical health, as well.

Pets are a good source of emotional support. They are wonderful companions for people suffering from loneliness. People who feel isolated from other people may enter more easily into a relationship with a pet because it is a non-judgmental and non-threatening relationship. Caring for pets can also give focus to the lives of pet owners by establishing a need for a daily routine and by providing opportunities for hobbies and club activities. In addition, pets provide comfort and a diversion from worries. Developing a relationship of trust with a pet can help relieve people suffering from anxiety.

There is also documentation that caring for pets can improve physical health. It has been shown that petting and talking to a pet lowers blood pressure and heart rate and improves survival rates from heart disease. Pets provide the opportunity for regular physical activity. Pets also provide the opportunity to play. It is well established that animals (including humans) who play live longer, healthier lives than those who do not. In fact, pet owners make up to 20% fewer visits to doctors' offices than non-pet owners.

Pet therapy is common practice in homes for the elderly. These institutions often keep resident cats and birds as pets. Volunteers often visit the homes with dogs and other types of pets, as well. It is now becoming more widely accepted that pet therapy can provide needed emotional support to people of all ages, and that there are physical benefits, as well.

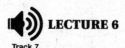 **LECTURE 6**

Track 7

Listen to the lecture and take notes on an idea map.

 **READING 7**

Read the passage and take notes on an idea map.

Pollution of our oceans is a serious problem. There are different sources of ocean pollution, and much of it results from activities that take place on land. In fact, 80% of ocean pollution originates on land. For example, oil is one of the major sources of ocean pollution, but only about 12% of this type of pollution results from oil spills at sea. Another 36% of it comes from waste from cities and factories which travels to the ocean through rivers and drains.

Fertilizers are another serious source of ocean pollution. Fertilizers wash off farms and lawns and eventually end up in the ocean. Once in the ocean, they allow algae to grow. The overgrowth of algae depletes the ocean of oxygen and suffocates other marine plants, resulting in dead areas. There are several large dead areas in the world's oceans, including the Gulf of Mexico and the Baltic Sea.

Garbage is another type of pollution in our oceans, and it can seriously harm marine animals. One of the worst culprits is plastic. This material does not break down easily. Animals often mistake it for food and eat it. Plastic bags can block an animal's breathing passage. The plastic rings that hold packs of cans together can choke birds and other small animals.

Toxic chemicals also cause serious pollution problems. Until the 1970s, toxic waste chemicals were freely dumped into the oceans. In the 1970s, laws were passed banning such activity. However, run-off from manufacturing and disposal sites as well as accidental leaks continue to pollute our oceans with toxic chemicals. These chemicals accumulate in the animals that ingest them and move up the food chain. They eventually end up in the seafood that we eat.

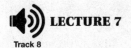

LECTURE 7

Track 8

Listen to the lecture and take notes on an idea map.

READING 8

Read the passage and take notes on an idea map.

The psychological effects of color have been of interest to people for a long time. The ancient Egyptians, Chinese, and Indians all used color as part of healing therapies. The psychology of color is still of interest in modern times. Interior decorators, graphic designers, and web designers all incorporate an understanding of the relationship between color and mood into their work.

In selecting color for an interior space, the designer considers what type of mood is compatible with the activities that will be carried out in that space. At least one study has found that office workers are able to concentrate better in rooms that are painted with cool blues or dark greens. Yellow might be considered suitable for a sales office because it contributes to a positive mood. Health care centers, on the other hand, are often painted with neutral colors, as these convey a sense of cleanliness and help the healthcare workers stay clear and focused. Restaurants are often painted orange or bright red as it is believed that these colors stimulate the appetite.

There is some research indicating that color may have an effect on the body as well. Some scientists believe that blue slows the heart rate and reduces blood pressure. Red, on the other hand, is believed to increase blood pressure.

While there is a great deal of interest in the psychology of color, many scientists remain skeptical. Although the effect of color on mood has been observed in many cases, research has shown that this effect is often temporary. In addition, observed psychological effects of a particular color may not hold up across cultures.

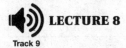

LECTURE 8

Track 9

Listen to the lecture and take notes on an idea map.

WRITE A THESIS STATEMENT

Your thesis statement is what you plan to write about. It is your main idea statement for the whole essay. For the Integrated Task, your thesis statement must refer to the main ideas of both the reading passage and the lecture and must say whether the ideas are similar or opposite.

POINT OF VIEW

In both the reading passage and the lecture, a point of view is explained. When you write your response for the Integrated Task you will have to restate these points of view. You can look at the main idea that you wrote in your notes. This should be a restatement or summary of the main point of view explained in the reading passage or the lecture.

   When you restate another person's ideas, you use reporting verbs. Here are a few common reporting verbs.

TIP

Some reporting verbs have special meanings. Look up these verbs in a dictionary so that you know what each one means.

REPORTING VERBS

believe	think	suggest	describe
propose	assert	tell	warn
state	say	point out	explain

Look at the following examples of restating a point of view.

EXAMPLES

Reading 1

The author <u>explains</u> that understanding learning styles can improve learning and training.

Lecture 1

The speaker <u>suggests</u> that understanding learning styles does not always provide a solution.

Tell and *Warn*

Tell is usually followed by an object.
   The author tells us *that students don't always care about learning styles.*

Warn is sometimes followed by an object, but not always.
   The author warns us *that students don't always care about learning styles.*
   The author warns *that students don't always care about learning styles.*

PRACTICE 1

Look at the main ideas in the notes you wrote in Step 1: Plan, Practice 1 and 2 on pages 35 and 39. Rewrite each idea as a restatement of point of view. Use reporting verbs.

Reading 1   The author states that _____

Lecture 1   The speaker explains that _____

Reading 2   The author believes that _____

Lecture 2   The speaker proposes that _____

Reading 3   The author _____

Lecture 3   The speaker _____

Reading 4   The author _____

Lecture 4   The speaker _____

Reading 5   The author _____

Lecture 5   The speaker _____

Reading 6   The author _____

Lecture 6   The speaker _____

Reading 7   The author _____

Lecture 7   The speaker _____

Reading 8   The author _____

Lecture 8   The speaker _____

COMPARE AND CONTRAST

When you write your response for the Integrated Task, you will be asked to compare the ideas in the reading passage and the lecture if they are similar in some way. You may be asked how the information in the lecture adds to, supports, or explains the information in the reading passage. Here are some words you can use when you compare ideas.

TIP

See page 138 for more examples of ways to compare and contrast.

Compare

like	similar to	also
and	similarly	likewise
in the same way	as	agree

You will be asked to contrast the ideas in the reading passage and the lecture if they are different or opposite to each other. You may be asked how the information in the lecture casts doubt on the information in the reading passage. Here are some words you can use when you contrast ideas.

Contrast

however	on the other hand	but
although	in contrast	disagree

In Practice 1 on page 43, you restated the main point of view of each reading passage and lecture. When you write your thesis statement, you will put these two ideas together and say whether they are similar or opposing points of view.

Look at these examples from the reading on pages 29–30.

EXAMPLES

Reading 1
The author explains that understanding learning styles can improve learning and training.

Lecture 1
The speaker suggests that understanding learning styles does not always provide a solution.

These ideas are opposite to each other. When you write the thesis statement, you will *contrast* them.

EXAMPLE

Thesis statement
The author explains that understanding learning styles can improve learning and training. The speaker, *however*, suggests that understanding learning styles does not always provide a solution.

This example uses the word *however* to show that the two points of view oppose each other. See page 138 for more examples of ways to compare and contrast.

PRACTICE 2

Look at the restated points of view you wrote in Practice 1 on page 43. Write a thesis statement that combines each pair of viewpoints.

1. Compare Reading 1 and Lecture 1 points of view.

   Thesis statement: _____

   _____

2. Contrast Reading 2 and Lecture 2 points of view.

   Thesis statement: _____

   _____

3. Contrast Reading 3 and Lecture 3 points of view.

   Thesis statement: _____

   _____

4. Compare Reading 4 and Lecture 4 points of view.

   Thesis statement: _____

   _____

5. Contrast Reading 5 and Lecture 5 points of view.

   Thesis statement: _____

   _____

6. Compare Reading 6 and Lecture 6 points of view.

   Thesis statement: _____

   _____

7. Compare Reading 7 and Lecture 7 points of view.

   Thesis statement: _____

   _____

8. Contrast Reading 8 and Lecture 8 points of view.

   Thesis statement: _____

   _____

WRITE THE SUPPORTING DETAILS

When you write your response for the Integrated Task, you must explain the ideas you read and heard. These are not your own, original ideas. They are your explanation or report of other people's ideas.

When you write the supporting details in your response, you should report the most important supporting details the author and speaker used. You can use **paraphrasing** and **citing** to do this.

Paraphrasing

When you paraphrase, you use your own words to express what another person wrote or said. When you paraphrase a sentence or a group of sentences, focus on the most important points. Restate them in your own words by using synonyms, changing the word order, using active instead of passive voice, and leaving out the less important details.

Original

People may be described as auditory learners, who learn best by listening; visual learners, who learn best by seeing; or kinesthetic learners, who learn best by doing.

Paraphrase

Some people learn more easily by listening, others by seeing, and still others by doing.

Original

Another system sees some people as active learners who process new information by doing something with it or using it in some way. Other learners are seen as reflective, preferring to process new information by thinking about it rather than by using it.

Paraphrase

Active learners understand new information by doing something with it. Reflective learners understand information by thinking about it.

Original

Similarly, learners might be described as either sequential or global. Sequential learners see new information in logically connected steps, whereas global learners understand things better by looking at the whole picture rather than focusing on the parts.

Paraphrase

Sequential learners look at information as a series of steps, but global learners prefer to look at the whole rather than the parts.

 **PRACTICE 3**

Read each original text. Then choose the best paraphrase.

READING 1

1. In the past, gardeners cultivated nonnative species for food or medicine. Gardeners still bring in plants from other parts of the world, sometimes because they want hardy or drought-resistant plants, in other cases because of the particular beauty of some species.

   Paraphrase

   (A) In the past, gardeners grew nonnative plants for food and medicine. Now they do not because these plants are neither hardy, drought resistant, nor beautiful.

   (B) Gardeners from around the world introduce each other to different species of plants. Each gardener tries to find the hardiest, most drought-resistant, or most beautiful plant in the world.

   (C) Gardeners have introduced nonnative plants for food and medicine. They may also plant them because they are hardy, drought resistant, or beautiful.

2. Then we call them invasive. They take over an area, pushing out the native species. They may shade out the local plants, strangle them with vines, or deplete the soil of nutrients.

   Paraphrase

   (A) Invasive plants harm native species by shading them out, strangling them, or using up all the nutrients in the soil.

   (B) Many local plants grow on vines and invade an area with shade.

   (C) In order to grow, invasive plants require plenty of shade and soil rich in nutrients.

3. The effects on the local ecology can be devastating. Native plants are reduced in number, and animals suffer loss of habitat and reduction of food supplies.

   Paraphrase

   (A) The local ecology devastates native plants and reduces food supplies.

   (B) The local ecology suffers because there are fewer native plants and animals lose their homes and food.

   (C) Large numbers of native plants and animals suffer a devastating loss of habitat.

READING 2

4. It has also been shown that children who have television sets in their bedrooms earn lower test scores than children with no television sets in their bedrooms.

   Paraphrase

   (A) Children who have TV sets in their bedrooms get low grades in school because they do not get enough sleep.

   (B) Children who have TV sets in their bedrooms do not do as well in school as their classmates.

   (C) Children who spend a lot of time watching TV spend less time preparing for their school tests.

5. There are those who see TV as a potential educational tool. However, there are actually very few programs on TV that teach children important academic or thinking skills. Most programs aimed at children, cartoons, for example, contain little valuable content.

Paraphrase

(A) Some people think of TV as educational, but most children's programs actually do not have much valuable or educational content.

(B) TV is not a useful academic tool because educators do not believe that children should watch cartoons.

(C) Children usually prefer to watch cartoons because the academic content of educational programs makes them think too hard.

6. Children who spend more time watching TV spend less time doing homework or interacting with other people. They learn to be passive rather than active.

Paraphrase

(A) TV watching is a passive activity while doing homework is active.

(B) Children should keep the TV turned off when they are doing their homework or interacting with other people.

(C) TV takes time away from important activities like doing homework or being with other people.

7. Research supports the view that parents interested in supporting their children's success in school should keep the television turned off.

Paraphrase

(A) Parents can help their children by turning off the television.

(B) Parents should do more research about school success and television.

(C) Parents are often interested in children's television programs.

READING 3

8. This program includes an advertising campaign, the implementation of no-smoking policies for places frequented by teens, and various community antismoking events.

Paraphrase

(A) The program frequently included teens who implemented a variety of events.

(B) The program included advertising, no-smoking policies, and antismoking events.

(C) The program implemented advertising in a variety of places throughout the community.

9. Close to 25% of teens surveyed said that they had participated in one of these events during the past year. More significantly, over 50% reported having seen the antismoking ads.

Paraphrase

(A) Many teens participated in the events and many more saw the ads.

(B) Almost 25% of teens had surveyed the program and heard about the events.

(C) A significant number of teens participated in an advertising campaign and reported on the events.

10. The public health department plans to continue and expand the campaign so as to reach more young people throughout the state. Clearly, such campaigns can go a long way toward addressing public health issues.

Paraphrase

(A) The public health department will continue to ask young people throughout the state about public health issues that affect them.

(B) The public health department plans to address more public health issues concerning young people.

(C) The public health department will continue with this successful campaign to improve public health among young people in the state.

READING 4

11. A shopper's mood, of course, may be influenced by many things. Something as uncontrollable as the weather can have a great effect on what and how much a person buys on any particular day. A person's work or personal life also influences the mood that he or she brings into the store, and, of course, retailers have no control over this, either.

Paraphrase

(A) A shopper may feel he or she has no control over his life when the weather is bad or when there are problems at work, and this puts retailers in a bad mood.

(B) A shopper usually does not buy much from retailers when the weather is bad or when there are problems at work or at home.

(C) A shopper's mood may be influenced by things that retailers cannot control, such as the weather or personal or work problems.

12. But retailers do have control over their store environment, and this has been shown to have a great impact on shoppers' moods and therefore on their behavior as consumers.

Paraphrase

(A) Retailers can influence shoppers' moods by controlling the store environment.

(B) Retailers feel the impact of consumers' behavior in the store environment.

(C) The behavior of moody shoppers has a great impact on the store environment.

13. Retailers spend a great deal of effort with such things as lighting, colors, music, and product displays in an effort to create an environment that will have a positive impact on shopper mood and thereby increase sales.

Paraphrase

(A) It takes a lot of effort to create a positive environment and increase sales.

(B) Shoppers buy more when retailers use lighting, color, and music to improve shopper mood.

(C) More effort is needed to determine the impact of the retail environment on shopper mood.

> **You can find more information on paraphrasing here.**
>
>
>
> *http://examples.yourdictionary.com/examples-of-paraphrasing.html*

 **PRACTICE 4**

Paraphrase the following original sentences from the lectures. Some of the paraphrases have been partially written for you.

LECTURE 1

1. Garlic mustard is a problem in several areas in the United States. It's a cool season plant, blooming in midspring. It's replacing several other spring-blooming species because it competes with them for light, nutrients, and space.

   Paraphrase

   _____ in the U.S. because it threatens _____ by taking up _____.

2. The West Virginia white butterfly is also threatened by this invasive plant. Garlic mustard pushes out certain native species of mustard, which the butterfly relies on for a food source.

   Paraphrase

   Garlic mustard also threatens _____. It competes with _____ which are the butterfly's _____.

3. Garlic mustard was first introduced to the United States in the nineteenth century as a food source. It was first recorded on Long Island but now thrives throughout the eastern and midwestern United States.

   Paraphrase

   Garlic mustard was first grown on _____ for _____ and has since spread to _____.

LECTURE 2

4. TV can expose children to new ideas and information that they might otherwise not have access to.

   Paraphrase

   _____

   _____

5. The key here is the amount of time spent in front of the TV.

   Paraphrase

   _____

   _____

6. Children who spend three hours a day or more in front of the TV do poorly in school, scoring lower on both math and reading tests than children who watch some, but less, TV.

   Paraphrase

   _____

   _____

LECTURE 3

7. Surveys taken near the end of this campaign, in March of last year, showed that well over half of those surveyed were aware of the campaign...and that 40% reported that they were unlikely to try smoking.

Paraphrase

_____

_____

8. Just three months after the campaign ended, this figure changed dramatically.

Paraphrase

_____

_____

9. At the end of June, 58% of survey participants reported that they were "very likely" to smoke in the next year. At the same time, less than 30% reported awareness of the anti-smoking campaign.

Paraphrase

_____

_____

LECTURE 4

10. The researchers found that restaurant patrons who heard music with a slow tempo tended to remain at the restaurant longer than patrons who heard fast music.... they [also] purchased more food, which of course is the effect desired by the restaurant owner.

Paraphrase

_____

_____

11. The study subjects were...college students. Some of them heard currently popular hit songs while shopping—the "familiar" music—while others heard music normally aimed at an older age group.

Paraphrase

_____

_____

12. [The students] who heard familiar music stayed in the store longer than those listening to unfamiliar music. They also expressed more positive opinions of the products offered for sale.

Paraphrase

_____

_____

TIP

Some sentences include ellipses (...). These show where unnecessary words were left out. Some sentences also have words in brackets ([ ]). These words were added to help the reader understand the sentences.

Quoting

When you paraphrase, you express another person's ideas using your own words. Sometimes you may also want to include a phrase or sentence using the exact words that were used by the source (the author or speaker). When you include the exact words written or spoken by another person, you need to put quotation marks (" ") around them. Whether you paraphrase or quote, you need to mention the source. This means that you acknowledge that you are reporting someone else's ideas or words, and that they are not your own.

EXAMPLE

Original
Sequential learners, for example, can make a habit of outlining new information.

Paraphrase with quote
The author proposes that sequential learners "make a habit of outlining new information."
Notice that the example has quotation marks around the words that were borrowed from the source, and that the source, *the author*, is mentioned.

You will need to use a reporting verb to introduce your paraphrase or quote. Here are several reporting verbs that you can use.

REPORTING VERBS

say	tell	state	remind
suggest	claim	remark	assert
report	explain	point out	contend
note	propose	believe	think
describe	warn	confirm	deny

Look at the following examples.

EXAMPLES

Original
People may be described as auditory learners, who learn best by listening.

Paraphrase with quote
The author <u>tells us</u> that auditory learners "learn best by listening."

Original
Global learners understand things better by looking at the whole picture.

Paraphrase with quote
The author <u>explains</u> that global learners prefer to look at "the whole picture."

Original
It is also true that many students simply are not interested in finding out about their learning style.

Paraphrase with quote
The speaker <u>suggests</u> that students "simply aren't interested" in information about learning styles.

TIP

Most of the reporting verbs are followed by a *that* clause. (*Describe* is often followed by an object and an *as* clause instead.) *Tell* and *remind* must have an object before *that*.

TIP

The topic itself and terms customarily used to discuss a topic do not need quotes. Common words do not usually need quotes unless they are used in some unusual way.

 **PRACTICE 5**

For each paraphrase below, add an appropriate reporting verb. Then put quotation marks around the quoted word or words.

1. **Original**   The effects on the local ecology can be devastating.

   Paraphrase   The author _____ that invasive plants may have devastating results.

2. **Original**   Most programs aimed at children, such as cartoons, for example, contain little valuable content.

   Paraphrase   The author _____ that most children's TV programs do not have valuable content.

3. **Original**   Smoking prevention campaigns, particularly those aimed at young people, have met with significant success all around the country.

   Paraphrase   The author _____ that antismoking campaigns for teens have had significant success.

4. **Original**   ... office assistants can devote themselves to other tasks. Offices can operate with fewer assistants, thus spending a great deal less on salaries and benefits.

   Paraphrase   The speaker _____ that offices save money because office workers can now devote themselves to other tasks.

5. **Original**   The fact is, research shows that children who watch an hour or so of TV daily... actually do better in school than children who do not watch TV at all.

   Paraphrase   The speaker _____ that when children watch TV, they actually do better in school.

6. **Original**   It is well established that animals (including humans) who play live longer, healthier lives than those who do not.

   Paraphrase   The author _____ that play helps people live longer, healthier lives.

7. **Original**   Health care centers, on the other hand, are often painted with neutral colors, as these convey a sense of cleanliness...

   Paraphrase   The author _____ that neutral colors are used in health care centers to convey a sense of cleanliness.

WRITE THE RESPONSE

Summarizing

A summary is a short description of the main idea and supporting information in a passage. When you write the response for the Integrated Task, you will summarize the main points of the reading passage and the lecture and compare or contrast them.

Your notes will give you the foundation to write a concise summary and comparison of the different ideas presented. You can use the notes you wrote in Step 1, and the thesis statement and rephrased sentences you have written in Step 2.

Look at the following notes for the sample reading passage and lecture on pages 29–30.

STEP 1 PLAN

Reading Notes

Topic/Main idea   Understanding learning styles can improve learning and training.

Paragraph 1	**Main idea**	Improve classrooms and training sessions
	Supporting details	(1) Individuals can study better.
		(2) Professors and trainers can instruct better.
Paragraph 2	**Main idea**	Different ways to describe learning styles
	Supporting details	(1) Auditory, visual, kinesthetic
		(2) Doing, reflecting
		(3) Sequential, global
Paragraph 3	**Main idea**	Improve study skills
	Supporting details	(1) Sequential—make outlines
		(2) Auditory—talk in study groups
		(3) Reflective—questions, summaries

Lecture Notes

Topic/Main idea	Understanding learning styles does not always provide a solution.
Supporting details	(1) Some things have to be taught in certain ways.
	(2) Some students are not interested in learning styles.
	(3) Some instructors are not interested in learning styles.

Now look at the way the notes were used to write a **thesis statement** and **paraphrased sentences**.

STEP 2 WRITE

Thesis Statement

The author explains that understanding learning styles can improve learning and training. The speaker, however, suggests that understanding learning styles does not always provide a solution.

Paraphrased Sentences

Reading

- Understanding learning styles helps individuals learn better and professors and trainers instruct better.
- Some people learn more easily by listening, others by seeing, and still others by doing.
- Active learners understand new information by doing something with it. Reflective learners understand information by thinking about it.
- Sequential learners look at information as a series of steps, but global learners prefer to look at the whole rather than the parts.
- Sequential learners, auditory learners, and reflective learners, for example, can each choose the study methods that best suit their individual learning styles.

Lecture

- Some subjects have to be taught in certain ways. Math has to be taught sequentially.
- The speaker suggests that students "simply aren't interested" in information about learning styles.
- Some professors are not interested in learning styles.

Finally, read this summary, which contrasts the reading passage and the lecture.

Summary

The author explains that understanding learning styles can improve learning and training. The speaker, however, suggests that understanding learning styles does not always provide a solution. *Thesis statement*

The author states that understanding learning styles helps individuals learn better and professors and trainers instruct better. He explains different ways to describe learning styles. Some people learn more easily by listening, others by seeing, and still others by doing. Active learners understand new information by doing something with it. Reflective learners understand information by thinking about it. Sequential learners look at information as a series of steps, but global learners prefer to look at the whole rather than the parts. The author believes that understanding learning styles can improve study skills. Sequential learners, auditory learners, and reflective learners, for example, can each choose the study methods that best suit their individual learning styles. *Rephrased sentences from Reading*

The speaker presents a different point of view. First, some subjects have to be taught in certain ways. Math has to be taught sequentially. In addition, the speaker suggests that students "simply aren't interested" in information about learning styles. Some professors are not interested in learning styles, either. *Rephrased sentences from Lecture*

 **PRACTICE 6**

Look at these notes, thesis statements, and rephrased sentences from the practice exercises. Use them to write summaries comparing or contrasting the main points in the reading passage and lecture.

SUMMARY 1

(based on Reading 1 and Lecture 1, page 35)

Reading Notes

Main idea	Invasive plants harm native plants.
Supporting details	(1) They are introduced to an area through gardening.
	(2) They escape from the garden and grow wild.
	(3) They push out native species, causing devastating effects on the local ecology.

Lecture Notes

Main idea	Garlic mustard is an invasive species that causes problems.
Supporting details	(1) It competes with other spring-blooming species.
	(2) The West Virginia white butterfly is threatened by this plant.
	(3) Garlic mustard was introduced to the United States as a food source.

Thesis Statement

The author states that invasive plants harm native plants, and the speaker explains that garlic mustard is an invasive species that causes problems.

Paraphrased Sentences

Reading

- Gardeners have introduced nonnative plants for food and medicine. They may also plant them because they are hardy, drought resistant, or beautiful.
- Invasive plants harm native species by shading them out, strangling them, or using up all the nutrients in the soil.
- The local ecology suffers because there are fewer native plants and animals lose their homes and food.

Lecture

- Garlic mustard threatens other spring-blooming plants by taking up light, nutrients, and space.
- Garlic mustard also threatens the West Virginia white butterfly. It competes with other types of mustard which are the butterfly's food source.
- Garlic mustard was first grown on Long Island for food and has since spread to other areas of the country.

SUMMARY 2

(based on Reading 2 and Lecture 2, page 36)

Reading Notes

Main idea	TV viewing has negative effects on children's school performance.
Supporting details	(1) Children who watch a lot of TV get lower grades and test scores.
	(2) Few TV programs teach academic or thinking skills.
	(3) When children spend time watching TV, they spend less time on homework, with other people, and being active.

Lecture Notes

Main idea	TV watching can actually improve school performance.
Supporting details	(1) TV exposes children to new ideas and information.
	(2) Children should watch some TV, but not too much.

Thesis Statement

The author believes that TV viewing has negative effects on children's school performance. The speaker, on the other hand, proposes that TV watching can actually improve school performance.

Paraphrased Sentences

Reading

- Children who have TV sets in their bedrooms do not do as well in school as their classmates.
- Some people think of TV as educational, but most children's programs actually do not have much valuable or educational content.
- TV takes time away from important activities like doing homework or being with other people.
- Parents can help their children by turning off the television.

Lecture

- Children can learn new things from TV.
- The amount of time spent watching TV is important.
- More than three hours a day of TV watching results in lower reading and math test scores.

SUMMARY 3

(based on Reading 3 and Lecture 3, page 36)

Reading Notes

Main idea   A particular smoking prevention campaign aimed at young people has been successful.

Supporting details
(1) Many teens participated in antismoking events, and many saw antismoking ads.
(2) Teens who saw the ads are less likely to start smoking.
(3) The public health department will continue and expand the campaign.

Lecture Notes

Main idea   The initial results of public health campaigns can be misleading.

Supporting details
(1) Surveys taken near the end of an antismoking campaign showed 40% unlikely to try smoking.
(2) Surveys taken three months later showed 58% very likely to try smoking.

Thesis Statement

The author tells us about a particular smoking prevention campaign aimed at young people that has been successful. In contrast, the speaker warns us that initial results of public health campaigns can be misleading.

Paraphrased Sentences

Reading

- The program included advertising, no smoking policies, and antismoking events.
- Many teens participated in the events and many more saw the ads.
- The public health department will continue with this successful campaign to improve public health among young people in the state.

Lecture

- Surveys made at the end of a recent antismoking campaign showed that 50% knew about the campaign and 40% would probably not smoke.
- Three months later, the numbers had changed.
- Many more said they would probably smoke and many fewer said they knew about the campaign.

SUMMARY 4

(based on Reading 4 and Lecture 4, page 37)

Reading Notes

Main idea	A good mood makes shoppers buy more.
Supporting details	(1) Mood can be affected by weather, personal life, and store environment.
	(2) Retailers create a store environment to have a positive impact on mood and therefore on sales.

Lecture Notes

Main idea	Studies show that mood can make consumers spend more time shopping.
Supporting details	(1) When listening to slow music, restaurant patrons remained longer and purchased more food.
	(2) When listening to familiar music, shoppers stayed in a store longer and expressed more positive opinions about the products.

Thesis Statement

The author proposes that a good mood makes shoppers buy more. Similarly, the speaker explains that studies show that music can make consumers spend more time shopping.

Paraphrased Sentences

Reading

- A shopper's mood may be influenced by things that retailers cannot control, such as the weather or personal or work problems.
- Retailers can influence shoppers' moods by controlling the store environment.
- Shoppers buy more when retailers use lighting, color, and music to improve shopper mood.

Lecture

- Research showed that slow music caused customers to stay at the restaurant longer and order more food.
- Some of the study subjects, college students, heard popular music in the store, and others heard older music.
- Those who heard familiar music shopped longer and said better things about the store's products.

USE THE REVISION CHECKLIST

Revision is an important part of the writing process. After you write your response, you need to check the content and language. You need to make sure that the content is well developed and well organized, and you need to make sure you have used correct language and punctuation. You can use the following revision checklist as a guide.

REVISION CHECKLIST

- **Content**
  - ☐ Thesis Statement
  - ☐ Topics that support the thesis
  - ☐ Main ideas
  - ☐ Supporting details
- **Fluency and Cohesion**
  - ☐ Transition words
  - ☐ Grammar and Spelling
  - ☐ Sentence variety

Read the following model task. Notice how it matches the items on the checklist.

MODEL TASK 1

Summarize the main points of the reading passage and explain how the points made in the lecture oppose them.

The author asserts that advances in technology do not always lead to increased productivity. The speaker, in contrast, suggests that investment in technology is paid back in increased productivity.

The author explains that because of technology, workers often stay at their desks all day, but this does not lead to increased productivity. It can cause back, neck, and eye pain. This is very uncomfortable and actually lowers productivity. Workers need to take breaks more often and go out for lunch. They also should have meetings in person instead of using email. In addition, companies can buy special equipment that is more comfortable to use.

The speaker has the opposite point of view. She believes that technology increases productivity. Photocopy machines, for example, can copy, collate, and staple much faster than a person. Because of this, workers can spend their time doing other things. Also an office can hire fewer people and save money on salaries. When people communicate by email, they do not have to go to so many meetings. They can spend more time working. The speaker does not mention the physical pains that using technology can cause. Clearly, technology solves some problems, but it causes others.

(based on Reading 5, page 38, and Lecture 5, page 39)

Content

> ## REVISION CHECKLIST
>
> ■ **Content**
> - ☑ Thesis Statement
> - ❑ Topics that support the thesis
> - ❑ Main ideas
> - ❑ Supporting details
>
> ■ **Fluency and Cohesion**
> - ❑ Transition words
> - ❑ Grammar and Spelling
> - ❑ Sentence variety

✓ CHECK FOR THESIS STATEMENT

The model essay has a thesis statement that shows understanding of the task. The task asks the writer to summarize points and explain how they oppose each other, that is, to contrast them. The first two sentences are the thesis statement. They summarize the main idea of the reading and of the lecture. The transition words *in contrast* let the reader know that these ideas are in opposition to each other.

Task: Summarize points and explain how they oppose each other

Contrast words: *in contrast*

> ## REVISION CHECKLIST
>
> ■ **Content**
> - ❑ Thesis Statement
> - ☑ Topics that support the thesis
> - ❑ Main ideas
> - ❑ Supporting details
>
> ■ **Fluency and Cohesion**
> - ❑ Transition words
> - ❑ Grammar and Spelling
> - ❑ Sentence variety

✓ CHECK FOR TOPICS THAT SUPPORT THE THESIS

The supporting topics are the main idea of the reading and the main idea of the lecture. They are presented in the thesis statement. The model essay summarizes the main points of the reading and of the lecture and explains how the author's ideas contrast with the speaker's ideas.

Main idea of the reading and lecture

Reading   Advances in technology do not always lead to increased productivity.

Lecture   Investment in technology is paid back in increased productivity.

> ## REVISION CHECKLIST
>
> ■ **Content**
> - ❑ Thesis Statement
> - ❑ Topics that support the thesis
> - ☑ Main ideas
> - ❑ Supporting details
>
> ■ **Fluency and Cohesion**
> - ❑ Transition words
> - ❑ Grammar and Spelling
> - ❑ Sentence variety

✓ CHECK FOR MAIN IDEAS

The second paragraph in the model essay supports the reading main idea by summarizing the main points of the reading. The third paragraph in the model essay supports the lecture main idea by summarizing the main points of the lecture.

Main Idea of the Reading and Lecture	Developed Further in...	Ideas That Are Developed
Advances in technology do not always lead to increased productivity.	Paragraph 2	Technology means workers stay at their desks all day. This causes discomfort.
Investment in technology is paid back in increased productivity.	Paragraph 3	Photocopy machines and email make work faster and more convenient.

REVISION CHECKLIST

■ **Content**
  ❑ Thesis Statement
  ❑ Topics that support the thesis
  ❑ Main ideas
  ☑ Supporting details

■ **Fluency and Cohesion**
  ❑ Transition words
  ❑ Grammar and Spelling
  ❑ Sentence variety

✓ CHECK FOR SUPPORTING DETAILS

The paragraphs in the model essay have topic sentences and supporting details. In the body of the response, the topic sentences of the paragraphs match the topics introduced in the first paragraph.

Paragraph 2: *Main Idea*

...because of technology, workers often stay at their desks all day, but this does not lead to increased productivity.

Supporting Details

- This is very uncomfortable and actually lowers productivity.
- Workers need to take breaks more often and go out for lunch.
- They also should have meetings in person instead of using email.
- In addition, companies can buy special equipment that is more comfortable to use.

Paragraph 3: *Main Idea*

...technology increases productivity.

Supporting Details

- Photocopy machines, for example, can copy, collate, and staple much faster than a person.
- When people communicate by email, they do not have to go to so many meetings. They can spend more time working.

Fluency and Cohesion

REVISION CHECKLIST

■ **Content**
- ❏ Thesis Statement
- ❏ Topics that support the thesis
- ❏ Main ideas
- ❏ Supporting details

■ **Fluency and Cohesion**
- ☑ Transition words
- ❏ Grammar and Spelling
- ❏ Sentence variety

✓ CHECK FOR TRANSITION WORDS

Transition words show how the ideas fit together. The model essay includes appropriate transition words.

Transition Word	Paragraph	Function
also	Paragraph 2	Adds information
In addition	Paragraph 2	Adds information
for example	Paragraph 3	Clarifies as point
Also	Paragraph 3	Adds information

TIP

See pages 137–139 for more information on transition words.

REVISION CHECKLIST

■ **Content**
- ❏ Thesis Statement
- ❏ Topics that support the thesis
- ❏ Main ideas
- ❏ Supporting details

■ **Fluency and Cohesion**
- ❏ Transition words
- ☑ Grammar and Spelling
- ❏ Sentence variety

✓ CHECK FOR GRAMMAR AND SPELLING

There are no grammar or spelling errors in the model essay.

REVISION CHECKLIST

■ **Content**
- ❏ Thesis Statement
- ❏ Topics that support the thesis
- ❏ Main ideas
- ❏ Supporting details

■ **Fluency and Cohesion**
- ❏ Transition words
- ❏ Grammar and Spelling
- ☑ Sentence variety

✓ CHECK FOR SENTENCE VARIETY

The model essay uses a variety of sentence structures.

Sentence Type	Paragraph	Example
Series	Paragraph 2	It can cause back, neck, and eye pain.
Adjective clause	Paragraph 2	In addition, companies can buy special equipment that is more comfortable to use.
Complex sentence	Paragraph 3	When people communicate by email, they do not have to go to so many meetings.
Simple sentence	Paragraph 3	They can spend more time working.
Compound sentence	Paragraph 3	Clearly, technology solves some problems, but it causes others.

PRACTICE 1

Read the following model tasks. Do the exercises that follow each one.

MODEL TASK 2

Summarize the main points of the reading passage, and explain how they are supported by the information presented in the lecture.

The author explains that animal-assisted therapy is used to improve emotional and physical health, and the speaker tells us about a study that showed positive effects of pet ownership on health.

The author explains how pets improve both emotional health and physical health. Pets are good companions for lonely people. They also give their owners things to do, like hobbies or club activities. In addition, pets are a comfort to anxious or worried people. Pets are good for physical health, as well. They help people with high blood pressure and heart problems. They help people stay physically active. They give people a chance to play. Finally, pet therapy is used with elderly people.

The speaker supports pet therapy. He describes a study where pets had a positive effect on the health of heart patients. Half the patients had a dog to take care of. The other half only got traditional treatment. After six months, the patients with pets had lower blood pressure, and they had lost more weight than the other patients. They felt happier, too. These are all things that can affect heart disease. This is a case that shows how pet therapy works to improve physical health.

(based on Reading 6, page 39, and Lecture 6, page 40)

REVISION CHECKLIST

■ **Content**
- ❏ Thesis Statement
- ❏ Topics that support the thesis
- ❏ Main ideas
- ❏ Supporting details

■ **Fluency and Cohesion**
- ❏ Transition words
- ❏ Grammar and Spelling
- ❏ Sentence variety

EXERCISES

1. Find the thesis statement. Underline it.
2. In the first paragraph, find the topics that support the thesis. Number them.
3. Put a check (✓) next to the main idea in the second paragraph. Mark each supporting detail with a letter: A, B, C, etc.
4. Put a check (✓) next to the main idea in the third paragraph. Mark each supporting detail with a letter: A, B, C, etc.
5. Underline all transition words in the second and third paragraphs.
6. Check grammar and spelling. Correct any errors.
7. Find and mark one simple sentence (ss), one compound sentence (cm/s) and one sentence with an adjective clause (adj.c).

MODEL TASK 3

Summarize the main points in the reading passage and explain how the information presented in the lecture adds to them.

The author warns that ocean pollution is a serious problem. In the same way, the speaker explains how plastic garbage threatens sea animals.

The author explains that different things cause ocean pollution. Oil from factories and cities enters the ocean through rivers and drains. **Similarly,** fertilizers wash into the ocean, and they cause large growths of algae. Toxic chemicals continue to pollute the ocean, **as well.** There are laws against dumping these chemicals, but the chemicals still leak into the ocean. Animals eat them, and when we eat seafood, we eat these chemicals, **too.** There is **also** a lot of garbage in the ocean. Plastic is the worst kind because it does not break down quickly. Animals think it is food. They eat it and choke on it.

While the author gives an overview of ocean pollution, the speaker specifically describes the problem of plastic garbage. People produce billions of pounds of plastic a year, and a lot of this ends up in the ocean. The water and wind break large pieces of plastic into smaller pieces. **Then** animals try to eat these pieces. An animal may choke on plastic. It may starve because it does not feel hungry after eating plastic. Animals are often caught in floating plastic. They are also strangled by it. There are many types of pollution in the ocean. Plastic garbage is one of the worst examples.

(based on Reading 7, page 40, and Lecture 7, page 41)

REVISION CHECKLIST

■ **Content**
- ❏ Thesis Statement
- ❏ Topics that support the thesis
- ❏ Main ideas
- ❏ Supporting details

■ **Fluency and Cohesion**
- ❏ Transition words
- ❏ Grammar and Spelling
- ❏ Sentence variety

EXERCISES

1. Find the thesis statement. Underline it.
2. In the first paragraph, find the topics that support the thesis. Number them.
3. Put a check (✓) next to the main idea in the second paragraph. Mark each supporting detail with a letter: A, B, C, etc.
4. Put a check (✓) next to the main idea in the third paragraph. Mark each supporting detail with a letter: A, B, C, etc.
5. Underline all transition words in the second and third paragraphs.
6. Check grammar and spelling. Correct any errors.
7. Find and mark one compound sentence (cm/s), one complex sentence (cx/s), and one simple sentence (ss).

MODEL TASK 4

Summarize the main points of the reading passage and explain how the points made in the lecture cast doubt on them.

The author explains that color has psychological effects. In contrast, the speaker tells us about a study that showed no effect of color on appetite.

The author describes different ways people have used the psychological effects of color. Ancient people used color for healing, and modern designers use color to create mood. Designers might use yellow to create a positive mood in an office. Likewise, they might use neutral colors to create a clean, clear, and focused mood in health care centers. Restaurants often use orange and red to stimulate the appetite. Some scientists say that blue lowers the heart rate and blood pressure. Red, on the other hand, raises blood pressure. Other scientists do not believe that color affects mood. They say the effect is temporary and also that it is different in every culture.

The speaker describes a study that showed no relationship between color and appetite. A fast-food restaurant chain had orange walls in half its restaurants and beige walls in the rest of its restaurants. It recorded all the food ordered for two years. There was no difference between the restaurants with orange walls and the restaurants with beige walls. People ordered the same food in both types of places. In other words, according to the company president, there is no effect of color on appetite. He said that the study proved it. In this case, at least, there was no psychological effect of color.

(based on Reading 8 and Lecture 8, page 41)

REVISION CHECKLIST

■ **Content**
- ❑ Thesis Statement
- ❑ Topics that support the thesis
- ❑ Main ideas
- ❑ Supporting details

■ **Fluency and Cohesion**
- ❑ Transition words
- ❑ Grammar and Spelling
- ❑ Sentence variety

EXERCISES

1. Find the thesis statement. Underline it.
2. In the first paragraph, find the topics that support the thesis. Number them.
3. Put a check (✓) next to the main idea in the second paragraph. Mark each supporting detail with a letter: A, B, C, etc.
4. Put a check (✓) next to the main idea in the third paragraph. Mark each supporting detail with a letter: A, B, C, etc.
5. Underline all transition words in the second and third paragraphs.
6. Check grammar and spelling. Correct any errors.
7. Find and mark one compound sentence (cm/s), one sentence with a noun clause (nc), and one simple sentence (ss).

 **PRACTICE 2**

Complete each essay by answering the questions that follow.

ESSAY 1

Summarize the main points of the reading passage and explain how they are strengthened by the information presented in the lecture.

The author explains why global warming is a serious problem. (1) _____, the speaker explains the impact of global warming in the northeastern United States.

(2) _____. Greenhouse gases, such as carbon dioxide, hold heat in the atmosphere and result in rising temperatures on Earth. As average temperatures rise, there are a number of effects. (3) _____, scientists predict that weather patterns will change. In addition, snow and ice will melt and sea levels will rise. This can lead to flooding, drought, and powerful storms. It can also affect the economy, particularly agriculture and transportation. (4) _____.

The speaker explains the effects of global warming in the northeastern part of the United States. This is a cold and snowy area. (5) _____. There are also fewer days with snow on the ground than there used to be. This has an effect on the economy because many people in this part of the world depend on the ski industry to make a living. The predicted effects of global warming that the author described are already coming true, at least in the northeastern United States.

1. Choose the best way to complete the thesis statement.

   (A) In contrast
   (B) As a result
   (C) Likewise

2. Choose the best main idea for this paragraph.

   (A) The author explains that human activity, such as industry and cutting down forests, has resulted in an artificial increase in greenhouse gases in Earth's atmosphere, with serious results.
   (B) The author explains that it is difficult for scientists to come to agreement about whether or not global warming is actually occurring in the world today.
   (C) The author explains that some people believe that greenhouse gases are very harmful, while others are sure that global warming is not such a very serious problem.

3. Choose the best transition word for this sentence.

   (A) Nevertheless
   (B) First
   (C) However

4. Choose the missing supporting detail.

   (A) People will be better off economically, especially farmers.

   (B) Economists predict that global warming will lead to a drop in gross national product and consumer consumption in countries around the world.

   (C) Warmer temperatures will result in people using transportation more often as they will take more frequent vacations.

5. Choose the missing supporting detail.

   (A) Since 1965, many people have moved to this part of the country.

   (B) Since 1965, there has been a decrease in employment in this area.

   (C) Since 1965, temperatures in this region have risen.

ESSAY 2

Summarize the main points of the reading passage and explain how they are supported by the information presented in the lecture.

The reading passage talks about camouflage as a key survival strategy used by many animals. (6) _____.

The author explains how camouflage helps animals survive. There are different kinds of camouflage. Some animals are similar in color to their surroundings. Deer, (7) _____, have brown fur, which helps them blend in with their forest habitat. Some arctic animals, such as the arctic hare, change color with the seasons. (8) _____. Striped zebras and fish with shiny scales are two examples of this. Some animals are mimics, taking on characteristics of another object or animal in their environment. The green anole, a type of lizard, looks like a leaf. The caterpillar of the hawk moth resembles a snake. Camouflage is important to both predators and prey. It helps predators to be invisible to their victims, and it helps prey animals to hide from the animals that hunt them.

The speaker talks about how camouflage helps certain animals hide in the arctic environment. Many of them are brown in the summer to match their summer environment and white in the winter when snow covers the ground. One example is the arctic fox. (9) _____. It is also a prey animal and needs to hide from its predators. When winter approaches, the fox sheds its brown fur and grows white fur. (10) _____ animal that does this is the lemming. It needs to be brown in the summer and white in the winter in order to hide from its main predator—the arctic fox.

6. Choose the best way to complete the thesis statement.

   (A) Additionally, the speaker discusses other survival tactics used by animals.

   (B) Similarly, the speaker talks about the way that several arctic animals use camouflage for survival.

   (C) In contrast, the speaker explains how predators attack their prey.

7. Choose the best transition word for this sentence.

   (A) for example

   (B) on the other hand

   (C) in addition

8. Choose the missing supporting detail.

(A) Some herd animals have patterns on their fur that make it very easy to see them in any season of the year.

(B) Some herd animals have patterns on their fur that make them very beautiful to look at.

(C) Some herd animals have patterns on their fur that make it difficult for predators to pick out one animal from the group.

9. Choose the missing supporting detail.

(A) It looks very nice in the winter when it plays in the snow.

(B) It is a predator, so it needs to be invisible to its prey while it hunts.

(C) In the summer it eats berries and other fruits and vegetation.

10. Choose the best transition word for this sentence.

(A) Another

(B) However

(C) Furthermore

ESSAY 3

Summarize the main points of the reading passage and explain how the points made in the lecture oppose them.

(11) _____. In contrast, the lecture reports evidence that girls and women do better in school than boys and men.

The author describes research done by a psychologist who claims that men have higher intelligence than women. The psychologist studied the results of intelligence tests taken by university students aged 17 and 18. (12) _____. Furthermore, more men than women qualify as geniuses. The psychologist suggests that the reason for men's higher intelligence is their larger brain size.

(13) _____. In the first place, study after study has shown that girls outperform boys in elementary school. (14) _____, in high schools all around the country there are far more girls than boys in advanced-level classes. (15) _____. Each year, 170,000 more women than men earn college degrees. The facts presented by the lecturer completely contradict the results of the study described in the reading passage.

11. Choose the best way to complete the thesis statement.

(A) The reading passage describes a study which claims that men are more intelligent than women.

(B) The reading passage describes a study proving that girls are better students than boys.

(C) The reading passage describes a study of different educational methods used in schools around the country.

12. Choose the missing supporting detail.

(A) Some researchers believe that IQ tests are not a valid measure of an individual's intelligence.

(B) Some schools these days use intelligence tests to evaluate their students' academic potential.

(C) The results showed that the IQs of the men averaged four points higher than the IQs of the women.

13. Choose the missing main idea.

   (A) The lecturer agrees that among school children, girls are generally smarter than boys.
   (B) The lecturer has a contradictory viewpoint, discussing evidence that girls are better students than boys.
   (C) The lecturer contradicts the author, stating that girls take more tests in school than boys do.

14. Choose the best transition word for this sentence.

   (A) In addition
   (B) In contrast
   (C) In other words

15. Choose the missing supporting detail.

   (A) Finally, the same number of women as men attend college.
   (B) Finally, more than 60% of college students are women.
   (C) Finally, both men and women have found success in college.

ESSAY 4

Summarize the main points of the reading passage and explain how the points made in the lecture cast doubt on them.

The reading passage describes the benefits of genetically modified foods. The lecture, (16) _____, discusses the disadvantages of these foods.

The author explains what genetically modified foods are and describes the advantages they have for food production and health. (17) _____. Some crops are genetically modified to be resistant to disease. As a result, they are easier to cultivate and farmers can grow larger crops. Other crops are genetically modified to contain more vitamins and minerals. Golden rice, (18) _____, has been modified to contain more vitamin A. Additionally, some genetically modified crops are used to develop new products. Scientists are currently working on a banana, for example, that can be used to produce vaccines against serious diseases.

(19) _____. In the first place, some crops have been genetically modified to be resistant to insects, but their genes could actually be transferred to those insects. Then the insects would be resistant to insecticides, and the crops would not be protected. (20) _____, the effects of genetically modified foods on our health are not yet known, but there are serious possibilities. Some examples are the development of allergies and of resistance to antibiotics. Finally, many people are concerned that widespread use of genetically modified foods would allow a few large companies to dominate food production. According to the speaker, genetically modified foods may cause more problems than they solve.

16. Choose the best way to complete the thesis statement.

   (A) on the other hand
   (B) therefore
   (C) similarly

17. Choose the missing supporting detail.

   (A) Genetically modified foods have a number of advantages and disadvantages.
   (B) Genetically modified foods are available for sale in most grocery stores.
   (C) Genetically modified foods come from crops that have had their genes altered by technology.

18. Choose the best transition word for this sentence.

   (A) for instance
   (B) however
   (C) likewise

19. Choose the missing main idea.

   (A) The speaker discusses some serious problems with genetically modified foods.
   (B) The speaker believes that genetically modified foods have many advantages.
   (C) The speaker mentions that corn and soybeans are crops that are often genetically modified.

20. Choose the best transition word for this sentence.

   (A) Consequently
   (B) Furthermore
   (C) Although

 **PRACTICE 3**

Read the following essay and use the revision checklist to identify what is missing or incorrect. Then revise the essay, adding the missing parts and correcting the errors. Write the revised essay on your computer or on a piece of paper.

REVISION CHECKLIST

■ **Content**
- ❏ Thesis Statement
- ❏ Topics that support the thesis
- ❏ Main ideas
- ❏ Supporting details

■ **Fluency and Cohesion**
- ❏ Transition words
- ❏ Grammar and Spelling
- ❏ Sentence variety

Summarize the main points of the reading passage and explain how they are supported by the information presented in the lecture.

The reading passage explains why farming is difficult in far northern regions in general. The lecture is similar.

In the first place, the growing season is very short. It might last three months or less, which is not enough time for most crops to mature. Additionally, few people live in northern regions because the cold weather is not attractive. Therefore, farmers have to pay to transport their crops long distances to cities where they can sell them to a larger market. Consequently, the harsh climate causes farm machinery to break down frequently. The cost to repair or replace specialized farm equipment can to be very high.

The speaker discusses farmers working in a particular northern province. He explains that many people have stopped farming in that area because they are no longer able to make a living that way. One reason is the disease affecting the rye crop, one of the few crops that can be grown so far north. Another reason is the rising cost of transportation. Fewer and fewer farmers can afford to ship their crops to cities. Although, because of the losses due to the rye disease, many farmers have difficulty paying the cost of maintaining their buildings and equipment. For reasons similar to those outlined in the reading passage, many people in this northern province is leaving their farms to look for jobs in towns and cities.

Missing items:

Paragraph 1: _____

Paragraph 2: _____

Paragraph 3: _____

Grammar and vocabulary errors:

Paragraph 1: _____

Paragraph 2: _____

Paragraph 3: _____

CHECK THE SPELLING AND PUNCTUATION
Spelling

Remember that there is no spell checker on the computer that you will use during the TOEFL iBT. You must work to improve your spelling before you take the test. Whenever you read in English, pay close attention to words. This will help you understand English spelling patterns. You should be able to spell the most common English words before you take the test.

Here are some hints for succeeding with spelling on the Integrated Task.

- Pay special attention to how key words in the Reading passage are spelled.
- Take careful notes on the spelling of these words.
- Listen for these same words as you take notes during the Lecture.
- When you revise your essay, check your spelling against your notes.

NOTE

You will not be penalized if you use a space between paragraphs instead of indents. Also, remember that proper nouns are capitalized.

Punctuation

Also, whenever you read in English, pay attention to punctuation. This will help you when writing your response. There are three important things to remember about punctuation when you write your responses.

- **Indent each paragraph or use a space between paragraphs.**
  This will help the reader determine when you are starting a new topic.

- **Capitalize the first word of each sentence.**
  This will help the reader determine when you are starting a new sentence.

- **Put a period or question mark at the end of each sentence or question.**
  This will help the reader determine when you are ending a sentence or question.

Here are some other forms of punctuation that will help make your response easier to read.

TIP

Commas help the reader follow your ideas, but be careful not to use them where they are not needed.

COMMA

Use a comma in a list of three or more things. It is optional to put a comma before the *and*.

Plants require sunlight, water, and soil.
It was an educational, interesting and entertaining program.

Use a comma between a noun and a following description.

The Baltic Sea, in northern Europe, is polluted with trash.
The study participants, teenagers sixteen to eighteen, were asked about smoking habits.

Use a comma to separate transition words, adjectives, or participles that are not part of the sentence or were added for emphasis.

Unfortunately, the success of the program did not last.
The effects on the local ecology, however, can be devastating, very devastating.

Use a comma between two independent clauses.

> Office workers need to take frequent breaks, and they should use ergonomic equipment.
> Many teens saw the ads, but only a few quit smoking.

Use a comma to separate a non-restrictive clause.

> Elderly people, who are often lonely, can benefit from pet therapy.
> The study, which included all of the company's restaurants, looked at color of the walls and how this affected sales.

Use a comma after a subordinate clause at the beginning of a sentence.

> If the store environment is pleasant, shoppers may spend more money.
> Because we produce so much plastic, it ends up in the oceans.

SEMICOLON

Use a semicolon to separate two closely related sentences.

> Some people thought the program was successful; others disagreed.

COLON OR DASH

Use a colon or dash in front of a list or explanation.

> There are three things retailers can use to improve the store environment: color, lighting, and music.
> Invasive vines are considered a threat for a very good reason—they strangle native plants.

TIP

You can find a list of commonly confused words here:

barronsbooks.com/ TP/TOEFL/Writing

 **PRACTICE 4**

Read the following sentences. Some have misspelled words. Revise the sentences, correcting the spelling. If a sentence has no misspelled words, write "correct."

1. Garlic mustard is a problm in the U.S. because it threatens other spring-bluming plants by taking up lite, nutrients, and espace.

   _____

   _____

   _____

2. Garlic mustard also thretens the West Virginia wite butterfly. It compeats with another type of mustard which is the butterfly's food sourse.

   _____

   _____

   _____

3. Garlic mustard was first grown on Long Island for food and has since spread to other areas of the country.

   _____

   _____

   _____

4. Childrens can learn new thins from TV.

   _____

   _____

   _____

5. The amownt of time spent waching TV is important.

   _____

   _____

   _____

6. More than three hours a day of TV watching results in louer reading and mathes test scors.

   _____

   _____

   _____

7. Surveys made at the end of an antiesmoking campane showed that more than 50% new about the campane and 40% would probably not smoke.

_____

_____

_____

8. Three months later, the numbers had changed.

_____

_____

_____

9. More than haf said they wood probaly smoke, and fewer than one-therd said they knew about the campaign.

_____

_____

_____

10. Reserch showd that slow music coused customers to stay at the restarant longer and order more food.

_____

_____

_____

11. Some of the study subjecs, college students, herd popular music in the store, and others heared older music.

_____

_____

_____

12. Those who heard familiar music shoped longer and said better things about the store's products.

_____

_____

_____

 **PRACTICE 5**

Read the following essays. Then revise the essays, adding punctuation and capitalization. Write on your computer or on a piece of paper.

ESSAY 1

Summarize the main points of the reading passage and explain how they are strengthened by the information presented in the lecture.

the author states that invasive plants harm native plants and the speaker explains that garlic mustard is an invasive species that causes problems.

gardeners have introduced nonnative plants for food and medicine. they have also planted them because they are hardy drought resistant or beautiful. however these plants escape from the garden and cause problems. invasive plants harm native species by shading them out strangling them or using up all the nutrients in the soil. the local ecology suffers because there are fewer native plants and animals lose their homes and food.

garlic mustard is an example of an invasive plant that harms the local ecology. it threatens other spring-blooming plants by taking up light nutrients and space. it also threatens the West Virginia white butterfly by competing with another type of mustard which is the butterfly's food source. garlic mustard was first grown on long island for food and has since spread to other areas of the country.

(based on Reading 1 and Lecture 1, page 35; see Summary 1 on page 56)

ESSAY 2

Summarize the main points in the reading passage and explain how the points made in the lecture oppose them.

the author believes that TV viewing has negative effects on children's school performance. The speaker on the other hand proposes that TV watching can actually improve school performance.

according to the author children who have TV sets in their bedrooms do not do as well in school as their classmates. some people think of TV as educational but the author asserts that most children's TV programs do not have "valuable content." in addition TV takes time away from important activities like doing homework or being with other people. parents can help their children by turning off the television.

the lecturer does not agree with this point of view. it is his opinion that children actually can learn new things from watching TV. he points out however that the amount of time spent watching TV is important. he says that more than three hours a day of TV watching can result in lower reading and math scores.

(based on Reading 2 and Lecture 2, page 36; see Summary 2 on page 57)

ESSAY 3

Summarize the main points in the reading passage and explain how the points made in the lecture cast doubt on them.

the author tells us about particular smoking prevention campaign aimed at young people that has been successful. in contrast the speaker warns us that initial results of public health campaigns can be misleading.

the antismoking campaign described in the passage included advertising no-smoking policies and antismoking events. many teens participated in the events and many more saw the ads. the public health department plans to continue with this successful campaign to improve public health among young people in the state.

the speaker warns us that we can be deceived by the initial results of public health campaigns He mentioned a recent antismoking campaign as an example. surveys made at the end of the campaign showed that 50% knew about the campaign and 40% would probably not smoke. three months later however the numbers had changed. many more said they would probably smoke and many fewer said they knew about the campaign. so a public health campaign that looks successful at first can look less successful a few months later.

(based on Reading 3 and Lecture 3, page 36; see Summary 3 on page 58)

ESSAY 4

Summarize the main points of the reading passage and explain how they are supported by the information presented in the lecture.

the author proposes that a good mood makes shoppers buy more. similarly the speaker explains that studies show that music can make consumers spend more time shopping.

the reading passage explains that a shopper's mood may be influenced by things that retailers cannot control such as the weather or personal or work problems. retailers can however influence shoppers' moods by controlling the store environment. shoppers buy more when retailers use lighting color and music to improve shopper mood.

the speaker describes research about the effect of music on consumers. research showed that slow music caused customers to stay at a restaurant longer and order more food. in another study some of the subjects college students heard popular music in a store and others heard older music. those who heard familiar music shopped longer and said better things about the store's products. these two studies show that restaurant and store owners can influence shoppers' moods and encourage them to buy more.

(based on Reading 4 and Lecture 4, page 37; see Summary 4 on page 59)

EXTRA PRACTICE

Study the model tasks on pages 60, 65, 66, and 67. Circle all the punctuation.

PRACTICE INTEGRATED TASK

Read the passage for three minutes.

Take notes as you read the passage and listen to the lecture. Then read the instructions and write an essay in response. Write 150–225 words. Remember to divide your writing time as follows:

STEP 1	PLAN	3 minutes
STEP 2	WRITE	14 minutes
STEP 3	REVISE	3 minutes

Many people agree that the most important invention of the late twentieth century was the cell phone. Cell phones have now become a regular part of daily life. Cell phones have made many things much more convenient, but they have also brought new dangers to our lives.

Cell phone use has risen dramatically everywhere over the past several years. In the United States alone, just fifteen years ago, there were 4.3 million cell phone users. Today more than 224 million people use cell phones in this country. Everywhere we go—restaurants, stores, buses, parks, offices, schools—people are talking on their cell phones.

Cell phones have made many things more convenient for people, but they have also raised some serious safety concerns, most notably for drivers. Talking on the phone distracts the driver's attention from the road, and cell phones have been blamed for many traffic accidents. In several cases, drivers in accidents involving cell phones have been successfully sued by the victims. Employers have also been held liable for accidents involving cell phones and caused by their employees.

In response to such concerns, laws have been passed restricting cell phone use while driving. In some places, talking on the phone while driving is completely prohibited. In other places, use of a headset is required. Some places allow talking on the phone while driving but fine drivers responsible for crashes involving phones. In other places, drivers may lose their automobile insurance if they were talking on the phone when involved in an accident. In as many as 40 countries around the world, there are laws restricting or prohibiting the use of cell phones while driving.

 **LECTURE**

Track 10

Listen to the lecture.

Summarize the main points of the reading passage and explain how the points made in the lecture cast doubt on them. Write on your computer or on a piece of paper. Write for no more than 20 minutes.

TIP

Need help with pronouns? See page 148 for information on using pronouns.

Writing Skills: Independent Task

4

WRITE A THESIS STATEMENT

The Independent Task is different from the Integrated Task because it is more personal. In the Integrated Task, you write about other people's ideas, but in the Independent Task, you write about your own ideas. In the Independent Task, you are asked to explain your own ideas about a topic. Your opinion about the topic is the thesis of your essay.

Before you write your thesis statement, you have to read the topic carefully and make sure you understand what it asks you to do. Following are the types of topics that generally appear on the TOEFL Independent Writing task.

POINT OF VIEW This is the most common type of topic. It asks you to describe and support your point of view about something. The question may be stated in one of several ways. Each one asks you to respond in a certain way. You may be asked to

- agree or disagree with a statement
- choose which point of view you agree with or which situation you prefer ·
- say whether you support or oppose something
- compare two points of view or preferences and explain which you agree with

EXPLAIN SOMETHING This type of topic asks you to describe a type of person, place, or situation and/or explain the reasons for something.

IMAGINARY SITUATION This type of topic asks you to imagine a situation and describe what you would do.

> **NOTE**
>
> Remember that a *thesis statement* is what you plan to write about—it is your main idea statement for the whole essay.

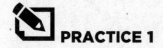 **PRACTICE 1**

Choose the topic type for each of the following topics. Write the correct letter next to each topic.

A. Agree or disagree with a statement
B. Choose which point of view you agree with or which situation you prefer
C. Say whether you support or oppose something
D. Compare two points of view or preferences and explain which you agree with
E. Explain Something
F. Imagine a Situation

1. ESSAY TOPIC 43

Some people say that physical exercise should be a required part of every school day. Other people believe that students should spend the whole day on academic studies. Which opinion do you agree with? Give specific reasons and details to support your answer. *D*

2. ESSAY TOPIC 24

If you could study a subject that you have never had the opportunity to study, what would you choose? *F*

3. ESSAY TOPIC 16

It has recently been announced that a new movie theater may be built in your neighborhood. Do you support or oppose this plan? Why? Use specific reasons and details to support your answer. *A*

4. ESSAY TOPIC 13

In general, people are living longer now. Discuss the causes of this phenomenon. Use specific reasons and details to develop your essay. *E*

5. ESSAY TOPIC 22

Do you agree or disagree with the following statement? Businesses should do anything they can to make a profit. Use specific reasons and examples to support your position. *C*

6. ESSAY TOPIC 31

Many students have to live with a roommate while going to school or university. What are some of the important qualities of a good roommate? Use specific reasons and examples to explain why these qualities are important. *E*

7. ESSAY TOPIC 39

Some people choose friends who are different from themselves. Others choose friends who are similar to themselves. Compare the advantages of having friends who are different from you with the advantages of having friends who are similar to you. Which kind of friend do you prefer for yourself? Why? *D*

8. ESSAY TOPIC 49

Imagine that you have received some land to use as you wish. How would you use the land? Use specific details to explain your answer. *F*

Once you understand the topic, you can write your thesis statement. The thesis statement focuses the direction of the essay. It tells the reader what your essay is about.

Look at these example topics to see how different thesis statements can come from the same topic.

ESSAY TOPIC 33

> **You have been told that dormitory rooms at your university must be shared by two students. Would you rather have the university assign a student to share a room with you, or would you rather choose your own roommate? Use specific reasons and details to explain your answer.**

Thesis Statement A

Since I would like to live with a neat and organized person like myself, I prefer to choose my own roommate.

From this statement, we can infer that the writer will discuss why he or she wants a neat and organized person as a roommate.

Thesis Statement B

The opportunity to meet new people is an important benefit of a university education, so I believe it is better to let the university choose my roommate for me.

From this statement, we can presume the writer will discuss the benefits of meeting new people at a university.

A thesis statement must be on the topic. Pay close attention to what the topic asks you to do.

ESSAY TOPIC 32

> **Some people think governments should spend as much money as possible exploring outer space (for example, traveling to the moon and to other planets). Other people disagree and think governments should spend this money for our basic needs on Earth. Which of these two opinions do you agree with? Use specific reasons and details to support your answer.**

Thesis Statement A

The moon is a better place to explore because it is nearer than the planets.

This is NOT a good thesis statement for the topic. It uses some words from the topic to make a statement about exploration possibilities. It does not do what the topic asks—to state which of the two opinions the writer agrees with.

Thesis Statement B

While there is still hunger, poverty, and illiteracy on Earth, our resources should be focused here and not in outer space.

This statement does what the topic asks—it says which of the two opinions the writer agrees with. From this statement, we can presume that the writer will discuss why she believes that hunger, poverty, and illiteracy are more worthy of attention than space exploration.

Thesis Statement C

Gaining psychological and scientific knowledge through space exploration will benefit us more than trying to solve problems here on Earth.

This statement also says which of the two opinions the writer agrees with. From this statement, we can presume that the writer will support the point of view that the psychological and scientific benefits we receive from space exploration are more important.

 **PRACTICE 2**

Choose the thesis statements that are appropriate to the topic. There can be more than one possible answer.

1. What is one of the most important decisions you have made? Why was this decision important? Use specific reasons and details to explain your answer.

   (A) Decisions are important because without them nothing would get done.

   (B) Deciding to leave home to attend school in the U.S. has been so far the most important decision I've made.

   (C) It is difficult to make important decisions, especially when you are young and have your whole future ahead of you.

2. Someone who was considered an educated person in the past (for example, in your parents' or grandparents' generation) would not be considered an educated person today. Do you agree or disagree? Use specific reasons and examples to support your answer.

   (A) If you define education as earning degrees, than I would have to agree that today people are more educated then they were in the past.

   (B) It was more difficult to get an education in the past since there weren't as many schools.

   (C) Both my grandfather and my grandmother attended university, which is where they met.

3. If you could make one important change in a school that you attended, what change would you make? Use reasons and specific examples to support your answer.

   (A) There have been many changes to the school I attended since I graduated three years ago.

   (B) If I could help change things at my old school with ideas, money, or time, I would be glad to do it.

   (C) If I could change one thing at my high school, it would be the size of the classes, which were much too large.

4. In the future, students may have the choice of studying at home by using technology such as computers or television or of studying at traditional schools. Which would you prefer? Use reasons and specific details to explain your choice.

   (A) Interaction with my fellow students is important to me so I would prefer to study in a more traditional setting.

   (B) Computers and television are two examples of technology that will change a lot in the future.

   (C) Technological advances have already made home education a real possibility for many people.

5. It has recently been announced that a large shopping center may be built in your neighborhood. Do you support or oppose this plan? Why? Use specific reasons and details to support your answer.

(A) Large shopping centers have been built in communities all around the world.

(B) While there would be both advantages and disadvantages to having a shopping center built in my neighborhood, I think that overall the advantages are greater.

(C) Many people still enjoy doing their shopping at large shopping centers, but more and more people are making most of their purchases on the Internet.

EXTRA PRACTICE

Do any or all of the following activities on your own or in a group. There are no answers provided.

1. Write your own thesis statement for the five topics above.
2. Write essays on the above topics. Allow yourself no more than 30 minutes to write each essay. Write about 300 words.

MAKE NOTES ABOUT GENERAL IDEAS AND SPECIFIC DETAILS

In the Integrated Task, you make notes about what you read in the reading passage and what you hear in the lecture. Your notes are about other people's ideas. In the Independent Task, you write your own ideas about your own opinion. You make notes as a way of organizing your ideas before you write. When you wrote your thesis statement, you wrote your opinion about a subject. Now you will write notes about your ideas that explain your opinion.

Just as in the Integrated Task, you can use either an outline or an idea map to organize your ideas for the Independent Task. Both outlines and idea maps help you organize your thoughts into a thesis, topics (general ideas), and details (supporting statements). Use whichever form works best for you.

As a rule, you should try to have three general ideas per essay and at least two supporting details per general idea. This will vary according to your topic and the way you choose to organize it.

Outlines

Look at the following examples of outlines and essays for specific topics.

ESSAY TOPIC 52

> The twentieth century saw great change. In your opinion, what is one change that should be remembered about the twentieth century? Use specific reasons and details to explain your choice.

Thesis	Medical advances are the most important change.	
Paragraph 1	**Main idea**	Vaccines and antibiotics have saved lives
	Supporting details	(1) Polio vaccine
		(2) Penicillin
Paragraph 2	**Main idea**	Increased access to health care
	Supporting details	(1) More clinics and hospitals
		(2) Easier to get treatment
Paragraph 3	**Main idea**	Improved surgical techniques
	Supporting details	(1) Microscopic and laser surgery easier to perform
		(2) Patients recover faster

Compare the outline with the following essay.

Medical Advances: An Important Change of the Twentieth Century

There were many important changes, both technological and cultural, during the twentieth century. In my opinion, the most important of these are the advances that were made in medical science. The development of vaccines and antibiotics, increased access to health care, and improvements in surgical techniques are all things that improved, and saved, the lives of people all around the world.

Vaccines and antibiotics have saved the lives of many people. Until the middle of the twentieth century, many people became crippled or died from polio. Now the polio vaccine is available everywhere. In the past, people could die from even simple infections. Now penicillin and other antibiotics make it easy to cure infections.

Increased access to health care has also improved the lives of millions of people. In the past, many people lived far from hospitals and clinics. Now hospitals, clinics, and health centers have been built in many parts of the world. More people have the opportunity to visit a doctor or nurse before they become very sick. They can be treated more easily. They are sick less, and this leads to a better quality of life.

Improved surgical techniques make it easier to treat many medical problems. Microscopic and laser surgery techniques are more efficient than older methods. It is easier for the doctor to perform them, and easier for the patient to recover. Surgery patients can return to their normal lives more quickly now than they could in the past.

Everybody needs good health in order to have a good quality of life. Advances in medical science have improved the lives of people all around the world. They are improvements that are important to everyone.

SAMPLE ESSAY TOPIC

> Think of the most important class you have ever had. Why did you enjoy this class so much? Use specific reasons and details to explain your answer.

Thesis		I learned a lot in Intro. to Art History, and it was inspiring.
Paragraph 1	**Main idea**	Art History teaches you about more than art.
	Supporting details	(1) History, religion, literature, mythology
		(2) I didn't learn these things in my engineering classes
Paragraph 2	**Main idea**	I had a very good teacher.
	Supporting details	(1) Experienced and well known
		(2) Enthusiastic and inspiring
Paragraph 3	**Main idea**	I learned about the history of engineering.
	Supporting details	(1) Buildings and bridges
		(2) City planning

Compare the outline with the following essay.

Art History

Even though I am an engineer, I have to say that Introduction to Art History is the most important class I have ever taken. In this class I had the opportunity to learn new things, not only about art, but about other areas as well. I had a teacher who inspired me. And, believe it or not, it was important to my career as an engineer.

The course not only had interesting content but also a very inspiring teacher. My art history professor had a lot of enthusiasm for her subject, and she was able to convey that enthusiasm to her students. Even though I am in a different field, this professor was a sort of role model for me. It is always inspiring to see people who love their work, no matter what it is. As I pursue my career as an engineer, I often think of this professor and hope that I bring the same enthusiasm to my own work.

Art History should be a required course for everyone because it teaches you about so many things. I learned not only about art, but also about history, religion, literature, and mythology. These are subjects I didn't learn about in my engineering classes, so it was a wonderful opportunity for me.

Studying art history taught me some things about the history of engineering. In old paintings, I saw how buildings and bridges were built in the past. I saw how cities were planned. I realized that I could learn about my own field in different ways.

I learned a lot of things in my art history class. I learned about art, about engineering, and about other things I hadn't imagined. Both the subject and the teacher inspired me to expand my mind. I am very glad that I took this class.

NOTE

Because the Independent Tasks are personal in nature, the sample responses include some contractions.

 **PRACTICE 3**

Read each essay. Then complete the missing parts of each outline.

ESSAY TOPIC 30

> Some people prefer to live in places that have the same weather or climate all year long. Others like to live in areas where the weather changes several times a year. Which do you prefer? Use specific reasons and examples to support your choices.

If I could choose a place to live according to climate alone, I would definitely live in a place that has warm weather all year. It would make my life much easier and more comfortable. I would be healthier, have more fun, and save money if I lived in a warm climate.

I would always be healthy if I lived in a warm climate. Where I live now the winters are long and cold, so I get sick every winter. I often miss days of school because I get bad colds. I wouldn't have this problem in a warm climate. Also, in a warm climate I would be able to be outside all year long. I would play sports and get exercise everyday. That would make me healthier, too.

I would have more fun if I lived in a warm climate. I really enjoy outdoor activities such as going to the beach, playing soccer, and riding my bicycle. I can't do these things when the weather is cold, which means I can't do them at all during the winter in a cold climate. In a warm climate, I would be able to enjoy my favorite activities all year.

I would save money if I lived in a warm climate. It costs money to heat the house during cold winters, and this can get very expensive. In a warm climate I would not have to worry about this expense. It also costs money to buy new clothes every time the season changes. This is another expense I wouldn't have to worry about in a warm climate because I could wear the same clothes all year.

My life would be better if I lived in a warm climate. My health, my free time activities, and my bank account would all improve. In fact, I plan to move to a warm climate as soon as I finish school.

Thesis		I prefer to live in a warm climate.
Paragraph 1	**Main idea**	(1) _____
	Supporting details	Now I get sick every winter
		I could be outside all year
Paragraph 2	**Main idea**	I would have more fun.
	Supporting details	(2) _____
		Favorite activities all year
Paragraph 3	**Main idea**	I would save money.
	Supporting details	(3) _____
		No need to buy new clothes

> Some people like doing work by hand. Others prefer using machines. Which do you prefer? Use specific reasons and examples to support your answer.

I prefer using machines to doing work by hand. Machines can work faster than I can work by hand. They can also work more neatly. Most of all, machines never get tired.

Machines are fast. If I want to make a dress, it would take me hours and hours working with a needle and thread to make each stitch by hand. If I use a sewing machine, however, I can make a dress in an hour or less. If I want to build something out of wood, I could cut each piece with a handsaw. That would take a very long time. But a power saw cuts much more quickly. When I bake a cake, I can stir in each ingredient by hand, or I can use an electric mixer, which makes the work go so much faster.

Machines are neat. They never make mistakes. Every line or cut is neat, straight, and in the right place. Machines don't get distracted and spill coffee all over the work or cut something the wrong size or add the wrong ingredients. Machines can do the same job over and over again, each time as neatly as the time before. I could never be as neat as a machine.

Machines never get tired. I can use my sewing machine to sew one seam or ten. The machine never gets tired of pushing the needle and thread through the fabric. The power saw doesn't slow down because it has cut too many pieces of wood. A machine keeps working with the same amount of energy until the job is done, and doesn't even need to stop for a rest break.

I can depend on machines to do the job right each time, but I can't always depend on myself to be fast, neat, and tireless.

Paragraph 1	**Main idea**	Machines are fast.
	Supporting details	Sew a dress
		Build with wood
		(4) _____
Paragraph 2	**Main idea**	(5) _____
	Supporting details	No mistakes
		Not distracted
		All jobs neat
Paragraph 3	**Main idea**	Machines don't get tired.
	Supporting details	Sewing machines
		(6) _____

PRACTICE 4

Create an outline for each of the following topics. Photocopy the blank outline on this page as many times as you need and use the copies for writing your outlines. You may have two or more main ideas for each topic and two or more supporting details for each main idea. Then write an essay from each of your outlines. Allow yourself no more than 30 minutes to write. Write about 300 words. Compare your essays with the essays for those topics in the Model Essay section beginning on page 177.

NOTE

In the Independent Task essay, there is no right or wrong opinion. The task measures your ability to express your opinion in writing, to explain your opinions clearly, and to back your opinion with supporting details.

Thesis _____

Paragraph 1   Main idea _____

        Supporting details   (1) _____

                         (2) _____

                         (3) _____

Paragraph 2   Main idea _____

        Supporting details   (1) _____

                         (2) _____

                         (3) _____

Paragraph 3   Main idea _____

        Supporting details   (1) _____

                         (2) _____

                         (3) _____

ESSAY TOPIC 7

> Do you agree or disagree with the following statement? Universities should give the same amount of money to their students' sports activities as they give to their university libraries. Use specific reasons and examples to support your opinion.

ESSAY TOPIC 6

> Some people prefer to live in a small town. Others prefer to live in a big city. Which place would you prefer to live in? Use specific reasons and details to support your answer.

ESSAY TOPIC 5

> How do movies or television influence people's behavior? Use reasons and specific examples to explain your answer.

ESSAY TOPIC 49

> Imagine that you have received some land to use as you wish. How would you use this land? Use specific details to explain your answer.

Idea Maps

Look at the following examples of idea maps and essays for specific topics.

SAMPLE ESSAY TOPIC

> When choosing a place to live, what do you consider most important—location, size, style, number of rooms, types of rooms, or other features? Use reasons and specific examples to support your answer.

Idea Map

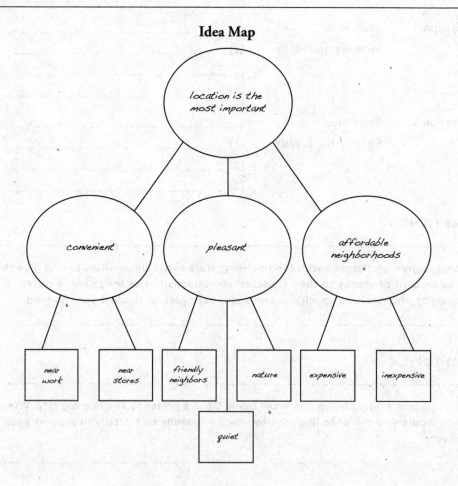

Compare the idea map with this essay.

House Hunting

When choosing a place to live, I look at several things. I need to consider price, size, and type of housing. However, the most important thing of all is location. I look for a house in a convenient and pleasant neighborhood that has rents I can afford to pay.

My apartment must be conveniently located. I don't have a car, so I want to be near my job. I want to be able to walk or take the bus to work. I don't have a lot of time for shopping, so I want to be near stores, too.

I want to live in a pleasant neighborhood. I like quiet areas with little traffic. I like to have nature around me, so I prefer a neighborhood with a lot of trees, gardens, and maybe even a park. Most of all, I want to have friendly neighbors.

Some neighborhoods are more expensive than others. I have to look for my apartment in neighborhoods that aren't too expensive. Some neighborhoods are very beautiful, but if the rents are too high, I can't afford to live there. If I only look in areas of the city that have affordable rents, I won't be disappointed.

The size of my apartment and the style of the building aren't important to me. I don't care if my apartment is small or if the building is old and in need of repair. If I can find an affordable place to live in a convenient and pleasant location, then I will have everything I need.

ESSAY TOPIC 1

People attend college or university for many different reasons. Why do you think people attend college or university? Use specific reasons and examples to support your answer.

Idea Map

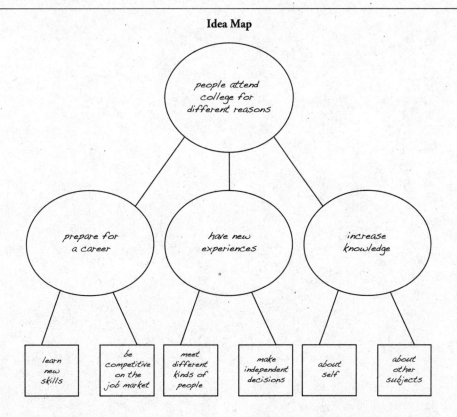

Compare the idea map with this essay.

Three Reasons People Attend College

People attend college for a lot of different reasons. I believe that the three most common reasons are to prepare for a career, to have new experiences, and to increase their knowledge of themselves and of the world around them.

Career preparation is probably the primary reason that people attend college. These days, the job market is very competitive. Careers such as information technology will need many new workers in the near future. At college, students can learn new skills for these careers and increase their opportunities for the future.

Students also go to college to have new experiences. For many, it is their first time away from home. At college, they can meet new people from many different places. They can see what life is like in a different city. They can learn to live on their own and take care of themselves without having their family always nearby.

At college, students have the opportunity to increase their knowledge. As they decide what they want to study, pursue their studies, and interact with their classmates, they learn a lot about themselves. They also, of course, have the opportunity to learn about many subjects in their classes. In addition to the skills and knowledge related to their career, college students also have the chance to take classes in other areas. For many, this will be their last chance to study different subjects.

Colleges offer much more than career preparation. They offer the opportunity to have new experiences and to learn many kinds of things. I think all of these are reasons why people attend college.

PRACTICE 5

Read each essay. Complete the missing parts of each idea map.

ESSAY TOPIC 37

> Some people prefer to spend time with one or two close friends. Others choose to spend time with a large number of friends. Compare the advantages of each choice. Which of these two ways of spending time do you prefer? Use specific reasons to support your answer.

We all need to have friends, and I think the more friends we have, the better. When you have a lot of friends, you are never alone. You always have people who will entertain you, people you can trust, and people who teach you about life.

I want to have a lot of people I can have fun with. If I have a lot of friends, I always have people to laugh and joke with me. I have people to go to the movies or the mall with me. I have people to go to parties with me. If I have only a few friends, they might be busy when I want to do these things, or they might not enjoy some of the things I enjoy.

I need to have a lot of people I can trust. If I have a problem, I want to share it with several friends. If I make a mistake or fail a test or have a fight with my parents, I need my friends to help me. I want to be able to pick up the phone and know I can easily find some friends to talk with. If I have only a few friends, they might not be available when I need them.

I like to have a lot of people who teach me about life. If I have a lot of friends, I have a lot of different people to learn from. Each person has different experiences and a different point of view. I can learn a lot of things from a lot of different people. If I have only a few friends, I will see only a few points of view.

I like to have a lot of friends around me. I like to have fun with them and to learn from them and to know that I can rely on them. My life is better because of all the friends I have.

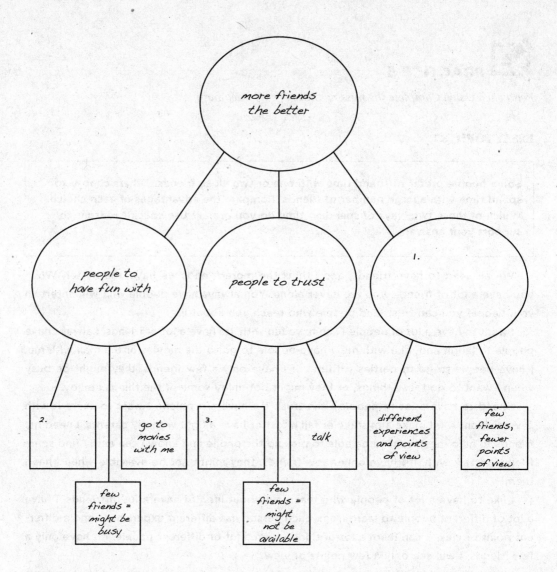

ESSAY TOPIC 29

A foreign visitor has only one day to spend in your country. Where should this visitor go on that day? Why? Use specific reasons and details to support your choice.

A foreign visitor with only one day to spend in my country should definitely spend that day in the capital. Spending time in the capital is the easiest way to see many aspects of our country in one place. In this city, the visitor can learn about our history, see examples of our culture, and buy our best products.

Our country's history is represented in several ways throughout the city. In the Government Palace, a visitor can learn about the history of our independence. In our National Museum, a visitor can see exhibits that show all the different stages of our history, from ancient times to the present. In parks all around the city, a visitor can see monuments to famous historical people and events.

It is also possible to see different representations of our culture throughout the city. Our art museums and galleries show paintings and sculptures by our artists. Plays written by national playwrights are performed in the theaters. Folk ballet performances show examples of our traditional dances. Many restaurants in the capital serve our native dishes.

The best products of our country are sold in the capital city. The large department stores sell clothes, furniture, and household items manufactured in our country. The Central Market sells fruit and vegetables from the surrounding agricultural region. Tourist and craft shops sell native handicrafts made in the countryside.

The capital city is the best place to learn about our country in one place. Of course, it is difficult to see all of the city's attractions in one day. With some planning, though, it is possible to see at least a few examples of our country's history, culture, and products in one day.

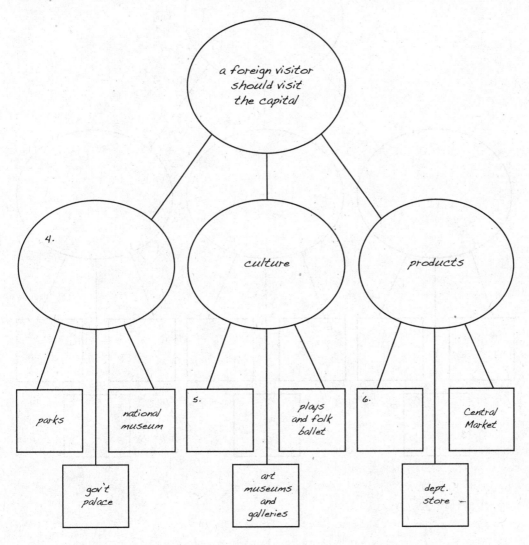

PRACTICE 6

Create an idea map for each of the following topics. Photocopy the blank idea map on this page as many times as you need and use the copies for making your idea maps. You may not need all parts of the map for every topic. Then write an essay from each of your idea maps. Allow yourself no more than 30 minutes to write. Write about 300 words. Compare your essays with the essays for those topics in the Model Essay section beginning on page 177.

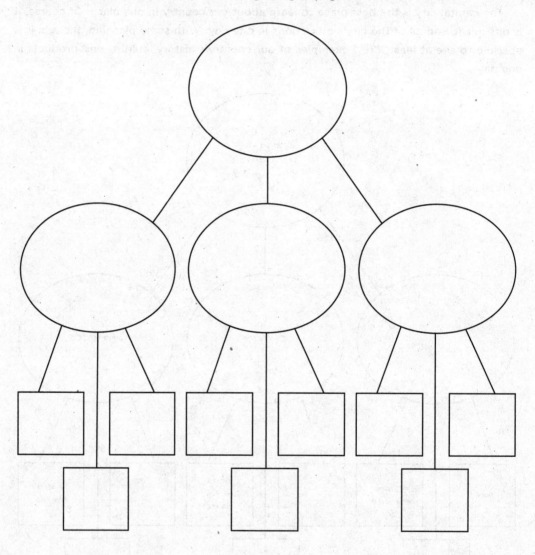

ESSAY TOPIC 42

Do you agree or disagree with the following statement? It is more important for students to study history and literature than it is for them to study science and mathematics. Use specific reasons and examples to support your opinion.

ESSAY TOPIC 50

In some countries, people are no longer allowed to smoke in many public places and office buildings. Do you think this is a good rule or a bad rule? Use specific reasons and details to support your position.

ESSAY TOPIC 24

If you could study a subject that you have never had the opportunity to study, what would you choose? Explain your choice, using specific reasons and details.

ESSAY TOPIC 25

Some people think that the automobile has improved modern life. Others think that the automobile has caused serious problems. What is your opinion? Use specific reasons and examples to support your answer.

EXTRA PRACTICE

Choose any model essay from the Appendix. Cover up the essay and look only at the topic. Create an outline or an idea map for the topic, then use it to write an essay. Compare your essay with the model. Do this with at least five model essays.

WRITE THE INTRODUCTION

You need two things to write a good introduction. You need to have an opinion on the topic and you need to have topic sentences for each of the paragraphs. Your opinion will tell the reader what you think about the subject; the summary of the topic sentences will guide your reader through your essay.

State Your Opinion

The introduction to your essay should tell the reader what your opinion is on the topic. The Independent Task is a personal essay. Your ideas on a topic are important. The readers are interested in what you have to say. There is, however, no right or wrong opinion. The readers look to see how you express your opinion, whatever it is.

You can express your opinion by using set phrases or by varying the verbs, adjectives, and adverbs you use. On the Independent Task, you must show a variety in your vocabulary and expression as well as your sentence types to score high. This section will help you give your writing more variety.

Here are some examples of set phrases that you can use to express your opinion.

Set Phrases	
In my opinion	It is my opinion that
	I believe
To my way of thinking	I think
In my view	It seems to me that
To me	It appears that
From my point of view	To my mind

EXAMPLES

In my opinion, university students must attend classes.
From my point of view, one must change with the times.
To me, there is nothing more important than good health.

It is my opinion that one learns by example.
It seems to me that a good neighbor is one who respects your privacy.
It appears that all the information one needs is available on computer.

 **PRACTICE 1**

Give your opinion about these topics. Use the phrases suggested.

1. People's lives (are/are not) easier today.
   In my opinion, *people's lives are easier today.*_____

2. Most people (prefer/do not prefer) to spend their leisure time outdoors.
   It seems to me that _____

3. An apartment building (is/is not) better than a house.
   To my mind, _____

4. It (is/is not) good that English is becoming the world language.
   From my point of view, _____

VERBS

You can use different verbs to show how strongly you feel about something. *Believe* and *think* are the most common verbs used to express a personal opinion.

agree	realize
believe	suppose
guess	think
hope	understand
imagine	

EXAMPLES

I agree that studying science is more important than studying literature.

I hope that people remember the special gifts I gave them.

I realize that most young people feel they have nothing to learn from older people.

I understand why people like to work with their hands.

 **PRACTICE 2**

Give your opinion about these topics. Use the verbs suggested.

1. High schools (should/should not) allow students to study what they want.
   I believe that _____

2. It is better to be a (leader/member) of a group.
   I guess that _____

3. People (should/should not) do things they do not enjoy doing.
   I agree that _____

4. I would rather have the university (assign/not assign) me a roommate.
   I suppose that _____

EXTRA PRACTICE

Read the introductions to some of the model essays in the Appendix. Look for examples of the verbs in the box on page 101. Find at least ten examples.

ADJECTIVES

You can use different adjectives to show how strongly you feel about something.

certain	positive
convinced	sure

EXAMPLES

I am certain that movies influence people's behavior.

I am convinced that having a pet can contribute to a child's development.

 **PRACTICE 3**

Give your opinion about these topics. Use the adjectives suggested.

1. Children (should/should not) spend a great amount of time practicing sports.
    I am sure that _____

2. A shopping center in my neighborhood (will/will not) be a benefit to our community.
    I am positive that _____

ADVERB PHRASES

You can use different adverb phrases to qualify your opinion. These adverb phrases show how strongly you feel about something.

Not Very Strongly	Somewhat Strongly	Very Strongly
apparently	probably	certainly
conceivably	presumably	undoubtedly
possibly	likely	definitely
perhaps		surely
maybe		
supposedly		

EXAMPLES

Presumably, playing games can teach us about life.

Daily exercise definitely should be a part of every school day.

Undoubtedly, helping a child to learn to read is important.

Individual sports are possibly better than team sports for some students.

PRACTICE 4

Give your opinion about these topics. Use the adverb phrases suggested.

1. A zoo (has/does not have) a useful purpose.

   Maybe, _____

2. The city/countryside is a better place to grow up.

   Probably, _____

3. Our generation (is/is not) different from that of our parents.

   Certainly, _____

4. A sense of humor can sometimes be (helpful/detrimental) in a difficult situation.

   Surely, _____

You can use different adverb phrases to make a general statement about how you feel about something.

all in all	basically	generally
all things considered	by and large	in general
altogether	essentially	on the whole
as a rule	for the most part	overall

EXAMPLES

All in all, it is better to learn from a teacher than on your own.

As a rule, it is better for students to wear uniforms to school.

For the most part, countries are more alike than different.

On the whole, higher education should be available to all.

PRACTICE 5

Give your opinion about these topics. Use the adverb phrases suggested to make a general statement.

1. The family (is/is not) the most important influence on young adults.

   All things considered, _____ .

2. Parents (are/are not) the best teachers.

   In general, _____

3. People (are never/are sometimes) too old to attend college.

   By and large, _____

You can use different adverb phrases to qualify your opinion. These adverb phrases show an idea is not completely true.

for all intents and purposes	to some extent
in a sense	up to a point
in a way	

EXAMPLES

Up to a point, people succeed because of hard work, not because of luck.

For all intents and purposes, television has destroyed communication among family members.

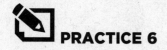 **PRACTICE 6**

Give your opinion about these topics. Use the adverb phrases suggested to show an idea is not completely true.

1. It is better to make a wrong decision than to make no decision.

   or

   It is better to make no decision than to make a wrong decision.

   In a way, _____

2. Watching movies (is/is not) more enjoyable than reading.

   To some extent, _____

3. You (can/cannot) learn as much by losing as winning.

   In a sense, _____

Guide the Reader

The introduction to your essay should also tell the reader how you plan to develop your topic. The topic sentences that you develop from your outline or idea map should be summarized in the introduction.

Compare these introductions.

INTRODUCTION TO TOPIC 1
Version A

I believe that people attend college for many different reasons. These reasons are personal to them.

Version B

People attend colleges or universities for a lot of different reasons. I believe that the three most common reasons are to prepare for a career, to have new experiences, and to increase their knowledge of themselves and the world around them.

Comment

Version A starts with the writer's opinion, but it does not tell us much. What are these reasons? We need to know the basic reasons so we can prepare ourselves to find supporting details in the body of the essay.

Version B gives three specific reasons that the writer believes are the most important ones: to prepare for a career, to have new experiences, and to increase their knowledge of themselves and the world around them. From this introduction, we will expect to see one paragraph for each of these three reasons.

INTRODUCTION TO TOPIC 4
Version A

I think there are changes necessary in my hometown. It is always the same. There has to be something different.

Version B

If I could change one thing about my hometown I think it would be the fact that there's no sense of community here. People don't feel connected, they don't look out for each other, and they don't get to know their neighbors.

Comment

Version A starts with the writer's opinion but doesn't say what changes are necessary. We need some guidance.

Version B narrows in on the topic and talks about the sense of community. The writer says that "People don't feel connected, they don't look out for each other, and they don't get to know their neighbors." From this introduction, we will expect to see one paragraph for each of these three reasons.

INTRODUCTION TO TOPIC 9

Version A

I believe that some people like to eat at food stands, and some like to eat in restaurants. There are different reasons for this.

Version B

Some people like to eat out at food stands and restaurants, while others like to prepare food at home. Often it depends on the kind of lifestyle people have. Those with very busy jobs outside the house don't always have time to cook. They like the convenience of eating out. Overall, though, I think it is cheaper and healthier to eat at home.

Comment

In Version A, the writer does not share what these reasons are. There are no general statements.

In Version B, the writer tells us that the choice depends on a person's lifestyle. The writer will probably give us more details about the reasons of convenience, costs, and health.

PRACTICE 7

Read the following introductions and tell us what the writer believes and the focus of each paragraph. You might not have three paragraphs for all introductions.

TIP

For extra practice, choose five model essays from the Appendix and analyze the introductions in the same way: identify the writer's opinion and the focus of each paragraph.

1. **Introduction to Topic 37**

   We all need to have friends, and I think the more friends we have, the better. Friendship helps us learn how to trust others, it helps us know what to expect from others, and it helps us profit from experiences. I want to have a lot of friends around me so I can learn more about myself from different people.

   Opinion: *I think the more friends we have, the better.*

   Paragraph focus: *learn how to trust others*

   Paragraph focus: *learn what to expect from others*

   Paragraph focus: *helps us profit from experiences*

2. **Introduction to Topic 48**

   Almost everyone, whether child or adult, loves games. The types of games we like may change as we grow up, but our enjoyment of them never does. I believe that playing games is both fun and useful because it teaches us the skills we need in life. Games teach us about cause and effect relationships, teamwork, and following rules.

   Opinion: _____

   Paragraph focus: _____

   Paragraph focus: _____

   Paragraph focus: _____

3. **Introduction to Topic 38**

   Although friends make an impression on your life, they do not have the same influence that your family has. Nothing is as important to me as my family. From them, I learned everything that is important. I learned about trust, ambition, and love.

   Opinion: _____

   Paragraph focus: _____

   Paragraph focus: _____

   Paragraph focus: _____

4. **Introduction to Topic 36**

There are people who say they prefer to be alone, but I cannot understand this. I always choose to spend time with friends whenever possible because friends bring so much to my life. They keep me company, they are enjoyable to talk with, and they teach me new things. I cannot imagine my life without them.

Opinion: _____

Paragraph focus: _____

Paragraph focus: _____

Paragraph focus: _____

5. **Introduction to Topic 21**

Traveling alone is the only way to travel. If you take someone with you, you take your home with you. When you travel alone, you meet new people, have new experiences, and learn more about yourself.

Opinion: _____

Paragraph focus: _____

Paragraph focus: _____

Paragraph focus: _____

EXTRA PRACTICE

Choose any model essay from the Appendix. Cover up the first paragraph and read the rest of the essay and the topic. Use these as a basis to write your own introduction for the essay. Then, uncover the first paragraph and see how it compares with yours. Do this with at least five model essays.

WRITE THE PARAGRAPHS

Once you have stated your opinion and shown the reader how you plan to develop your essay, the rest is easy. You simply turn the supporting details in your outline or idea map into sentences. Of course, you must make sure your sentences are written correctly, and you must show variety in your vocabulary and sentence types. (See Part 4, Writing Skills—Both Tasks for further practice with sentence writing.)

Look at these examples of how an outline and an idea map become paragraphs.

SAMPLE 1

Paragraph 3 from Essay Topic 47

Paragraph 3   **Main idea**   The foreign language program needs well-trained instructors.

Supporting details
(1) Current teachers don't speak well
(2) Teachers make frequent errors
(3) Well-trained teachers are good models

The foreign language program should be staffed with well-trained instructors. The current teachers in the program don't speak the language well enough. In our classes, teachers frequently make errors that the students repeat. If the teachers were well trained, they would be good models for the students.

SAMPLE 2

Paragraph 2 from Essay Topic 43

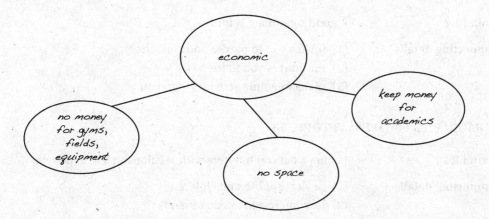

Another issue is economic. Many schools simply do not have the money to provide gym facilities, playing fields, and athletic equipment for their students. Other schools are located in cities where that kind of space just isn't available. A few schools would rather keep money for academic purposes.

 **PRACTICE 8**

Look at the following outlines and idea maps. Use each one to write a paragraph on a separate piece of paper or on your computer. Compare your paragraphs with the cited paragraphs for those topics in the Model Essay section beginning on page 177 of the Appendix.

PARAGRAPH 3 FROM ESSAY TOPIC 9

Main idea	Eating at home is better than eating at restaurants.
Supporting details	(1) Restaurant meals high in fat and calories
	(2) At home you control ingredients
	(3) Restaurants big plates of food
	(4) At home you control portion size

PARAGRAPH 4 FROM ESSAY TOPIC 31

Main idea	A good roommate is fun.
Supporting details	(1) invites you to parties and concerts
	(2) introduces you to friends
	(3) plans free time activities with you

PARAGRAPH 3 FROM ESSAY TOPIC 56

Main idea	Loving a pet can interfere with relationships with people.
Supporting details	(1) neglect spouse and children
	(2) lose interest in making friends
	(3) less complicated than relationships with people

PARAGRAPH 2 FROM ESSAY TOPIC 14

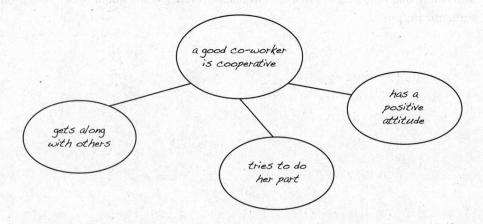

PARAGRAPH 2 FROM ESSAY TOPIC 26

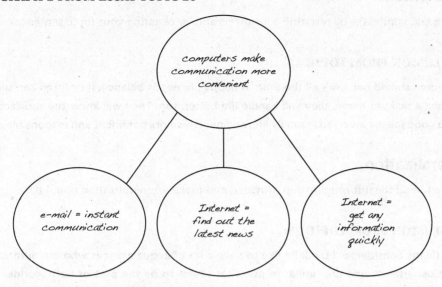

PARAGRAPH 2 FROM ESSAY TOPIC 53

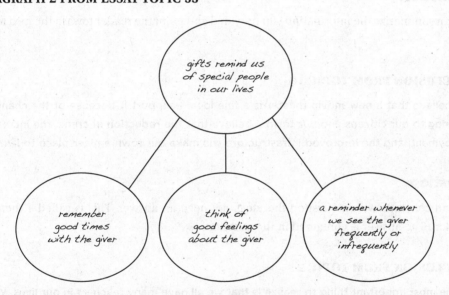

EXTRA PRACTICE

Choose any model essay from the Appendix. Cover up the main part of the essay and read only the topic and the introduction. Use these as a basis to write your own body paragraphs for the essay. Then, uncover the essay and see how it compares with your paragraphs. Do this with at least five model essays.

WRITE THE CONCLUSION

A good essay should have a good conclusion. A conclusion has a few sentences that support your thesis and remind the reader of your intentions. There are a few different ways to write a conclusion. Look at these conclusions from the essays in this book. You can review the complete essay in the Model Essay section.

Restatement

You can end your essay by restating your thesis and/or restating your topic sentences.

CONCLUSION FROM TOPIC 45

Children should not work all the time. A happy life needs balance. If children can successfully handle tasks at home, they will handle life better, too. They will know the satisfaction of doing a good job, be involved in family life, and become more confident and responsible adults.

Generalization

You can use all the information you provided and make a generalization about it.

CONCLUSION FROM TOPIC 39

All things considered, I think I'd like to have a lot of acquaintances who are different and a few close friends who are similar to me. That seems to be the best of both worlds.

Prediction

You can summarize the information you provided and point the reader toward the next logical step.

CONCLUSION FROM TOPIC 16

I believe that a new movie theater is a fine idea. I support it because of the changes it will bring to our citizens and our town. I believe that the reduction in crime, the increase in employment, and the improved infrastructure will make our town a nicer place to live.

Question

You can conclude with a question that does not need an answer. This is called a rhetorical question. The answer is contained in the question.

CONCLUSION FROM TOPIC 2

The most important thing to realize is that we all have many teachers in our lives. Where would we be without our parents, teachers, and our peers to guide us? What would we do without books, newspapers, and television to inform us? All of them are very valuable.

Recommendation

You can urge your readers to do something with the information you provided.

NOTE

Your conclusion does not have to be long. Two or three sentences may be enough for your summary.

CONCLUSION FROM TOPIC 9

Both eating at restaurants and cooking at home can be satisfying. Both can taste good and be enjoyed with family and friends. I prefer cooking at home, because of the money and health issues. I encourage my friends to eat out less, but it's up to them to make the choice that fits their lifestyles best.

PRACTICE 9

What kind of a conclusion is each of these sentences or paragraphs? Refer to the whole essay, in the Appendix, beginning on page 177, to help you decide.

1. CONCLUSION FROM TOPIC 20

If you give up, you might as well die. My advice is to always look for another opportunity, another goal, or another option. There is always something else. Don't give up.

(A) Restatement
(B) Generalization
(C) Prediction
(D) Question
(E) Recommendation

2. CONCLUSION FROM TOPIC 40

Clothes don't change you into a different person, but they can make you behave differently. If you are dressed inappropriately for a situation, people will react to you in a different way. This reaction can, in turn, change your behavior. If you want good reactions from people, make sure to dress appropriately for every situation.

(A) Restatement
(B) Generalization
(C) Prediction
(D) Question
(E) Recommendation

3. CONCLUSION FROM TOPIC 15

On the whole, though, I think my neighborhood should support having a shopping center built here. It would bring more variety to our shopping, give us the opportunity to amuse ourselves at movie theaters and restaurants, and bring more jobs into the area.

(A) Restatement
(B) Generalization
(C) Prediction
(D) Question
(E) Recommendation

4. CONCLUSION FROM TOPIC 41

If we all based our final opinion of others on first impressions, it would be hard to get to know anyone. We would probably miss many opportunities to make good friends. Isn't it important to give everyone the chance to show us who they really are? And don't you want other people to do the same for you?

(A) Restatement
(B) Generalization
(C) Prediction
(D) Question
(E) Recommendation

5. CONCLUSION FROM TOPIC 18

The more I moved the more I would experience change. I would meet new people in every place I lived; I could move to sample countries with four seasons or even a continent like Antarctica, which only has two. Wherever I lived, I would experience living in housing particular to that area. I would then be a citizen of the world, wouldn't I? Could you call me a foreigner if I called everyplace my home?

(A) Restatement
(B) Generalization
(C) Prediction
(D) Question
(E) Recommendation

EXTRA PRACTICE

1. Choose at least five model essays from the Appendix. Identify the type of conclusion each contains.

2. Choose any model essay from the Appendix. Cover up the conclusion. Read the essay and write your own conclusion. Then, uncover the conclusion and see how it compares with yours. Do this with at least five model essays.

USE THE REVISION CHECKLIST

After you write your essay, you need to check the content and language. You need to make sure that the content is well developed and well organized, and that you have used correct language and punctuation. You can use a revision checklist similar to the one for the Integrated Task.

REVISION CHECKLIST

■ **Content**
- ❑ Thesis Statement
- ❑ Main ideas
- ❑ Supporting details

■ **Fluency and Cohesion**
- ❑ Transition words
- ❑ Grammar and Spelling
- ❑ Sentence variety

Read the following model essay. Notice how it follows the items on the checklist.

ESSAY TOPIC 2

> **Do you agree or disagree with the following statement? Parents are the best teachers. Use specific reasons and examples to support your answer.**

Parents shape their children from the beginning of their children's lives. They develop close emotional ties with their children. They share their interests with them. They teach them values. Parents can be very important teachers in their children's lives; however, they are not always the best teachers. *[main ideas / thesis statement]*

Parents may be too close to their children emotionally. For example, they may limit a child's freedom in the name of safety. A teacher may organize an educational trip to a big city, but a parent may think this trip is too dangerous. A school may want to take the children camping, but a parent may be afraid of the child getting hurt.

Another problem is that parents sometimes expect their children's interests to be similar to their own. If the parents love science, they may try to force their child to love science too. But what if the child prefers art? If the parents enjoy sports, they may expect their child to participate on different teams. But what if the child prefers to read?

Finally, although parents want to pass on their values to their children, values can change. The children of today are growing up in a world different from their parents' world. Sometimes parents, especially older ones, can't keep up with rapid social or technological changes. A student who has friends of different races at school may find that his parents have narrower views. A student who loves computers may find that her parents don't understand or value the digital revolution.

Parents are important teachers in our lives, but they aren't always the best teachers. Fortunately, we have many teachers in our lives. Our parents teach us, our teachers teach us, and we learn from our peers. Books and newspapers also teach us. All of them are valuable.

Content

> ## REVISION CHECKLIST
>
> ■ **Content**
>   - ☑ Thesis Statement
>   - ❑ Main ideas
>   - ❑ Supporting details
>
> ■ **Fluency and Cohesion**
>   - ❑ Transition words
>   - ❑ Grammar and Spelling
>   - ❑ Sentence variety

✓ CHECK FOR THESIS STATEMENT

The task asks the writer to agree or disagree with a statement. In the first paragraph, the writer clearly expresses disagreement with the statement.

Task: Agree or disagree

Thesis: Parents...are not always the best teachers.

> ## REVISION CHECKLIST
>
> ■ **Content**
>   - ❑ Thesis Statement
>   - ☑ Main ideas
>   - ❑ Supporting details
>
> ■ **Fluency and Cohesion**
>   - ❑ Transition words
>   - ❑ Grammar and Spelling
>   - ❑ Sentence variety

✓ CHECK FOR MAIN IDEAS

The first paragraph mentions three topics that support the thesis. These will become the main ideas of the paragraphs in the body of the essay.

Thesis: Parents...are not always the best teachers.

Location	Main Idea
Paragraph 1, Sentence 2	...develop close emotional ties...
Paragraph 1, Sentence 3	...share their interests...
Paragraph 1, Sentence 4	...teach them values

> ## REVISION CHECKLIST
>
> ■ **Content**
>   - ❑ Thesis Statement
>   - ❑ Main ideas
>   - ☑ Supporting details
>
> ■ **Fluency and Cohesion**
>   - ❑ Transition words
>   - ❑ Grammar and Spelling
>   - ❑ Sentence variety

✓ CHECK FOR SUPPORTING DETAILS

The paragraphs have topic sentences and supporting details. In the body of the essay, the topic sentences of the paragraphs match the topics introduced in the first paragraph.

Paragraph 2: *Main Idea*

Parents may be too close to their children emotionally.

Supporting Details

- For example, they may limit a child's freedom in the name of safety.

Paragraph 3: *Main Idea*

Another problem is that parents sometimes expect their children's interests to be similar to their own.

Supporting Details

- If the parents love science, they may try to force their child to love science too.
- If the parents enjoy sports, they may expect their child to participate on different teams.

Paragraph 4: *Main Idea*

Finally, although parents want to pass on their values to their children, values can change.

Supporting Details

- A student who has friends of different races at school may find that his parents have narrower views.
- A student who loves computers may find that her parents don't understand or value the digital revolution.

Fluency and Cohesion

REVISION CHECKLIST

■ **Content**
- ❑ Thesis Statement
- ❑ Main ideas
- ❑ Supporting details

■ **Fluency and Cohesion**
- ☑ Transition words
- ❑ Grammar and Spelling
- ❑ Sentence variety

✓ CHECK FOR TRANSITION WORDS

This essay uses appropriate transition words.

Transition Word	Paragraph	Function
however	Paragraph 1	Shows contrast
Another	Paragraph 3	Adds information
But	Paragraph 3	Shows contrast
Finally	Paragraph 4	Shows order of ideas

TIP

See pages 137–139 for more information on transition words.

REVISION CHECKLIST

■ **Content**
  ❑ Thesis Statement
  ❑ Main ideas
  ❑ Supporting details

■ **Fluency and Cohesion**
  ❑ Transition words
  ☑ Grammar and Spelling
  ❑ Sentence variety

✓ CHECK FOR GRAMMAR AND SPELLING

There are no grammar or spelling errors in this essay.

REVISION CHECKLIST

■ **Content**
  ❑ Thesis Statement
  ❑ Main ideas
  ❑ Supporting details

■ **Fluency and Cohesion**
  ❑ Transition words
  ❑ Grammar and Spelling
  ☑ Sentence variety

✓ CHECK FOR SENTENCE VARIETY

This essay uses a variety of sentence structures.

Sentence Type	Paragraph	Example
Simple sentence	Paragraph 1	They share their interests with them.
Compound sentence	Paragraph 2	A teacher may organize an educational trip to a big city, but a parent may think this trip is too dangerous.
Complex sentence	Paragraph 3	If the parents love science, they may try to force their child to love science too.
Adjective clause	Paragraph 4	A student who has friends of different races at school may find that his parents have narrower views.
Series	Paragraph 5	Our parents teach us, our teachers teach us, and we learn from our peers.

 **PRACTICE 1**

Read the following model essays. Do the exercises that follow each one.

ESSAY TOPIC 9

> Some people prefer to eat at food stands or restaurants. Other people prefer to prepare and eat food at home. Which do you prefer? Use specific reasons and examples to support your answer.

Although many people prefer to eat at restaurants because it is easier than cooking at home, I prefer to prepare food at home. I believe it is much cheaper and healthier to eat at home, and it can be more convenient, too.

While eating in restaurants is fast, the money you spend can add up. When I have dinner at a restaurant, the bill is usually $25 or more. I can buy a lot of groceries with that much money. Even lunch at a food stand can easily cost seven or eight dollars. That's enough to feed a whole family at home.

Eating at home is better for you, too. Meals at restaurants are often high in fat and calories. When you cook at home, however, you can control what you eat. You can cook with low-fat and low-calorie ingredients. Restaurants also often serve big plates of food. You may eat a big plate of food at a restaurant because you paid for it, while at home you can control your portion size. You can serve yourself as little as you want.

It may seem more convenient to eat at a restaurant because you don't have to shop, cook, or clean up. All you do is eat. Cooking at home, however, can actually be more convenient. There are a lot of simple meals that don't take long to prepare. In addition, when you eat at home, you don't have to drive to the restaurant, look for a parking space, wait for a table, and wait for service.

People often choose to eat at restaurants because it seems more convenient. I find, however, that cooking at home is actually easier, and it is cheaper and healthier as well.

REVISION CHECKLIST

■ **Content**
- ☐ Thesis Statement
- ☐ Main ideas
- ☐ Supporting details

■ **Fluency and Cohesion**
- ☐ Transition words
- ☐ Grammar and Spelling
- ☐ Sentence variety

EXERCISES

1. The topic asks the writer to state a preference. Look at the first paragraph of the essay. Find the thesis statement, which states a preference, and underline it.

2. In the first paragraph, find the topics that support the thesis. Number them. They will become the main ideas of the paragraphs in the body of the essay.

3. Put a check (✓) next to the main idea in the second paragraph. Mark each supporting detail with a letter: A, B, C, etc.

4. Put a check (✓) next to the main idea in the third paragraph. Mark each supporting detail with a letter: A, B, C, etc.

5. Put a check (✓) next to the main idea in the fourth paragraph. Mark each supporting detail with a letter: A, B, C, etc.

6. Underline all transition words in the second, third, fourth, and fifth paragraphs.

7. Check grammar and spelling. Correct any errors.

8. Find and mark one simple sentence (ss), one complex sentence (cx/s) and one sentence with an adjective clause (adj.c).

ESSAY TOPIC 10

It has recently been announced that a new restaurant may be built in your neighborhood. Do you support or oppose this plan? Why? Use specific reasons and details to support your answer.

I can see both advantages and disadvantages to having a new restaurant built in our neighborhood. I believe, however, that the disadvantages outweigh the advantages. A new restaurant would bring more traffic problems to the area. In addition, it could attract undesirable people. Most of all, I think there are other types of businesses that would be more beneficial to the neighborhood.

Traffic congestion is already a problem in our neighborhood, and a new restaurant would just add to the problem. Most restaurant customers would arrive by car and crowd our streets even more. In addition, they would occupy parking spaces and make it even harder for residents to find places to park near their homes.

I'm also concerned about the type of patrons that a new restaurant would bring into our neighborhood. If the restaurant serves drinks and has dancing, there could be problems. The restaurant would stay open late and people leaving the restaurant might be drunk. They could be noisy, too. That is not the kind of thing I want to see in my neighborhood.

Finally, there are other types of businesses that we need in our neighborhood more. We already have a restaurant and a couple of coffee shops. We don't have a bookstore or pharmacy, however, and we have only one small grocery store. I would prefer to see one of these businesses established here rather than another restaurant. Any one of them would be more useful to the residents and would maintain the quiet atmosphere of our streets.

A new restaurant could disrupt the quiet lifestyle of our neighborhood. It might bring jobs, but it would also bring traffic and noise. Moreover, it would use space that might be better used for another type of business. This is why I would oppose a plan for a new restaurant.

REVISION CHECKLIST

■ Content
  ❑ Thesis Statement
  ❑ Main ideas
  ❑ Supporting details

■ Fluency and Cohesion
  ❑ Transition words
  ❑ Grammar and Spelling
  ❑ Sentence variety

EXERCISES

1. The topic asks the writer to support or oppose a plan. Look at the first paragraph of the essay. Find the thesis statement, which states support for or opposition to a plan, and underline it.

2. In the first paragraph, find the topics that support the thesis. Number them. They will become the main ideas of the paragraphs in the body of the essay.

3. Put a check (✓) next to the main idea in the second paragraph. Mark each supporting detail with a letter: A, B, C, etc.

4. Put a check (✓) next to the main idea in the third paragraph. Mark each supporting detail with a letter: A, B, C, etc.

5. Put a check (✓) next to the main idea in the fourth paragraph. Mark each supporting detail with a letter: A, B, C, etc.

6. Underline all transition words in the second, third, fourth, and fifth paragraphs.

7. Check grammar and spelling. Correct any errors.

8. Find and mark one complex sentence (cx/s), one simple sentence (ss), and one compound sentence (cm/s).

ESSAY TOPIC 11

Some people think that they can learn better by themselves than with a teacher. Others think that it is always better to have a teacher. Which do you prefer? Use specific reasons to develop your essay.

Most people can learn to do something simple on their own with just a set of instructions. However, to learn something more complex, it's always best to have a teacher. Teachers help you find the way that you learn best. They help you stay focused on what you're learning. They provide you with a wider range of information than you might find on your own. In short, teachers provide you with a lot more support and knowledge than you can usually get by yourself.

Teachers can help students learn in the way that is best for each student because teachers understand that different people have different learning styles. For example, some students learn better by discussing a topic. Others learn more by writing about it. A teacher can help you follow your learning style, while a book can give you only one way of learning something.

Teachers help you focus on what you are learning. They can help you keep from becoming distracted. They can show you which are the most important points in a lesson to understand. If you have to study on your own, on the other hand, it might be difficult to keep your attention on the material or know which points are most important.

Teachers bring their own knowledge and understanding of the topic to the lesson. A book presents you with certain information, and the teacher can add more. The teacher might also have a different point of view from the book and can provide other sources of information and ideas, as well.

There is nothing wrong with studying on your own. For the best possible learning, though, a teacher is the biggest help you can have.

EXERCISES

1. The topic asks the writer to state a preference. Look at the first paragraph of the essay. Find the thesis statement, which states a preference, and underline it.

2. In the first paragraph, find the topics that support the thesis. Number them. They will become the main ideas of the paragraphs in the body of the essay.

3. Put a check (✓) next to the main idea in the second paragraph. Mark each supporting detail with a letter: A, B, C, etc.

4. Put a check (✓) next to the main idea in the third paragraph. Mark each supporting detail with a letter: A, B, C, etc.

5. Put a check (✓) next to the main idea in the fourth paragraph. Mark each supporting detail with a letter: A, B, C, etc.

6. Underline all transition words in the second, third, fourth, and fifth paragraphs.

7. Check grammar and spelling. Correct any errors.

8. Find and mark one complex sentence (cx/s), one simple sentence (ss), and one compound sentence (cm/s).

ESSAY TOPIC 14

> We all work, or will work, in jobs with many different kinds of people. In your opinion, what are some important characteristics of a good co-worker (someone you work closely with)? Use reasons and specific examples to explain why these characteristics are important.

I've worked in several offices, and I've found there are certain characteristics that all good co-workers have in common. They tend to be cooperative people, they adapt well to changes, and they are helpful to others in the office. People who have these characteristics are easy to work with.

A good co-worker is very cooperative. She does her best to get along with others. She tries to do her work well because she knows that if one person doesn't get her work done, it affects everyone else. She also has a positive attitude that creates a pleasant working environment.

A good co-worker is adaptable. She is not stubborn about changes in schedules or routines. She doesn't object to having her job description revised. She has no problem with new procedures. In fact, she welcomes changes when they come.

A good co-worker is helpful. For instance, she lends a hand when someone falls behind in his or her work. She is willing to change her schedule to accommodate another worker's emergency. She doesn't keep track of how often she has to take on extra work.

We spend more time with our co-workers during the week than we do with our family. Thus, it's important for our co-workers to be people we can get along with. When co-workers are cooperative, adaptable, and helpful, everyone gets along better and can get their jobs done well.

REVISION CHECKLIST

■ **Content**
- ❑ Thesis Statement
- ❑ Main ideas
- ❑ Supporting details

■ **Fluency and Cohesion**
- ❑ Transition words
- ❑ Grammar and Spelling
- ❑ Sentence variety

EXERCISES

1. The topic asks the writer to describe something. Look at the first paragraph of the essay. Find the thesis statement, which tells us what the writer will describe, and underline it.

2. In the first paragraph, find the topics that support the thesis. Number them. They will become the main ideas of the paragraphs in the body of the essay.

3. Put a check (✓) next to the main idea in the second paragraph. Mark each supporting detail with a letter: A, B, C, etc.

4. Put a check (✓) next to the main idea in the third paragraph. Mark each supporting detail with a letter: A, B, C, etc.

5. Put a check (✓) next to the main idea in the fourth paragraph. Mark each supporting detail with a letter: A, B, C, etc.

6. Underline all transition words in the second, third, fourth, and fifth paragraphs.

7. Check grammar and spelling. Correct any errors.

8. Find and mark one complex sentence (cx/s), one simple sentence (ss), and one sentence with a noun clause (nc).

 **PRACTICE 2**

Complete each essay by answering the questions that follow.

TOPIC 23

TIP

Reading ahead in
the essay will help
you choose the
best answer.

Many teachers assign homework to students every day. Do you think that daily homework is necessary for students? Use specific reasons and details to support your answer.

(1) _____. Students already spend most of the day in school. They need time to spend with their families, to work, and to just relax. They can learn their lessons with homework two or three times a week, but every day isn't necessary.

(2) _____. They are still young, and they need the guidance and support their parents can give them. They need the companionship of their brothers and sisters. (3) _____, many families rely on their older children to help out at home. They take care of the younger children and help with the cooking and cleaning. If students have too much homework, they won't have time for their families.

Many high school students have jobs. They go to their jobs after school and on weekends. Some work in order to help their families. (4) _____. Students' jobs are important to them. If they have too much homework, they won't have time and energy to go to work.

Students need time to relax. They study hard in school all day, and many work at jobs after school. But they are still young. They need to spend time with their friends and have fun. When students relax with friends, they then have more energy for school and work. (5) _____. Having free time is important for a child's development. If students have too much homework, they won't have time for relaxation.

Homework is important for students, but other things are important, too. Some homework is good, but daily homework can take time away from a student's family, job, and relaxation. There needs to be a balance.

1. Choose the best thesis statement.

   (A) Teachers often assign homework.
   (B) I believe that daily homework is not necessary.
   (C) Homework may involve solving math problems or writing essays.

2. Choose the best main idea for this paragraph.

   (A) All students need to spend time with their families.
   (B) Many students have to work.
   (C) Some families believe that homework is important.

3. Choose the best transition word for this sentence.

   (A) For example
   (B) Although
   (C) In addition

4. Choose the missing supporting detail.

   (A) Others work to save money for college.
   (B) Others spend time relaxing with friends.
   (C) Others do homework all evening.

5. Choose the missing supporting detail.

   (A) They should spend their energy getting a job.
   (B) They never have time for their families.
   (C) They have a chance to develop social skills or to pursue their own interests.

TOPIC 22

> **Do you agree or disagree with the following statement? Businesses should do anything they can to make a profit. Use specific reasons and examples to support your position.**

After I get my degree, I plan to start my own business. Like any business owner, my goal is to make as much money as I can. (6) _____. I must always keep in mind that the success of my business depends on (7)_____, the customers I serve, and the community I live in.

My employees are a very important part of my business. Without them, my company would not be able to function. I depend on my employees to carry out the day-to-day operations of the business, and I rely on them for their advice on what to sell and how to sell it. Naturally, I have to compensate them for their contributions to the company. I can't take a large profit without sharing it with the people who made it possible.

(8) _____, I would not have a business without my customers. I can never forget that they could take their business somewhere else. Therefore, I have to give them good value for their money and not overcharge them just because I want to make a few more pennies. (9) _____.

My employees and I are part of the social life of our community. We have an obligation to be active community members. (10)_____. We need to support local programs to support our neighbors, for example, summer jobs for high school students, campaigns to clean up city parks, and efforts to make the shopping area more attractive.

A business must make profits, of course, but we all—workers customers, community members—must profit from a successful business, as well.

6. Choose the best thesis statement.

   (A) To clarify, making a profit means earning money rather than losing it.
   (B) In fact, earning a profit is the most important aspect of a business.
   (C) However, I can't forget that there are more important things in life than earning a profit.

7. Choose the missing topic that supports the thesis.

   (A) the money I earn
   (B) the people I work with
   (C) the product or service I provide

8. Choose the best transition word for this sentence.

   (A) Therefore
   (B) Similarly
   (C) Otherwise

9. Choose the missing supporting detail.

   (A) I want my customers to trust me and keep coming back.
   (B) If some customers leave, I can always find others.
   (C) I should earn as much profit from my customers as possible.

10. Choose the missing supporting detail.

    (A) Taking part in community activities is an enjoyable way to spend free time.
    (B) If I am active in the community, I will get more customers and earn higher profits.
    (C) I feel it is important that some of the profits my business earns from the community be returned to the community.

TOPIC 6

> Some people prefer to live in a small town. Others prefer to live in a big city. Which place would you prefer to live in? Use specific reasons and details to support your answer.

I grew up in a small town and then moved to a big city. I didn't think I would like living here, but I was wrong. (11) _____. Transportation is much more convenient, everything is more exciting, and there is a greater variety of people. I can't imagine ever living in a small town again.

Transportation is easier in a city. In a small town, you have to have a car to get around because there isn't any kind of public transportation. In a city, (12) _____, there are usually buses and taxis, and some cities have subways. Cities often have heavy traffic and expensive parking, but it doesn't matter because you can always take the bus. Using public transportation is usually cheaper and more convenient than driving a car, (13) _____ you don't have this choice in a small town.

City life is more exciting than small town life. In small towns usually nothing changes. You see the same people every day, you go to the same two or three restaurants, everything is the same. (14) _____. You see new people every day. There are many restaurants, with new ones to choose from all the time. New plays come to the theaters, and new musicians come to the concert halls.

(15) _____. There are fewer people in a small town, and usually they are all alike. In a city you can find people from different countries, of different religions, of different races—you can find all kinds of people. This variety of people is what makes city life interesting.

Life in a city is convenient, exciting, and interesting. After experiencing city life, I could never live in a small town again.

11. Choose the best thesis statement.

    (A) I think life is much better in a big city.

    (B) However, I still prefer living in a small town.

    (C) Big cities are busy and noisy, while small towns are quiet and peaceful.

12. Choose the best transition word for this sentence.

    (A) consequently

    (B) for example

    (C) on the other hand

13. Choose the best transition word for this sentence.

    (A) but

    (B) also

    (C) so

14. Choose the missing supporting detail.

    (A) In a city, life can be very confusing.

    (B) In a city, things change all the time.

    (C) In a city, most people follow a routine.

15. Choose the best main idea for this paragraph.

    (A) Cities have many of the same types of people that you can find in a small town.

    (B) Cities have a larger population than small towns do.

    (C) Cities have a diversity of people that you don't find in a small town.

TOPIC 27

> **Do you agree or disagree with the following statement? Boys and girls should attend separate schools. Use specific reasons and examples to support your answer.**

    (16) _____. They will not be separated when they finish school and start their careers, so why should they be separated in school? When boys and girls study together, they are assured of getting equal quality of education, (17) _____, and they learn how to become friends. It is a much better preparation for life than studying in separate schools.

    When boys and girls attend the same school, they get equal education. They are in the same classrooms with the same teachers studying from the same books. (18) _____. One school might be better than the other. By studying together, girls get the same education as boys. This helps them work toward having equality in society.

    By attending the same schools, boys and girls learn how to work together. Some people say that they should study separately because they have different learning styles. I think it's better to study together, (19) _____. It gives them the chance to learn to work together despite their differences. This will help them in the future when they have to work together professionally.

When boys and girls see each other in school every day, they have the chance to become friends. (20) _____. If they attend separate schools, they don't know each other. It's easy to misunderstand, or even fear, each other. When boys and girls have the chance to become friends, their lives are much richer. They will have better relationships in the future.

By studying together, boys and girls get equal education, they learn to work together, and they become friends. This prepares them for adult life where men and women live and work together every day.

16. Choose the best thesis statement.

   (A) I agree that education is as important for girls as it is for boys.
   (B) I don't think it's a good idea for boys and girls to attend separate schools.
   (C) In many countries, boys and girls attend separate schools.

17. Choose the missing topic that supports the thesis.

   (A) they learn how to work together
   (B) they attend the same school
   (C) they do the same kind of homework

18. Choose the missing supporting detail.

   (A) If they attend separate schools, they could still study the same subjects.
   (B) If they attend separate schools, they will learn more.
   (C) If they attend separate schools, the quality of the schools might be different.

19. Choose the best transition word for this sentence.

   (A) however
   (B) for instance
   (C) moreover

20. Choose the missing supporting detail.

   (A) Children should have a lot of friends.
   (B) They see each other as normal people, not as strangers.
   (C) Friends can help each other with their schoolwork.

 **PRACTICE 3**

Read the following essay and use the revision checklist to identify what is missing or incorrect. Then write your revision of the essay on a separate piece of paper or on your computer, adding the missing parts and correcting the errors.

REVISION CHECKLIST

■ **Content**
- ❑ Thesis Statement
- ❑ Main ideas
- ❑ Supporting details

■ **Fluency and Cohesion**
- ❑ Transition words
- ❑ Grammar and Spelling
- ❑ Sentence variety

TOPIC 12

> It is better for children to grow up in the countryside than in a big city. Do you agree or disagree? Use specific reasons and examples to develop your essay.

Yes, I think so. When children grow up in the countryside, they have a healthier life. They also have a safer life. Children also learn to appreciate nature when they grow up in the countryside.

Life in the countryside is healthier for children than life in the city. Drinking water in the city is usually dirty. In the countryside, on the other hand, the drinking water are clean and pure.

They don't have to worry about crime because there are fewer criminals in the countryside than in the city. They don't have to worry about traffic accidents, either, because there are fewer cars in the countryside. Furthermore, they don't have to worry about strangers who might hurt them because in the countryside almost everybody knows everybody else.

Life in the countryside help children appreciate nature. There are few plants in the city. In the countryside, for instance, children see trees and flowers around them all the time. They also have opportunities to see wild animals, while in the city they can only see animals in zoos. In addition, they know where there food comes from. In the countryside children are surrounded by farms, but in the city they only see fruits and vegetables in the grocery stores.

Life in the countryside is definitely much better for children than life in the city. It is cleaner, safer, and closer to nature. When I have children, I plan to let they grow up far away from any city.

Missing items:

Paragraph 1: _____

Paragraph 2: _____

Paragraph 3: _____

Paragraph 4: _____

Paragraph 5: _____

TIP

You can find a list of commonly misspelled words here:

*barronsbooks.com/
TP/TOEFL/Writing*

Grammar and vocabulary errors:

Paragraph 1: _____

Paragraph 2: _____

Paragraph 3: _____

Paragraph 4: _____

Paragraph 5: _____

CHECK THE SPELLING AND PUNCTUATION

Just as you did in the Integrated Task, you will have to check the punctuation and spelling on the essay you write for the Independent Task.

Spelling

Remember that there is no spell checker on the computer that you will use during the TOEFL iBT. You should be able to spell the most common English words before you take the test. On the test, try to use words that you are sure how to spell.

Punctuation

There are three important things to remember about punctuation when you write your responses.

■ **Indent each paragraph or use a space between paragraphs.**
  This will help the reader determine when you are starting a new topic.
■ **Capitalize the first word of each sentence.**
  This will help the reader determine when you are starting a new sentence.
■ **Put a period or question mark at the end of each sentence or question.**
  This will help the reader determine when you are ending a sentence or question.

Here are some other forms of punctuation that will help make your response easier to read.

> **NOTE**
> You will not be penalized if you use a space between paragraphs instead of indents. Also, remember that proper nouns are capitalized.

COMMA

Use a comma in a list of three or more things. It is optional to put a comma before the *and*.

    I want to have a kitchen, living room and bedroom.
    I want a large, airy, inexpensive house.

Use a comma between a noun and a following description.

    Central Park, the huge expanse of green space in the center of New York City, is
    visited by thousands of people every day.

Use a comma to separate transition words, adjectives, or participles that are not part of the sentence or were added for emphasis.

    On the other hand, I think eating at home saves money.
    The apartment was very, very expensive.
    Excited, I signed the lease without reading the fine print.

Use a comma between two independent clauses.

    It is important to get along with co-workers, and it is important to get along with
    bosses as well.

Use a comma to separate a non-restrictive clause.

    All the neighbors, who are very friendly, get together for parties and picnics.

Use a comma after a subordinate clause at the beginning of a sentence.

> After I've chosen an area, I decide whether I want to live in a house or an apartment.

SEMICOLON

Use a semicolon to separate two closely related sentences.

> I wanted a renovated townhouse; none was available.

COLON OR DASH

Use a colon or dash in front of a list or explanation.

> I looked at three kinds of apartments: studio, one-bedroom, and two-bedroom.
> My needs are simple—a nice neighborhood and a park nearby.

PRACTICE 4

Read the following essay. Then write your revision of the essay on a separate piece of paper or on your computer, adding punctuation.

ESSAY TOPIC 13

people are living to be much older these days than ever before. the main reasons for this are greater access to health care improved health care and better nutrition.

basic health care is available to many more people now than it was in the past. when someone is ill nowadays he or she can go to a public hospital instead of having to pay for private care. there are also more clinics and more trained doctors and nurses than there used to be. years ago health care was not available to everyone. people who didn't live in big cities often did not have easy access to doctors or hospitals and many people couldn't afford to pay for the medical care they needed.

in addition to increased access to health care the quality of that health care has greatly improved over the years. doctors now know much more about diseases and how to cure them. in the past people died young because of simple things such as an infection or a virus. now we have antibiotics and other medicines to cure these diseases. furthermore advances in medical science have made it possible to cure certain types of cancer and to treat heart disease. this has prolonged the lives of many many people.

the quality of nutrition has also improved over time. because of this people tend to be healthier than they used to be. now we know how to eat more healthfully. we know that eating low fat food can prevent heart disease. we know that eating certain fruits and vegetables can prevent cancer. we have information about nutrition that can help us live longer healthier lives.

improved health care and healthy eating habits are allowing us to live longer. now we need to make sure that everyone in the world has these benefits.

EXTRA PRACTICE

Study the model essays on pages 117, 121, 122, 123, and 124. Circle all the punctuation.

PRACTICE INDEPENDENT TASK

On your computer or on a separate piece of paper, write an essay on the following topic. Write at least 300 words. Remember to divide your writing time as follows:

STEP 1	PLAN	5 minutes
STEP 2	WRITE	20 minutes
STEP 3	REVISE	5 minutes

ESSAY TOPIC 54

Some famous athletes and entertainers earn millions of dollars every year. Do you think these people deserve such high salaries? Use specific reasons and examples to support your opinion.

REVISION CHECKLIST

■ **Content**
- ❑ Thesis Statement
- ❑ Main ideas
- ❑ Supporting details

■ **Fluency and Cohesion**
- ❑ Transition words
- ❑ Grammar and Spelling
- ❑ Sentence variety

Writing Skills—Both Tasks 5

A well-written essay has good organization of ideas. It also has well-written sentences. In a well-written essay, transition words and phrases are used to make connections between ideas. There is variety of sentence structure and vocabulary. The reader can easily follow the writer's ideas and stays interested in them.

TRANSITION: CONNECTING AND LINKING

Transition Words

Transition words and phrases help the reader follow your ideas from sentence to sentence and paragraph to paragraph. They show the relationships between ideas and connect the ideas to your thesis.

In this section, you will learn about transition words and phrases that show different kinds of relationships between ideas. Transition words can be used to show time, degree, comparison and contrast, cause and effect, and the addition of new information.

TIP

See pages 74 and 133 for information about using commas with transition words.

TIME

When you are explaining the sequence of events, you may want to use these expressions.

before	first	while	after
then	second	meanwhile	once
next	finally	at the same time	when

EXAMPLE

The school counselors should help students who are new to a school. *Before the first day* of school, they should give an orientation to the building. *When* school opens, they should introduce the students to the teachers. *After* the students have gotten used to their classes, the counselors should find out about the student's hobbies and recommend some extracurricular clubs. *At the same time*, the counselor should invite the parents to visit the school so they can meet the teachers and administrators.

DEGREE

When you are explaining why one thing is more or less important than another thing, you may want to use these expressions.

most important	even more	in the first place	primarily
more importantly	even less	to a certain extent	principally
less important	above all	to a greater/lesser degree	chiefly

EXAMPLE

A pet is one of the *most important* things psychologists can recommend to patients suffering from loneliness. Pets can do many things for lonely people, but *above all* they provide companionship. To a *lesser* degree, they provide a distraction from anxieties. But *primarily*, they help isolated people stay emotionally connected with the world.

Comparison and Contrast

When you are explaining how two or more things are similar or how they are different, you may want to use these expressions.

TO COMPARE

too	likewise	similarly	by the same token
also	compared to	similar to	in a like manner
just as	by comparison	in the same way	in a similar fashion

TO CONTRAST

yet	whereas	conversely	in contrast to
but	unlike	nevertheless	on the other hand
while	however	although	otherwise

EXAMPLE

Although my friend chose to buy a car with his gift, I would have gone on vacation. He said he needed the car to go to work, *but* I think he should take the bus. He also wanted the car for convenience. *However*, a taxi is *just* as convenient and doesn't have to be serviced. We are both alike in that neither of us knows how to drive. *Otherwise*, I might have bought a car, too.

Cause and Effect

When you are explaining how something caused a change in something else, you may want to use these expressions.

so	thus	consequently	therefore
for this reason	as a result	because, because of	owing to
since	due to	accordingly	as a consequence

EXAMPLE

Effective advertising wants to change people's behaviors. Some public service ads show coffins of people who died of lung cancer; *as a result* many people have quit smoking. Other ads show glamorous people smoking; *consequently* young people start to smoke. *Owing to* the influence of advertising on youth, many cigarette ads are not allowed near schools or on TV.

Explanation

If you are explaining what something is by giving an example or if you are restating something for emphasis, you may want to use these expressions.

in other words	to clarify	to explain	for one thing
I mean	specifically	that is	for example
such as	for instance	to illustrate	namely

EXAMPLE

People are never too old to attend college. *For example*, there are many women who stayed at home to raise their families and now have time to return to school. There are other examples *such as* retired people who move to a college town just so they can take occasional classes or even working people in their sixties, *for instance*, who want to take some night classes. *In other words*, you are never too old to learn.

Adding More Information

If you are adding more information to make your point stronger, you may want to use these expressions.

in addition	besides	furthermore	as well as
moreover	in fact	also	what's more

EXAMPLE

In addition to music, retailers can use lighting to improve the store environment. *Besides* helping customers see the products better, certain types of lighting can create different moods. Soft music creates a relaxed atmosphere. *Similarly*, soft lighting helps customers feel at ease. Relaxed customers stay in the store longer. *What's more*, they make a greater number of purchases.

 **PRACTICE 1**

Choose the best transition word or phrase to complete each sentence.

1. City living is expensive. _____, many people move to the suburbs when they start having children.

   (A) Because
   (B) As a result
   (C) In addition

2. Many people enjoy the excitement of city life, _____ I prefer the peace and quiet of the countryside.

   (A) but
   (B) and
   (C) therefore

3. When you travel, you have the chance to see new places and meet new people. _____, you have the opportunity to learn about the customs and ideas of other cultures.

   (A) Next
   (B) Furthermore
   (C) However

4. I read whenever I have the chance. I always have a book with me when riding the bus to work. I usually read during my lunch hour _____.

   (A) in contrast
   (B) nevertheless
   (C) also

5. There are many ways to learn a foreign language. _____, you can buy a computer program and study in the comfort of your own home.

   (A) Since
   (B) Similarly
   (C) For example

6. I find living in the city to be very stressful. I don't like the noise and crowds. I can't afford the high prices. The high rate of crime makes me nervous. _____, city life is not for me.

   (A) In other words
   (B) Even more
   (C) Meanwhile

7. It isn't hard to plan a fun vacation. First, decide how much money you can spend. _____, think about what kind of place you would like to visit.

   (A) Finally
   (B) Then
   (C) Specifically

PRACTICE 2

Read the following paragraphs. Choose the appropriate transition words or phrases to complete each sentence.

1. If I chose my own roommate, I'd (1) _____ pick some candidates from the list supplied by the university. (2) _____ I'd write to them and they'd write back. Through our letters, we'd find out if we shared common interests, (3) _____ sports or movies. (4) _____ we'd find out if we had similar habits. (5) _____ my investigation, I'd probably find someone compatible with me.

next	first	as a result of
in addition	such as	

2. Billions of tons of plastic are produced every year, and it takes hundreds of years for plastic to break down. (1) _____, the ocean is filled with plastic trash. Many birds, (2) _____ seagulls, commonly eat fish eggs. These birds eat small pieces of plastic that look like fish eggs. (3) _____ eating a big meal of plastic, a bird might starve to death. This is because the plastic has no nutritional value. (4) _____ many birds choke when they try to swallow plastic pieces. (5) _____ whenever we throw plastic away, we are contributing to the threats to ocean life.

moreover	such as	consequently
in other words	after	

3. A major part of adapting to life in a new country is learning that country's language. Generally, children have an easier time with this than adults do. (1) _____, children's young brains are ready to learn many new things, including language. (2) _____, they spend most of the day in school using their new language in class and on the playground. Adults, (3) _____, have many other things to fill their time and their minds. They have to find ways to make a living and take care of their families, (4) _____. Since they aren't in school all day long, they have fewer opportunities to make new friends who speak the country's language. (5) _____, adults may take longer learning the language of their new country.

moreover	in the first place	on the other hand
as a result	for example	

4. Decorators may choose certain colors for rooms in order to create certain moods. (1) _____, they may use blue in a bedroom to create a relaxing atmosphere or red in a kitchen to stimulate the appetite. (2) _____, a decorator may choose yellow for a sitting room to give it a cheerful air. Beige is a color that gives a feeling of cleanliness. (3) _____, it is often used in doctors' offices. This neutral color helps the doctors and nurses stay clear and focused, (4) _____. (5) _____ many people believe that color has a strong influence on mood, scientists are skeptical.

as well	for example	similarly
because of this	although	

5. People often say that it is always important to be honest, but I don't agree with this. (1) _____, I feel that sometimes honesty is not the best policy. You wouldn't want to tell your best friend that her expensive new dress doesn't look good on her, (2) _____. That would only hurt her feelings and possibly damage your friendship. (3) _____, you wouldn't tell your neighbors that you don't like the way they redecorated their house. That would just cause bad feelings between you. (4) _____, honesty isn't always a good thing. (5) _____, it can lead to problems that could easily be avoided by telling people what they want to hear.

so	on the contrary	by the same token
in fact	in fact	

TIP

One of the best ways to increase your vocabulary is to read a lot. The more you read, the more opportunities you have to learn new words in context.

VARIETY: WORDS AND SENTENCES

A good essay holds the reader's interest. One way you can keep your reader interested is by varying your vocabulary. You can learn to express similar ideas in different ways by using synonyms. Learning about word families is another way to vary your vocabulary. You can also avoid repetition by using pronouns.

A good essay also has a variety of sentence structures that keep the ideas clear and interesting to the reader. You can develop variety in your prose by using parallel structures, making your paragraphs cohesive, and writing sentences that vary in type, length, subject, and voice.

Synonyms

When you are writing on one topic, you don't want to repeat the same verb or adverb, noun or adjective in every sentence. You should try to use words that are similar in meaning, and that will carry the meaning of the sentence. Synonyms are important because they help you link closely related words or ideas. Synonyms provide coherence in your essay.

Read the paragraph on page 143. Look for these synonyms of *discuss* and *discussion*.

Verb	Synonyms
discuss	argue, confer, debate, dispute, elaborate, examine, explain, hash over, reason

Noun	Synonyms
discussion	argument, conversation, discourse, explanation

EXAMPLE

Last month, I had a *dispute* with my parents. It started as a simple *conversation* that turned into an *argument*. I wanted to take a year off from school. Of course, my parents *argued* that I should stay in school. I tried to *reason* with them; I tried to *persuade* them that taking a year off from school and working would be valuable experience. My *explanation* fell on deaf ears, and they refused to let me continue the *discussion*. They felt I had not thoroughly *examined* the issue and saw no reason to *debate* the subject any longer. I *conferred* with my sister who felt we could *hash* it *over* later when my parents were in a better mood.

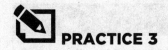

PRACTICE 3

Match the words in List A with their synonyms in List B. There may be more than one synonym for each word.

List A		List B
1. beautiful	_____	aid
2. begin	_____	alternative
3. belief	_____	assist
4. big	_____	attractive
5. calm	_____	automobile
6. car	_____	buses and trains
7. choice	_____	correct
8. choose	_____	costly
9. depend on	_____	count on
10. expensive	_____	decide on
11. famous	_____	enormous
12. fast	_____	fresh
13. help	_____	go
14. new	_____	huge
15. popular	_____	make a trip
16. public transportation	_____	mass transit
17. right	_____	opinion
18. travel	_____	option
		peaceful
		pick
		pretty
		private vehicle
		quick
		rapid
		recent
		rely on
		select
		spacious
		speedy
		start
		well-known
		well-liked

PRACTICE 4

Read the following topic and essay. Then revise the essay, replacing the underlined words with synonyms. Write your revision on your computer or on a separate piece of paper. You can find a revised version of this essay in the Model Essay section of the Appendix beginning on page 177.

TOPIC 35

> You need to travel from your home to a place 40 miles (64 kilometers) away. Compare the different kinds of transportation you could use. Describe which method you would choose. Give specific reasons for your choice.

When I think about the different methods of transportation I could choose to travel 40 miles from my home, I have three <u>choices</u>: bicycle, car, or public transportation. In order to <u>choose</u> the best method of transportation, I have to consider how much it will cost, how long it will take, and why I need to make the trip. Then I can <u>choose</u> the best method for the circumstances.

Bicycle is the least expensive <u>choice</u>. The only cost is the physical energy I need to pedal for 40 miles. This method, however, is extremely time consuming. I imagine it would take me all day to make the trip. On the other hand, biking is excellent exercise, so if my only goal is to burn calories and get stronger, then bicycle is my best choice.

Public transportation is another method that is inexpensive, since the fares in my area are low. On the other hand, you cannot depend on <u>public transportation</u> where I live. The schedules are inconvenient, and it might take me all day to make my 40-mile trip if I include waiting time. <u>Public transportation</u> is good for the environment since it causes less pollution than cars. But, I can't <u>depend on</u> it to get me to my destination on time, so I don't like to use it.

Private car is the most <u>expensive</u> way to travel. Since I don't own a <u>car</u>, I would need to borrow one from my parents. I would have to pay for the gasoline, which costs a lot, and I would also have to pay for parking at my destination. A <u>car</u> is the most dependable way to <u>travel</u> if you need to get somewhere fast. If convenience is my goal, I should choose to <u>travel</u> by this type of transportation.

When I consider these points, I must confess that I am spoiled. I prefer the convenience of the car over the exercise of a bicycle and the virtues of public transportation. I like to come and go as I please without waiting, even if it costs me more.

TIP

You can learn more about synonyms with an online thesaurus such as this one.

www.thesaurus.com

Word Families

Word families are groups of words that are related to each other by meaning. Each word in the word family has a different suffix, or ending. The suffix lets you know the part of speech of the word—noun, verb, adjective, or adverb.

Noun	Verb	Adjective	Adverb
beauty	beautify	beautiful	beautifully

When you learn a new word, you can also learn the other words in its word family. It's an easy way to expand your vocabulary and to learn to express your ideas in different ways.

EXAMPLE

The flowers fill the park with **beauty.**

The flowers **beautify** *the park.*

The flowers make the park look **beautiful.**

The flowers improve the park **beautifully.**

These sentences each express the same idea in a slightly different way.

Here are some more examples of word families.

Noun	Verb	Adjective	Adverb
attraction	attract	attractive	attractively
	broaden	broad	broaden
competition	compete	competitive	competitively
decision	decide	decisive	decisively
delight	delight	delightful	delightfully
dependence	depend	dependent	dependently
difference	differ	different	differently
familiarity	familiarize	familiar	familiarly
hesitation	hesitate	hesitant	hesitantly
popularity	popularize	popular	
profession		professional	professionally
rest	rest	restful	restfully
	suit	suitable	suitably

 **PRACTICE 5**

Complete each sentence with the correct word from the word family.

Noun	Verb	Adjective	Adverb
attraction	attract	attractive	attractively

1. The park is very _____ designed, and tourists enjoy walking there.
2. The cherry blossoms in the park _____ a large number of tourists every spring.
3. Many tourists find the city very _____ in the spring when the cherry blossoms bloom.
4. The cherry blossoms are a big _____ for tourists in the spring.

Noun	Verb	Adjective	Adverb
differences	differ	different	differently

5. Auditory learners _____ from their peers in several ways.
6. Teachers have noticed a number of _____ in these students' learning behavior.
7. Auditory learners process new information in a _____ way.
8. Students behave _____ in class, depending on their learning style.

Noun	Verb	Adjective
popularity	popularize	popular

9. Soccer is a sport that enjoys _____ in places all around the world.
10. Soccer is _____ everywhere, and many people like to play and watch it.
11. I believe that building a new stadium in my city would help _____ soccer in my country.

Noun	Adjective	Adverb
profession	professional	professionally

12. Education together with experience will help you do well in your _____.
13. It is important to act _____ at all times in the workplace.
14. If you have a _____ job, you must dress and act in a certain way.

Noun	Verb	Adjective	Adverb
rest	rest	restful	restfully

15. Vacations are important because even dedicated workers need to _____ sometimes.
16. A beach is a _____ place to spend a vacation.
17. It is important to take a _____ every so often and go on vacation.
18. Everyone can sleep _____ at the beach.

> **You can find more examples and information about word families here.**
>
>
>
> **barronsbooks.com/TP/TOEFL/Writing**

Pronouns

Pronouns replace nouns. They help you add variety to your writing. By using pronouns, you avoid repeating the same words over and over.

Pronouns that replace a subject

he	she	it	they
this	that	those	

Pronouns that replace an object

his	her	them
this	that	those

Pronouns that replace a possessive

his	her	its	their

NOTE

This in the last sentence refers to the whole paragraph. *This* equals *hiring a health worker.*

EXAMPLE

My community should hire a health worker. I worked in a rural area one summer with a community health worker and saw the wonderful ways she helped the people in the area. She worked with mothers teaching *them* how to keep *their* children healthy. She worked with school teachers helping *them* recognize early signs of illness. She worked with restaurant personnel showing *them* proper food handling techniques. A community needs help in many ways. *This* is one way its citizens can make it healthier.

 **PRACTICE 6**

Rewrite the paragraph, replacing each underlined word with an appropriate pronoun.

Different colors may create different moods. Colors can make people feel excited and ener-getic. Colors can also help people feel relaxed. In hospital waiting rooms, for example, people often feel nervous. People may feel better if the room is painted with a soothing color such as blue or gray. Some people like to paint people's bedrooms green. People feel that green helps people sleep better because green is a relaxing color. Yellow is an energizing color. Yellow is a good color for a kitchen because yellow helps people feel awake in the morning. My brother, however, didn't paint my brother's kitchen yellow. My brother painted the kitchen orange. My brother says that this color makes my brother feel hungry.

Parallel Structures

Parallelism gives your essay rhythm. It makes it easier to read and understand. Your structures must be parallel. That is, the subjects, verbs, adjectives, adverbs, and gerunds, when listed in a sentence, must have the same word form.

PARALLEL SUBJECTS

Work and play should be more evenly divided in my day.

Both *work* and *play* are the same kind of nouns. The subjects are parallel.

Working and play should be more evenly divided in my day.

Here *working* is a gerund, *play* is not. The subjects are not parallel.

Working and playing should be more evenly divided in my day.

Here both *working* and *playing* are gerunds. The subjects are parallel.

PARALLEL VERBS

We press a button, wait a short time, and remove the food from the microwave.

All three verbs are in the present tense. The verbs are parallel.

We press a button, wait a short time, and can remove the food from the microwave.

The third verb uses the auxiliary *can*, while the first and second do not. The verbs are not parallel.

We can press a button, wait a short time, and remove the food from the microwave.

Here, because *can* precedes the first verb, it does not have to be repeated for the remaining verbs in the list. All the verbs are now parallel.

PARALLEL ADJECTIVES

I found the movie <u>long</u> and <u>boring</u>.

The adjectives are both parallel.

I found the movie <u>long</u> and <u>it bored me</u>.

The sentence is not wrong, but it is not parallel.

PARALLEL ADVERBS

Athletes often move <u>gracefully</u>, <u>easily</u>, and <u>powerfully</u>.

The three adverbs all end in *-ly*. They are all parallel.

Athletes often move with <u>grace</u>, <u>easily</u> and <u>powerfully</u>.

The first description is a prepositional phrase. The adverbs are not parallel.

Athletes often move <u>gracefully</u>, <u>carefully</u>, and <u>powerfully</u>.

The second adverb *easily* was replaced with another adverb carefully. The meanings of *easily* and *carefully* are not the same, but *carefully* could be used to describe how an athlete moves. In this sentence, *carefully* adds to the rhythm of the sentence since the suffix *-fully* is used three times.

Athletes move with <u>grace</u>, <u>ease</u>, and <u>power</u>.

This sentence can also be made parallel by using three prepositional phrases. The objects of the preposition *with* are all parallel nouns: *grace, ease,* and *power*.

PARALLEL GERUNDS

I enjoy <u>shopping</u> and <u>keeping up</u> with the latest styles, but not <u>paying</u> the bills.

Shopping, keeping up, and *paying* are gerunds. The gerunds are parallel.

I enjoy <u>shopping</u> and to <u>keep up</u> with the latest styles, but not <u>to pay</u> the bills.

To keep up and *to pay* not only are not parallel with *shopping,* they are incorrect. The verb *enjoy* must be followed by a gerund, not an infinitive.

PARALLEL SENTENCES

<u>While</u> there are advantages and disadvantages to both machine-made, and hand-made products, <u>I</u> prefer machine-made products. <u>While</u> hand-made products are generally high quality, <u>I</u> find them expensive. <u>While</u> I appreciate high-quality products, <u>I</u> can't afford them.

These three sentences are parallel. They all begin with an adverb clause introduced by *While*. The subject of the independent clause in all three sentences is *I*. Each sentence after the first one takes an idea from the previous sentence and carries it forward using the same construction. There is a nice rhythm to these sentences. Be careful though. There is a narrow line between rhythmic parallels and boring repetitions.

While there are advantages and disadvantages to both, given my type of personality, I prefer machine-made products. While hand-made products are generally high quality, they are also very expensive. While I do appreciate high quality, my status as a student makes me appreciate low cost as well.

In this version, the basic parallel construction remains. The last two sentences have been changed. In these two sentences, the parallelism is within the sentences as well as between the sentences.

Hand-made products are high quality.
Hand-made products are very expensive.

I appreciate high quality.
I appreciate low cost.

The writer draws a similarity between adjectives *high quality* and *very expensive*, and contrasts the products with the adjectives *high quality* and *low cost*.

 **PRACTICE 7**

Read the sentences and decide if the underlined word or phrase should be changed. Some underlined words are incorrect; others are grammatically correct, but not well-written. If the word should be changed, rewrite it.

1. Dogs provide older people an important chance to learn or <u>maintaining</u> *maintain* social skills.

2. My parents didn't have time to analyze their feelings or <u>thinking</u> about themselves.

3. I believe zoos are useful both in terms of educating and <u>they can advance</u> scientific research.

4. I prefer a combination of living <u>at</u> a small, suburban town and working in a big city.

5. Agricultural research improves individual citizen's lives, whereas successful businesses <u>to improve</u> a country's economy.

6. Heated debate is interesting, and <u>interest</u> things are easier to learn about.

7. <u>One</u> might think that it is a waste of time to go out to see a movie when you can watch DVDs at home.

8. Teachers can instruct tomorrow's leaders; doctors can make those leaders healthier; and <u>engineering</u> can guarantee that future generations have good housing.

9. I could see the house where my grandmother grew up and <u>where my cousins still live in that house</u>.

10. Many people want to travel abroad to see new places and things; people also want to travel abroad <u>so that they can</u> improve their educational opportunities.

Coherence

Transition words help the reader see the relationship between sentences and ideas. They are one way to provide coherence in an essay. There are two other ways to provide coherence: repeating words and rephrasing ideas.

REPEATING

Repeating words can provide a rhythm to a paragraph. In the example below, notice how the phrase *She worked with* is repeated three times to show ways a community health worker helped people.

EXAMPLE

She *worked with* mothers teaching them how to keep their children healthy. She *worked with* school teachers helping them recognize early signs of illness. She *worked with* restaurant personnel showing them proper food handling techniques. A community needs help in many ways.

Repeating words can also link ideas that may be several sentences apart. Look at the Pronoun example on page 148. The second sentence in the example ends with *she helped the people in the area*. The next to the last sentence, *A community needs help in many ways*, emphasizes the need of the community for help.

REPHRASING

We can rephrase words and sentences to provide coherence to the essay. Rephrasing gives the reader a second chance to understand the idea. Synonyms are one way to rephrase.

EXAMPLE

The countryside where I grew up is very *isolated*. You can drive for miles without seeing another car. It seems in all directions you look at a *breathtaking vista*. The scenery near the ocean is especially *dramatic, with giant dark* cliffs rising out of the water.

Rephrased Version
Such a *secluded, remote* environment is a perfect place to relax. The *spectacular views* bring out the artist in me. I often take my paints and a canvas and try to capture the exciting *feel of the shoreline*.

Notice the ideas that are rephrased

The countryside where I grew up is very *isolated*. You can drive for miles without seeing another car.
Such a *secluded, remote* environment is a perfect place to relax.
It seems in all directions you look at a *breathtaking* vista.
The *spectacular* views bring out the artist in me.
The *scenery near the ocean* is especially *dramatic, with giant dark* cliffs rising out of the water.
I often take my paints and a canvas and try to capture the exciting *feel of the shoreline*.

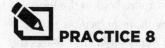 **PRACTICE 8**

Choose which phrase or sentence best completes the paragraph and makes the paragraph cohesive.

Paragraph 1. An effective advertisement matches images and music to its product and (1) _____. For instance, if it's selling cars to young men, it uses the image of speed and rock music. If it's selling cars to families, it uses the image of practicality and pleasant melodies. (2) _____.

   1. (A) its market
      (B) the market it wants to reach
      (C) to those who will buy the product

   2. (A) If it's trying to sell a more expensive car, it uses classical music to suggest elegance and comfort.
      (B) If the car is for the rich, advertisers will want to emphasize elegance and wealth.
      (C) If it's selling cars to wealthy executives, it uses the image of wealth and classical music.

Paragraph 2. Our parents studied grammar, a subject that a lot of schools don't teach today. They studied penmanship, a skill that today few people have mastered. (3) _____. They didn't have to learn advanced mathematics, but (4) _____ how to do basic math without the help of a calculator.

   3. (A) A foreign language, which is optional today, was a required subject.
      (B) They were taught to communicate in a foreign language.
      (C) They studied a foreign language, something that is not a requirement in many schools today.

   4. (A) they had to learn
      (B) it was important to learn
      (C) they felt they should know

Paragraph 3. The contributions scientists make to society are more obvious. The cars we drive, the computers we use at home and at work, (5) _____ —all of these come from the ideas and hard work of scientists. Because of scientific contributions, we're living longer and healthier lives. Scientists also (6) _____ the arts. Movies are the result of science, as are television, radio, and compact discs.

   5. (A) and the stove and cleaning machine
      (B) the appliances we have to help us cook our meals and clean our houses
      (C) the cooking and cleaning inventions

   6. (A) contribute to
      (B) help fund
      (C) support

 **PRACTICE 9**

Choose which sentence or phrase best completes the paragraph, rephrasing the underlined sections.

Paragraph 1. Zoos are also important for the research opportunities they provide. Because zoos are controlled environments, research is safer and easier to conduct. (1) _____. They may not be as secure in the wild. For example, while conducting a medical experiment in an animal's natural environment, scientists have to worry about both the animals they are working with and other animals nearby (2) _____. In zoos, however, they need only focus on the research subject.

1. (A) Scientists can feel protected in the confined area of the zoo.
   (B) Scientists are better able to manage their resources at the zoo.
   (C) Scientists carry out their work more effectively at the zoo.

2. (A) in hiding
   (B) in the bush
   (C) in proximity

Paragraph 2. Not everyone learns in the same way. For instance, some students learn better by discussing a topic while others (3) _____ by writing about it. Teachers know this and have been trained to teach using whatever methods help their students learn the most about a subject. A textbook can only give one way of learning something, but a teacher can help students learn (4) _____.

3. (A) study much harder
   (B) absorb more knowledge
   (C) enjoy the experience more

4. (A) using a different style
   (B) faster and more efficiently
   (C) in the ways that work best for them

Paragraph 3. Both art and music help students express themselves. Students who have never before drawn a picture or tried playing the piano may be surprised to find that they enjoy these methods of (5) _____. It is also always satisfying to try something new. It usually takes a while to develop skills in art and music, but the process of (6) _____ can be as satisfying as producing a perfect piece of art at the end.

5. (A) communicating their inner feelings
   (B) learning about art and music
   (C) improving their talents

6. (A) being part of a class
   (B) starting a new project
   (C) acquiring new abilities

Sentences

Both the Integrated Task and Independent Task want you to demonstrate syntactic variety. You can vary the types of sentences you use, the length of the sentences, the subject of the sentences, and the voice of the sentences.

SENTENCE TYPES

There are four types of sentences: simple, compound, complex, and compound-complex.

Simple Sentence

A simple sentence has one subject and one verb.

Television <u>commercials</u> <u>are</u> the most effective form of advertising.
            subject   verb

Compound Sentence

A compound sentence consists of two or more simple sentences linked by a coordinating conjunction: *and, or, but, yet, so.*

<u>Newspaper ads are often ignored,</u> and <u>radio ads are quickly forgotten.</u>
     simple sentence 1   conjunction   simple sentence 2

Complex Sentence

A complex sentence is made up of a simple sentence (independent clause) and one or more subordinate clauses, with a subordinating conjunction such as: *because, since, after, before, when, although, even though, if.*

<u>Most people listen to radio</u> <u>when they're driving to work.</u>
     simple sentence   subordinate clause

Compound-Complex Sentences

A compound-complex sentence has two or more simple sentences (independent clauses) and one or more subordinate clauses.

Although families may listen to a radio during the day, <u>the parents listen only for news reports,</u> and <u>the children use it for background noise.</u>

SENTENCE LENGTH

Some students think they have to use compound-complex sentences to show they are very proficient in English. This makes the essay very heavy and very difficult to read. It is better to mix up the type of sentences you use. For example, a complex sentence followed by several simple sentences can be very effective.

EXAMPLE

As the number of pets increase, the amount of money being spent on pets is also increasing. Pet owners buy special toys for their pets. They order them special clothes. They put them in day care centers. They treat them like children.

PRACTICE 10

Label the sentences by their type in the following essay.

Simple = S	Complex = Cx
Compound = C	Compound–Complex = C-Cx

TOPIC 8

Why People Visit Museums

1. _S_
2. _____
3. _____
4. _____
5. _____

People visit museums for a number of reasons. They visit museums when traveling to new places because a museum tells them a lot about the culture of those places. They also go to museums to have fun. People also are usually interested in museums that feature unusual subjects. It's impossible to get bored in a museum.

6. _____
7. _____
8. _____
9. _____
10. _____
11. _____

When visiting someplace new, you can find out about the culture of that place by going to a movie or a place of worship or a nightclub. Another option is to sit in the park and listen to the people around you. The easiest way to learn about a place, though, is by visiting its museums. Museums will show you the history of the place you're visiting. They will show you what art the locals think is important. If there aren't any museums, that tells you something, too.

12. _____
13. _____
14. _____
15. _____

Museums are fun. Even if you're not interested in art or history, there is always something to get your attention. Many museums now have "hands-on" exhibits. These exhibits usually involve activities like pushing a button and hearing more about what you're looking at, or using similar materials to create your own work of art, or trying on clothes like those on the models in the museum.

16. _____
17. _____
18. _____
19. _____

People also enjoy museums about unusual subjects. For instance, in my hometown there's a museum devoted to the potato. This museum has art made out of potatoes, it tells all about the history of the potato, and it sells potato mementos, like key chains and potato dolls. People enjoy this museum because it's so unusual.

20. _____
21. _____
22. _____

People everywhere like museums. They like learning about interesting and unusual things. No matter who you are or what you like, there is a museum that will amaze and interest you.

 **PRACTICE 11**

Combine each group of sentences into one new sentence. Use the conjunctions provided.

1. **Compound Sentence**
   City streets are crowded and noisy.
   City people are always in a hurry.
   (and)

   _____

2. **Compound Sentence**
   Most children like to watch TV.
   They don't usually watch educational programs.
   (but)

   _____

3. **Complex Sentence**
   People don't like to go shopping.
   The weather is bad.
   (when)

   _____

4. **Complex Sentence**
   Many native plants die.
   Invasive species take over.
   (after)

   _____

5. **Complex Sentence**
   You will feel more energized.
   You walk around the room for five minutes.
   (if)

   _____

6. **Compound-Complex Sentence**
   I prefer living in the countryside.
   I grew up in a city.
   Most of my relatives still live there.
   (even though, and)

   _____

Subject

You can vary your writing by varying the subjects of your sentences. Compare the following two versions of the same paragraph. In Version A, all the sentences have the same subject. In Version B, the sentences have been rewritten so that the subjects vary.

VERSION A

Games are more than entertainment. Games teach us important life skills. For example, games teach us about rules. Most games have rules that the players must follow. Games teach us how rules work, and they show us what happens when we don't follow the rules.

VERSION B

Entertainment is important, but games are much more than that. Games teach us important life skills. For example, rules are an important part of most games, so playing games is an opportunity to learn about rules. We can learn about how rules work and about what happens when we don't follow them.

When you write your sentences, you need to make sure that the subject of each sentence or clause agrees with the verb. A singular subject needs a singular verb and a plural subject needs a plural verb.

Most count nouns may be either singular or plural.

> This <u>game</u> <u>is</u> fun to play. (singular subject, singular verb)
> Most <u>games</u> <u>are</u> fun to play. (plural subject, plural verb)

Non-count nouns are singular and take singular verbs.

> <u>Entertainment</u> <u>helps</u> us relax.
> This <u>equipment</u> <u>needs</u> repair.

When the subject is a gerund, it takes a singular verb.

> <u>Playing</u> <u>keeps</u> us young.
> <u>Exercising</u> regularly <u>is</u> important for good health.

Words that begin with *every* and *no* take singular verbs.

> <u>Everybody</u> <u>agrees</u> that games are fun.
> <u>Nothing</u> <u>relaxes</u> me as much as playing a game.

 **PRACTICE 12**

For each sentence or clause, underline the subject and choose the correct form of the verb.

1. Doing housework (help/helps) children build skills.
2. When young children (do/does) simple tasks, they (develop/develops) motor skills.
3. Simple tasks, such as sweeping, (are/is) suitable for older children.
4. Older children (learn/learns) other kinds of skills.
5. They (learn/learns) skills that will be useful when they (grow up/grows up).
6. Completing housework (take/takes) effort.
7. Effort (have/has) its own rewards.
8. Children (feel/feels) proud when they (see/sees) the results of their work.
9. Nothing (are/is) as rewarding as a job well done.
10. Everybody (want/wants) their children to learn responsibility.

Voice

There are two voices in English: active and passive.

ACTIVE VOICE

Parents must teach their children computer skills.
subject   action   object

PASSIVE VOICE

Children must be taught computer skills by their parents.
subject   action   agent

The active voice emphasizes the agent (the one who performs the action). The agent is the subject of the sentence. The passive voice emphasizes the recipient of the action or the action itself. The recipient is the subject of the sentence. Most of the time we use active voice. It is a very direct way of writing and is often clearer and easier to read than passive voice.

We use passive voice when the agent is unknown or unimportant. The passive voice is useful for changing the emphasis of a sentence or for avoiding the need to mention unknown or unimportant information.

Look at these comparisons of active and passive voice.

ACTIVE VOICE

Fifty years ago, somebody built a factory in my town.

PASSIVE VOICE

Fifty years ago, a factory was built in my town.

The first sentence sounds awkward and strange. Who is "somebody?" We don't know and it doesn't matter. The important information is the building of the factory, not the person or people who built it.

ACTIVE VOICE

Many people lost their jobs when the owners closed the factory last year.

PASSIVE VOICE

Many people lost their jobs when the factory was closed last year.

The first sentence is possible, but the second sentence is better. We don't need to mention the agent, "the owners," because it is obvious that it was they who closed the factory. In this case, mentioning the agent takes emphasis away from the important information: the fact that the factory was closed.

 **PRACTICE 13**

Underline the verbs in the following essay and tell whether they are active or passive.

TOPIC 3

No Factory!

1. *active*

People <u>like</u> factories because they bring new jobs to a community. In my opinion, however, the benefits of a factory are outweighed by the risks. Factories cause pollution, and they bring too much growth. In addition, they destroy the quiet lifestyle of a small town. That is why I oppose a plan to build a factory near my community.

2. _____
3. _____
   _____
4. _____
5. _____

Factories cause smog. If we build a new factory, the air we breathe will become dirty. Everything will be covered with dust. Factories also pollute rivers and streams. Our water will be too dirty to drink. The environment will be hurt and people's health will be affected.

6. _____
7. _____
   _____
   _____
8. _____
9. _____
10. _____
11. _____
    _____

Some people will say that more jobs will be created by a factory. However, this can have a negative result. Our population will grow quickly. Many new homes and stores will be built. There will be a lot of traffic on the roads. Fast growth can cause more harm than good.

12. _____
    _____
13. _____
14. _____
15. _____
16. _____
17. _____

Our city will change a lot. It is a pleasant place now. It is safe and quiet. Everybody knows everybody else. If a factory brings growth to the city, all of this will change. The small-town feel will be lost.

18. _____
19. _____
20. _____
21. _____
22. _____
    _____
23. _____

A factory would be helpful in some ways, but the dangers outweigh the benefits. Our city would be changed too much by a factory. I cannot support a plan to build a new factory here.

24. _____
    _____
25. _____
26. _____

PRACTICE 14

Choose the active sentence that has the same meaning as the passive sentence.

1. Our lives have been dramatically improved by changes in food preparation.

    (A) Changes in food preparation have dramatically improved our lives.
    (B) Our lives are changing dramatically and so have changes in food preparation.
    (C) Our food preparation improvements have been dramatic changes.

2. Young people will be helped to overcome the fear of aging by associating with older people.

    (A) Our fear of associating with older people can overcome young people.
    (B) Young people can associate with older people who fear aging.
    (C) Association with older people will help young people overcome the fear of aging.

3. I do not like the fact that these products are made by machines.

    (A) I do not like the fact that these are machine-made products.
    (B) Products made by machine are not liked; it's a fact.
    (C) It's not a fact that these products were made by machines.

4. Large sums of money are earned by entertainers who do little to contribute to society.

    (A) Society earns a little from entertainers' contributions.
    (B) Entertainers earn large sums of money yet contribute little to society.
    (C) Money is contributed to society by entertainers who earn a lot.

Model Tests

6

This chapter contains four model tests. Each test includes one Integrated Task and one Independent Task. After you complete a model test, you can use the revision checklist to check your work. Before you fill in the checklist, follow the suggested steps to make sure you have covered everything. Then, look for the corresponding model essay in the Appendix, read it, and check it, following the same steps. See how your essay compares with the model. Remember, there is no one correct way to write any of these essays, but reading the model essays and using the revision checklists will help you see the strengths and weaknesses of your writing.

INTEGRATED TASK

Steps

1. Find the thesis statement. Underline it.
2. In the first paragraph, find the topics that support the thesis. Number them.
3. Put a check (✓) next the main idea in the second paragraph. Mark each supporting detail with a letter: A, B, C, etc.
4. Put a check (✓) next the main idea in the third paragraph. Mark each supporting detail with a letter: A, B, C, etc.
5. Underline all transition words in the second and third paragraphs.
6. Check grammar and spelling. Correct any errors.

REVISION CHECKLIST

■ **Content**
- ❏ Thesis Statement
- ❏ Topics that support the thesis
- ❏ Main ideas
- ❏ Supporting details

■ **Fluency and Cohesion**
- ❏ Transition words
- ❏ Grammar and Spelling
- ❏ Sentence variety

INDEPENDENT TASK

Steps

1. Find the thesis statement and underline it.
2. In the first paragraph, find the topics that support the thesis. Number them. They should become the main ideas of the paragraphs in the body of the essay.
3. Put a check (✓) next to the main idea in the second paragraph. Mark each supporting detail with a letter: A, B, C, etc.
4. Put a check (✓) next to the main idea in the third paragraph. Mark each supporting detail with a letter: A, B, C, etc.

5. Put a check (✓) next to the main idea in the fourth paragraph. Mark each supporting detail with a letter: A, B, C, etc.
6. Underline all transition words in the second, third, fourth, and fifth paragraphs.
7. Check grammar and spelling. Correct any errors.

REVISION CHECKLIST

■ **Content**
- ❏ Thesis Statement
- ❏ Main ideas
- ❏ Supporting details

■ **Fluency and Cohesion**
- ❏ Transition words
- ❏ Grammar and Spelling
- ❏ Sentence variety

MP3 files and audioscripts also available online at

barronsbooks.com/TP/TOEFL/Writing

Model Test 1

INTEGRATED TASK

 **READING**

Read the passage for three minutes.

The presence of technology in schools has greatly increased over the past two decades. More and more classrooms are equipped with computers and wireless technology, with the aim of boosting academic achievement. How far has technology gone toward reaching this goal?

The perceived benefits of classroom technology are several. According to many educators, one of the greatest advantages is that it provides a variety of learning tools, making it easy to address different learning styles. It allows students to experience a topic in verbal, written, spatial, quantitative, and graphical ways. Students can take in and use information in the ways that make most sense to them. Technology also helps teachers expand the boundaries of the classroom. Through use of the Internet, students can connect with people and ideas anywhere in the world.

In order to receive these benefits, however, technology must actually be used. Surveys have found that only a low percentage of teachers use technology on a regular basis, and that as many as half of all teachers never use it at all. Many teachers who do use technology do not use it to its fullest advantage. Rather, the tendency is to use computers to do the same things that can be done with pencil and paper.

Studies have shown that, properly used, technology does boost academic achievement. It has also been shown that teacher training can make the difference. In one study, teachers who received training in classroom use of technology used it regularly and used it in ways that developed higher-order thinking skills in their students. This study also showed that students in these classrooms scored higher on math tests than their peers in other classrooms. School systems, therefore, need to focus on training teachers in addition to equipping classrooms with computers.

Note: Models for these practice tasks can be found in the Appendix. Remember, there is no one correct response. If you follow the steps outlined in the previous chapters, you will be able to write an appropriate response that is your own, original work.

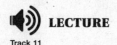 **LECTURE**

Track 11

Listen to the lecture.

Summarize the main points in the reading passage and explain how they are strengthened by the information presented in the lecture. Write on your computer or on a separate piece of paper.

Write 150–225 words. Remember to divide your writing time as follows:

STEP 1	PLAN	3 minutes
STEP 2	WRITE	14 minutes
STEP 3	REVISE	3 minutes

INDEPENDENT TASK

Write an essay on the following topic. Write on your computer or on a separate piece of paper.
Write at least 300 words. Remember to divide your writing time as follows:

STEP 1	PLAN	5 minutes
STEP 2	WRITE	20 minutes
STEP 3	REVISE	5 minutes

ESSAY TOPIC 28

Is it more important to be able to work with a group of people on a team or to work independently? Use reasons and specific examples to support your answer.

Model Test 2

INTEGRATED TASK

READING

Read the passage for three minutes.

The study of animal intelligence has long been of interest to humans. In studying the question of whether or not animals can be said to have intelligence, researchers look at such areas as emotions and self-recognition, among other things. The topic of animal intelligence has generated a great deal of controversy.

In one study designed to look at emotions, chimpanzees watched videos of other chimpanzees in different situations which might cause feelings of fear or happiness. The behavioral reactions of the chimpanzees watching the video were observed to be appropriate for each situation. Their brain activity was also shown to change according to the different emotions demonstrated on the videos.

Mirrors have been used in experiments to determine whether or not animals recognize themselves. In one study, dolphins were marked on different parts of their bodies. The fact that they raced to the mirror to look at their image as soon as they felt the markers demonstrated to researchers that the dolphins did indeed recognize themselves in their mirror images. Similar studies have been done with elephants and chimpanzees. Researchers have also looked at language, tool use, memory, and problem-solving ability in attempts to define intelligence in animals.

Research on animal intelligence raises a number of difficulties. For one, there is disagreement about what we actually mean by the word "intelligence." There is also disagreement about the correct way to interpret animal behavior observed in experiments. And, it is difficult to separate actual feelings and cognitive reasoning from instinctual behavior.

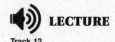 **LECTURE**

Track 12

Listen to the lecture.

Summarize the main points of the reading passage and explain how they are supported by the information presented in the lecture. Write on your computer or on a separate piece of paper.

Write 150–225 words. Remember to divide your writing time as follows:

STEP 1	PLAN	3 minutes
STEP 2	WRITE	14 minutes
STEP 3	REVISE	3 minutes

INDEPENDENT TASK

Write an essay on the following topic. Write on your computer or on a separate piece of paper. Write at least 300 words. Remember to divide your writing time as follows:

STEP 1	PLAN	5 minutes
STEP 2	WRITE	20 minutes
STEP 3	REVISE	5 minutes

ESSAY TOPIC 17

Do you agree or disagree with the following statement? People should sometimes do things they do not enjoy doing. Use specific reasons and examples to support your answer.

Model Test 3

INTEGRATED TASK

 **READING**

Read the passage for three minutes.

William Shakespeare (1564–1616) is considered to be one of the greatest writers of English literature. But did he really write *Romeo and Juliet*, *Hamlet*, *Macbeth*, and the other plays attributed to him? Scholars have long questioned the authenticity of the claim that these works were written by William Shakespeare of Stratford-on-Avon, England. There are a number of reasons why.

In the first place, William Shakespeare was a man of humble origins. He was not a wealthy aristocrat or nobleman. Rather, he was the son of a tradesman, and there is no record that he ever went to school. Yet many of his plays deal with the lives of nobility and show an understanding of politics, science, literature, and foreign languages that only an aristocrat or an educated person would have had.

In addition, very few concrete facts about Shakespeare's life are known. There are very few written records containing information about him. This seems unusual for someone who became as well known as Shakespeare did. Some scholars take this as evidence that records were destroyed to hide the true identity of the author of the plays attributed to Shakespeare.

Several contemporary writers have been suggested as the possible true author of Shakespeare's works. One of the more popular theories is that they were written by Sir Francis Bacon, a prominent scholar, diplomat, and writer. This claim is based in part on perceived similarities between some of Bacon's writing and certain phrases found in the plays attributed to Shakespeare. Other well-known writers, including playwright Christopher Marlowe and Edward de Vere, 17th Earl of Oxford, have also been put forth as possible authors of the plays.

 **LECTURE**
Track 13

Listen to the lecture.

Summarize the points in the reading passage and explain how they are challenged by points raised in the lecture. Write on your computer or on a separate piece of paper.

Write 150–225 words. Remember to divide your writing time as follows:

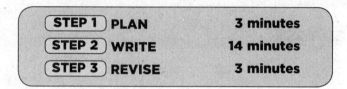

STEP 1	PLAN	3 minutes
STEP 2	WRITE	14 minutes
STEP 3	REVISE	3 minutes

INDEPENDENT TASK

Write an essay on the following topic. Write on your computer or on a separate piece of paper. Write at least 300 words. Remember to divide your writing time as follows:

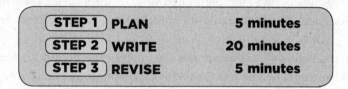

STEP 1	PLAN	5 minutes
STEP 2	WRITE	20 minutes
STEP 3	REVISE	5 minutes

ESSAY TOPIC 44

> If you could invent something new, what product would you develop? Use specific details to explain why this invention is needed.

Model Test 4

INTEGRATED TASK

READING

Read the passage for three minutes.

The bubonic plague, also known as the Black Plague or the Black Death, swept through the world during the Middle Ages. Originating in China, it left behind a lasting legacy.

The worst outbreak of the plague occurred in the mid-1300s. The deadly disease appeared in China in the early 1330s. Since China was a busy trading nation, the plague was soon carried from its ports to the rest of the world. The disease was transmitted to people by fleas. Rats, which infested trading ships, were the means of transporting the disease-ridden fleas throughout the world.

In 1347, several Italian trading ships returned from the Black Sea and docked in Sicily. Unbeknownst to the crew, the cargo they carried included plague-carrying rats, and a number of the sailors were dying, or already dead, from the disease. The plague spread quickly from the port to the surrounding countryside, and then throughout Italy. By the following year it had reached northern Europe. During the cold season, the plague seemed to recede, but it returned each spring with renewed vigor when fleas awakened from their winter dormancy.

It is estimated that 75 million people worldwide fell victim to the disease within the next five years. In Europe, 25 million people—one third of the continent's population—died. The widespread death led to breakdowns in the existing social order. Among other effects, the authority of the church weakened and there were peasant uprisings. There continued to be recurrences of the plague every generation or so for the next several centuries, though none as terrible as the outbreak of the 1300s. The plague finally disappeared in the 17th century.

Listen to the lecture.

Summarize the points in the reading passage and explain how they are challenged by points raised in the lecture. Write on your computer or on a separate piece of paper.

Write 150–225 words. Remember to divide your writing time as follows:

> STEP 1 PLAN   3 minutes
> STEP 2 WRITE   14 minutes
> STEP 3 REVISE   3 minutes

INDEPENDENT TASK

Write an essay on the following topic. Write on your computer or on a separate piece of paper. Write at least 300 words. Remember to divide your writing time as follows:

> STEP 1 PLAN   5 minutes
> STEP 2 WRITE   20 minutes
> STEP 3 REVISE   5 minutes

ESSAY TOPIC 19

> You have received a gift of money. The money is enough to buy either a piece of jewelry you like or tickets to a concert you want to attend. Which would you buy? Use specific reasons and details to support your answer.

Appendix

Model Essays

The Model Essay sections of the Appendix contain 10 model essays for the Integrated Task and 144 model essays for the Independent Task. They are provided as examples of ways to respond to the TOEFL essay writing tasks. There is no one correct way to respond to any of the writing task questions. These are models of well-organized essays that are clear, coherent, and address the question. These models show one possible way of responding to the particular question.

You can study these models as examples of ways to respond to the tasks. You can also use them to compare with your own writing.

For the Integrated Task essays, you can complete a practice task in the exercises or model tests, then compare your essay with the corresponding model essay in the Appendix. Notice how the lecture and reading are summarized and compared in the model essay and in your own. You might not have used the exact same words, but your essay should follow the same general points as the model essay.

For the Independent Task essays, choose one of the questions and write your own response to it before looking at the model essay. Since the Independent Task asks you to express your own ideas and opinions, your essay will be very different from the model essay. The model essay, however, will show you how to develop a theme with a main idea, supporting ideas, and details. Notice how this is done in the model essay, then check your essay to make sure it follows the same type of structure.

A good practice technique is to write out the essays by hand. This will help you become familiar with the structure of a sentence, the words used, and the organization of the essay. You can write them over several times. It is important to do this by hand. There is a correlation between the hand and the brain. This will help you internalize the patterns.

You can also use the essays to practice typing. This will help you with spelling and the formatting of the essay.

MODEL ESSAYS: INTEGRATED TASKS

These model Integrated Tasks are based on reading passages and lectures used in the Self-Tests and exercises in this book. Each task is identified so that you can easily find the reading passages and lectures that correspond to each model. These are examples only so that you can see ways to respond to the Integrated Task.

MODEL 1 (SELF-TEST, pages 23–24)

The author explains why global warming is a serious problem. Likewise, the speaker explains the impact of global warming in the northeastern United States.

The author explains that human activity, such as industry and cutting down forests, has resulted in an artificial increase in greenhouse gases in Earth's atmosphere, with serious results. Greenhouse gases, such as carbon dioxide, hold heat in the atmosphere and result in rising temperatures on Earth. As average temperatures rise, there are a number of effects. First, scientists predict that weather patterns will change. In addition, snow and ice will melt and sea levels will rise. This can lead to flooding, drought, and powerful storms. It can also affect the economy, particularly agriculture and transportation. Economists predict that global warming will lead to a drop in gross national product and consumer consumption in countries around the world.

The speaker explains the effects of global warming in the northeastern part of the United States. This is a cold and snowy area. Since 1965, temperatures in this region have risen. There are also fewer days with snow on the ground than there used to be. This has had an effect on the economy for people who depend on the ski industry to make a living. The predicted effects of global warming that the author described are already coming true, at least in the northeastern United States.

MODEL 2 (TASK 1, page 60)

Summarize the main points of the reading passage and explain how the points made in the lecture oppose them.

The author asserts that advances in technology do not always lead to increased productivity. The speaker, in contrast, suggests that investment in technology is paid back in increased productivity.

The author explains that because of technology, workers often stay at their desks all day, but this does not lead to increased productivity. It can cause back, neck, and eye pain. This is very uncomfortable and actually lowers productivity. Workers need to take breaks more often and go out for lunch. They also should have meetings in person instead of using email. In addition, companies can buy special equipment that is more comfortable to use.

The speaker has the opposite point of view. She believes that technology increases productivity. Photocopy machines, for example, can copy, collate, and staple much faster than a person. Because of this, workers can spend their time doing other things. Also an office can hire fewer people and save money on salaries. Moreover, when people use email, they don't have to go to so many meetings. Instead, they can spend more time working. The speaker does not mention the physical pains that using technology can cause. Clearly, technology solves some problems, but it causes others.

MODEL 3 (TASK 2, page 65)

Summarize the main points of the reading passage and explain how they are supported by the information presented in the lecture.

The author explains that animal-assisted therapy is used to improve emotional and physical health, and the speaker tells us about a study that showed positive effects of pet ownership on health.

The author explains how pets improve both emotional health and physical health. Pets are good companions for lonely people. They also give their owners things to do, like hobbies or club activities. In addition, pets are a comfort to anxious or worried people. Pets are good for physical health, as well. They help people with high blood pressure and heart problems. They help people stay physically active. They give people a chance to play. Finally, pet therapy is used with elderly people.

The speaker supports pet therapy. He describes a study where pets had a positive effect on the health of heart patients. Half the patients had a dog to take care of. The other half only got traditional treatment. After six months, the patients with pets had lower blood pressure, and they had lost more weight than the other patients. They felt happier, too. These are all things that can affect heart disease. This is a case that shows how pet therapy works to improve physical health.

MODEL 4 (TASK 3, page 66)

Summarize the main points in the reading passage and explain how the information presented in the lecture adds to them.

The author warns that ocean pollution is a serious problem. In the same way, the speaker explains how plastic garbage threatens sea animals.

The author explains that different things cause ocean pollution. Oil from factories and cities enters the ocean through rivers and drains. Similarly, fertilizers wash into the ocean, and they cause large growths of algae. Toxic chemicals continue to pollute the ocean, as well. There are laws against dumping these chemicals, but the chemicals still leak into the ocean. Animals eat them, and when we eat seafood, we eat these chemicals, too. There is also a lot of garbage in the ocean. Plastic is the worst kind because it does not break down quickly. Animals think it is food. They eat it and choke on it.

While the author gives an overview of ocean pollution, the speaker specifically describes the problem of plastic garbage. People produce billions of pounds of plastic a year, and a lot of this ends up in the ocean. The water and wind break large pieces of plastic into smaller pieces. Then animals try to eat these pieces. An animal may choke on plastic. It may starve because it does not feel hungry after eating plastic. Animals are often caught in floating plastic. They are also strangled by it. There are many types of pollution in the ocean. Plastic garbage is one of the worst examples.

MODEL 5 (TASK 4, page 67)

Summarize the main points of the reading passage and explain how the points made in the lecture cast doubt on them.

The author explains that color has psychological effects. In contrast, the speaker tells us about a study that showed no effect of color on appetite.

The author describes different ways people have used the psychological effects of color. Ancient people used color for healing, and modern designers use color to create mood. Designers might use yellow to create a positive mood in an office. Likewise, they might use neutral colors to create a clean, clear, and focused mood in health care centers. Restaurants often use orange and red to stimulate the appetite. Some scientists say that blue lowers the heart rate and blood pressure. Red, on the other hand, may raise blood pressure. Other scientists do not believe that color affects mood. They say the effect is temporary and also that it is different in every culture.

The speaker describes a study that showed no relationship between color and appetite. A fast-food restaurant chain had orange walls in half its restaurants and beige walls in the rest of its restaurants. It recorded all the food ordered for two years. There was no difference between the restaurants with orange walls and the restaurants with beige walls. People ordered the same food in both types of places. In other words, according to the company president, there is no effect of color on appetite. He said that the study proved it. In this case, at least, there was no psychological effect of color.

MODEL 6 (PRACTICE INTEGRATED TASK, page 80)

The author discusses the dangers of cell phone use while driving. The speaker, however, believes that cell phones are not any more dangerous to drivers than other distractions.

The author explains that talking on the phone while driving is dangerous because it distracts the driver. Because of this, drivers in accidents involving cell phones have been held responsible for the accidents. The author also discusses laws that prohibit the use of cell phones while driving.

The speaker disagrees with these laws. He points out that drivers can be distracted by things other than talking on the phone, such as eating, talking to passengers, taking care of children, putting on make up, and other things. He cites a study that found that cell phone use actually causes fewer accidents than other distractions. He mentions another study that used video tapes. The tapes showed that drivers were less distracted by their phones than by other activities. Finally, the speaker emphasizes that cell phones contribute to our safety. People use cell phones to report accidents and dangerous drivers on the road.

MODEL 7 (MODEL TESTS, INTEGRATED TASK 1, page 167)

The author explains that technology in the classroom can improve academic achievement, but only when it is used properly. The speaker agrees that adequate teacher training is necessary.

The author talks about the ways that technology can improve learning, by addressing different learning styles and by connecting to the rest of the world through the Internet. Unfortunately, teachers do not always use technology in the best way possible, so their students do not benefit from it. Academic achievement can be improved through technology if teachers are trained to use it.

The speaker completely supports this point of view by discussing two studies. A survey of teachers found that they often do not receive enough training to use technology, so they feel very uncomfortable with it. The majority do not use computers in their classrooms. The speaker then mentioned a special program in one school district. The teachers received 200 hours of training. They used technology in their classrooms to help their students develop thinking skills. These students scored much higher on achievement tests than other students in the school district.

MODEL 8 (MODEL TESTS, INTEGRATED TASK 2, page 169)

The author gives an overview of the study of animal intelligence and points out that there is a lot of controversy around such research. Likewise, the speaker discusses research on animal intelligence, specifically on self-recognition, and also mentions that not all scientists agree with interpretations of the results.

The author especially mentions emotions and self-recognition as two things researchers look at when studying animal intelligence. She describes a particular study with dolphins.

After scientists placed marks on the dolphins' bodies, the dolphins rushed to the mirror to look at the marks. So, scientists say, the animals recognized themselves in the mirror. The author adds that there is a lot of disagreement among scientists researching animal intelligence, including disagreement about how results should be interpreted.

The speaker describes specific research on animal intelligence. She talks in more detail about how studies are done with mirrors. Certain animals react to their reflection in a mirror. For example, they try to touch it. The only animals that do this are apes, dolphins, and elephants. In a self-recognition test, a mark is painted on the animal's face. When the animal looks in the mirror, it might try to wipe the mark off its face. This means that it recognizes itself in the mirror, scientists say. But not all scientists agree. The animal might be interested in the mark but that doesn't mean it connects the mirror image with itself.

MODEL 9 (MODEL TESTS, INTEGRATED TASK 3, page 171)

The author describes reasons why scholars believe that William Shakespeare was not the true author of his plays. In contrast, the speaker says there is not evidence to support this idea.

The author explains several reasons for doubting that Shakespeare wrote the plays. First, William Shakespeare was not wealthy and was probably not educated. The plays contain a lot of information that only a wealthy or educated person would know. Second, there are not many written records about Shakespeare's life. It is possible that records about him were destroyed to hide the fact that another person actually wrote the plays. Who was that other person? There have been several suggestions. Some people think it was Francis Bacon because there are some similarities between his writing and Shakespeare's plays.

The speaker disagrees with the theory that Shakespeare did not write the plays. He explains that Shakespeare could have had the knowledge to write the plays. He may have attended a school in his town, and he actually did have contact with wealthy people because of his theater work. The lack of records is also not evidence because records may have been lost over time. He also states that Bacon could not have written the plays because his writing style is very different from Shakespeare's.

MODEL 10 (MODEL TESTS, INTEGRATED TASK 4, page 173)

The author asserts that the bubonic plague originated in China during the Middle Ages and disappeared in the seventeenth century. The speaker, on the other hand, explains that the plague may actually have originated in ancient Egypt and that outbreaks still occur today.

According to the author, the worst outbreak of the bubonic plague occurred in the 1300s. The disease started in China and was transported to other parts of the world by rats. The rats carried disease-ridden fleas onto ships. The plague arrived in Europe through Italy in 1347. Over the next five years, it killed 25 million people in Europe and 75 million people worldwide. This led to a breakdown of the social order. The plague continued to recur every generation until the seventeenth century, when it disappeared.

The speaker presents a different theory of the origins of the bubonic plague. She describes the work of an archeologist who found evidence of the plague in ancient Egypt. The archeologist found the remains of fleas at the site of an ancient village. The archeologist then turned up evidence that ancient Egyptians had experienced epidemics which may have been the bubonic plague. The speaker says that rats may have carried the disease from Africa to Europe on ships. She also points out that the bubonic plague has not disappeared. There are still several thousand new cases reported around the world every year.

MODEL ESSAYS: INDEPENDENT TASKS

The model essays on the following pages are provided as examples so that you can see a variety of topics and ways to respond to them. The topics are similar to the topics actually used in the TOEFL. You can prepare for the test by using these topics for writing practice and by studying the model essays. Here are some ways you can use this section of the book for practice.

- Choose any model essay. Cover it up and look at the task only. Write your own response, then compare your essay to the model. They will not be the same, of course, but they should follow a similar general pattern of organization.
- Choose any model essay. Cover up the main part of the essay. Look only at the task and the introductory paragraph. Use the points presented in the introduction as the basis for writing your own version of the body of the essay. Then compare it to the model. Check to make sure you covered all the points mentioned in the introduction.
- Choose any model essay. Identify the topics presented in the introduction, the corresponding main ideas in each paragraph, and the supporting details for each main idea.

1

People attend college or university for many different reasons. Why do you think people attend college or university? Use specific reasons and examples to support your answer.

People attend college for a lot of different reasons. I believe that the three most common reasons are to prepare for a career, to have new experiences, and to increase their knowledge of themselves and of the world around them.

Career preparation is probably the primary reason that people attend college. These days, the job market is very competitive. Careers such as information technology will need many new workers in the near future. At college, students can learn new skills for these careers and increase their opportunities for the future.

Students also go to college to have new experiences. For many, it is their first time away from home. At college, they can meet new people from many different places. They can see what life is like in a different city. They can learn to live on their own and take care of themselves without having their family always nearby.

At college, students have the opportunity to increase their knowledge. As they decide what they want to study, pursue their studies, and interact with their classmates, they learn a lot about themselves. They also, of course, have the opportunity to learn about many subjects in their classes. In addition to the skills and knowledge related to their career, college students also have the chance to take classes in other areas. For many, this will be their last chance to study different subjects.

Colleges offer much more than career preparation. They offer the opportunity to have new experiences and to learn many kinds of things. I think all of these are reasons why people attend college.

2

> Do you agree or disagree with the following statement? Parents are the best teachers. Use specific reasons and examples to support your answer.

Parents shape their children from the beginning of their children's lives. They develop close emotional ties with their children. They share their interests with them. They teach them values. Parents can be very important teachers in their children's lives; however, they are not always the best teachers.

Parents may be too close to their children emotionally. For example, they may limit a child's freedom in the name of safety. A teacher may organize an educational trip to a big city, but a parent may think this trip is too dangerous. A school may want to take the children camping, but a parent may be afraid of the child getting hurt.

Another problem is that parents sometimes expect their children's interests to be similar to their own. If the parents love science, they may try to force their child to love science too. But what if the child prefers art? If the parents enjoy sports, they may expect their child to participate on different teams. But what if the child prefers to read?

Finally, although parents want to pass on their values to their children, values can change. The children of today are growing up in a world different from their parents' world. Sometimes parents, especially older ones, can't keep up with rapid social or technological changes. A student who has friends of different races at school may find that his parents have narrower views. A student who loves computers may find that her parents don't understand or value the digital revolution.

Parents are important teachers in our lives, but they aren't always the best teachers. Fortunately, we have many teachers in our lives. Our parents teach us, our teachers teach us, and we learn from our peers. Books and newspapers also teach us. All of them are valuable.

3

> A company has announced that it wishes to build a large factory near your community. Discuss the advantages and disadvantages of this new influence on your community. Do you support or oppose the factory? Explain your position.

People like factories because they bring new jobs to a community. In my opinion, however, the benefits of a factory are outweighed by the risks. Factories cause pollution and they bring too much growth. In addition, they destroy the quiet lifestyle of a small town. That is why I oppose a plan to build a factory near my community.

Factories cause smog. If we build a new factory, the air we breathe will become dirty. Everything will be covered with dust. Factories also pollute rivers and streams. Our water will be too dirty to drink. The environment will be hurt and people's health will be affected by a factory.

Some people will say that more jobs will be created by a factory. However, this can have a negative result. Our population will grow quickly. Many new homes and stores will be built. There will be a lot of traffic on the roads. Fast growth can cause more harm than good.

Our city will change a lot. It is a pleasant place now. It is safe and quiet. Everybody knows everybody else. If a factory brings growth to the city, all of this will change. The small-town feel will be lost.

A factory would be helpful in some ways, but the dangers outweigh the benefits. Our city would be changed too much by a factory. I cannot support a plan to build a new factory here.

4

> If you could change one important thing about your hometown, what would you change? Use reasons and specific examples to support your answer.

If I could change one thing about my hometown, I think it would be the fact that there is no sense of community. People don't feel connected, they don't look out for each other, and they don't get to know their neighbors.

The people who live here don't feel connected to the community. Many of them have jobs in nearby towns, so they spend most of the day somewhere else and are home only in the evenings and on weekends. Also, they tend to change jobs frequently and move away. This means they don't put down roots, and they don't do things that would mean making a commitment to the community, such as joining community organizations, participating in school events, or beautifying the neighborhoods. They don't feel like community members.

People in my hometown generally don't try to support their neighbors. They don't have the habit of watching out for each other's children or checking in on the elderly or keeping an eye on the house next door when the owner is on vacation. They would have no way of knowing if a neighbor suffered an accident or lost a loved one. There just isn't much community support for individuals.

Neighbors in my hometown don't seem interested in getting to know each other. There isn't much casual visiting among neighbors, and neighborhood events such as block parties are not the custom. Also, when there is a problem, such as children riding their bikes uninvited through someone's garden, there is no casual, friendly way of working it out. A simple problem can easily become a major disagreement because there is not a sense of friendliness or trust.

My hometown is a nice place to live in many ways. It is pretty and peaceful and very safe, but it would be much nicer if we had that sense of community.

5

> How do movies or television influence people's behavior? Use reasons and specific examples to support your answer.

Television is a big influence in most of our lives. We spend hours every week watching television programs, so of course it has effects on our behavior. Unfortunately, those effects are usually negative. Television makes people less sensitive to violence, less active, and less imaginative.

Many programs and movies on television are violent, and the more we see this violence, the less sensitive we become to it. Eventually, violence stops seeming wrong or bad. This is especially true because violence on television doesn't seem to have consequences. We might see an actor killed one week on one television program and then appear alive and well the next week on another program. Even though we know the violence and killing aren't real, if we see enough of it on television, it's easy to start confusing it with reality. It's easy to forget that violence in real life has real consequences and that killing someone is permanent.

Another effect of television is that it makes us less active, mentally as well as physically. Watching television requires almost no effort on the part of the watcher. We just push buttons to turn the television on and change the channels. In addition, all the time we spend sitting in front of the television is time we aren't spending moving around, playing a sport, or talking a walk. It's time we aren't spending reading books, conversing with our friends, or studying. It's time we aren't exercising our bodies or minds in meaningful ways.

Finally, television can stifle the imagination. On television, all the stories are told for us. We don't have to imagine what a character or place looks like, as we do when we read books, because everything is shown to us. Furthermore, since we can turn on the television so easily, we don't have to invent ways to spend leisure time. Any time we have a few free moments, we can just sit down and watch and let the television do the entertaining for us.

Television is a big influence in modern life, and it can be a valuable educational tool. The other side, however, is that it has strong negative effects on our behavior, encouraging us to accept violence and to be inactive and unimaginative.

6

> **Some people prefer to live in a small town. Others prefer to live in a big city. Which place would you prefer to live in? Use specific reasons and details to support your answer.**

I grew up in a small town and then moved to a big city. I didn't think I would like living here, but I was wrong. I think life is much better in a big city. Transportation is much more convenient, everything is more exciting, and there is a greater variety of people. I can't imagine ever living in a small town again.

Transportation is easier in a city. In a small town, you have to have a car to get around because there isn't any kind of public transportation. In a city, on the other hand, there are usually buses and taxis, and some cities have subways. Cities often have heavy traffic and expensive parking, but it doesn't matter because you can always take the bus. Using public transportation is usually cheaper and more convenient than driving a car, but you don't have this choice in a small town.

City life is more exciting than small town life. In small towns usually nothing changes. You see the same people every day, you go to the same two or three restaurants, everything is the same. In a city things change all the time. You see new people every day. There are many restaurants, with new ones to choose from all the time. New plays come to the theaters and new musicians come to the concert halls.

Cities have a diversity of people that you don't find in a small town. There are much fewer people in a small town and usually they are all alike. In a city you can find people from different countries, of different religions, of different races—you can find all kinds of people. This variety of people is what makes city life interesting.

Life in a city is convenient, exciting, and interesting. After experiencing city life, I could never live in a small town again.

7

> Do you agree or disagree with the following statement? Universities should give the same amount of money to their students' sports activities as they give to their university libraries. Use specific reasons and examples to support your opinion.

I disagree strongly with the idea that the same amount of money should go to university sports activities as to university libraries. Although playing sports is an important part of education, libraries are fundamental. Students cannot study without them and they require a lot of financial support to maintain up-to-date technology, to keep new books and magazines on the shelves, and to keep them operating.

Students need up-to-date library facilities to get a good education. They need computerized programs and access to Internet research databases. It costs money to have these things available, but they are fundamental to education. If a university offers its students only resources of a decade ago, it deprives those students of a tremendous amount of information.

Although we get a lot of information from computers and the Internet, university libraries still need to maintain a complete book and magazine collection. Every day new information is published on every subject, and every university wants to have this information available to its students. Again, this requires money.

It also costs money for universities to operate their libraries. University libraries are usually open for long hours and during this time they use heat and electricity. Most important, a university library needs a well-educated, knowledgeable staff. In order to be able to hire the best people, they have to be able to pay good salaries.

University students are only going to benefit from their education if they can get all the tools they need to learn. Sports are secondary to the resources that students need from university libraries. For this reason, libraries should always be better funded than sports activities.

8

> Many people visit museums when they travel to new places. Why do you think people visit museums? Use specific reasons and examples to support your answer.

People visit museums for a number of reasons. They visit museums when traveling to new places because a museum tells them a lot about the culture of those places. They also go to museums to have fun. People also are usually interested in museums that feature unusual subjects. It's impossible to get bored in a museum.

When visiting someplace new, you can find out about the culture of that place in many ways. The easiest way to learn about a culture, though, is by visiting its museums.

Museums will show you the history of the place you're visiting. They'll show you what art the locals think is important. If there aren't any museums, that tells you something, too.

Museums are fun. Even if you're not interested in art or history, there is always something to get your attention. Many museums now have what they call "hands-on" exhibits. These exhibits have activities such as pushing a button to hear more about what you're looking at, or creating your own work of art. Everyone, from child to adult, enjoys these hands-on activities in museums.

People also enjoy visiting museums about unusual subjects. For instance, in my hometown there's a museum devoted to the potato. This museum has art made out of potatoes. It also tells the history of the potato, and sells unusual items such as potato dolls. People enjoy visiting this museum because it is so unusual. There is no other place like it.

People everywhere like museums. They like learning about interesting and unusual things. No matter who you are or what you like, there is a museum that will amaze and interest you.

9

> Some people prefer to eat at food stands or restaurants. Other people prefer to prepare and eat food at home. Which do you prefer? Use specific reasons and examples to support your answer.

Although many people prefer to eat at restaurants because it is easier than cooking at home, I prefer to prepare food at home. I believe it is much cheaper and healthier to eat at home, and it can be more convenient, too.

While eating in restaurants is fast, the money you spend can add up. When I have dinner at a restaurant, the bill is usually $25 or more. I can buy a lot of groceries with that much money. Even lunch at a food stand can easily cost seven or eight dollars. That's enough to feed a whole family at home.

Eating at home is better for you, too. Meals at restaurants are often high in fat and calories. When you cook at home, however, you can control what you eat. You can cook with low-fat and low-calorie ingredients. Restaurants also often serve big plates of food. You may eat a big plate of food at a restaurant because you paid for it, while at home you can control your portion size. You can serve yourself as little as you want.

It may seem more convenient to eat at a restaurant because you don't have to shop, cook, or clean up. All you do is eat. Cooking at home, however, can actually be more convenient. There are lots of simple meals that don't take long to prepare. In addition, when you eat at home, you don't have to drive to the restaurant, look for a parking space, wait for a table, and wait for service.

People often choose to eat at restaurants because it seems more convenient. I find, however, that cooking at home is actually easier, and it is cheaper and healthier as well.

10

> It has recently been announced that a new restaurant may be built in your neighborhood. Do you support or oppose this plan? Why? Use specific reasons and details to support your answer.

I can see both advantages and disadvantages to having a new restaurant built in our neighborhood. I believe, however, that the disadvantages outweigh the advantages. A new restaurant would bring more traffic problems to the area. In addition, it could attract undesirable people. Most of all, I think there are other types of business that would be more beneficial to the neighborhood.

Traffic congestion is already a problem in our neighborhood, and a new restaurant would just add to the problem. Most restaurant customers would arrive by car and crowd our streets even more. In addition, they would occupy parking spaces and make it even harder for residents to find places to park near their homes.

I'm also concerned about the type of patrons the new restaurant would bring into our neighborhood. If the restaurant serves drinks and has dancing, there could be problems. The restaurant would stay open late and people leaving the restaurant might be drunk. They could be noisy too. This is not the kind of thing I want to see in my neighborhood.

Finally, there are other types of businesses that we need in our neighborhood more. We already have a restaurant and a couple of coffee shops. We don't have a bookstore or a pharmacy, however, and we have only one small grocery store. I would prefer to see one of these businesses established here rather than another restaurant. Any one of them would be more useful to the residents and would maintain the quiet atmosphere of our streets.

A new restaurant could disrupt the quiet lifestyle of our neighborhood. It might bring jobs, but it would also bring traffic and noise. Moreover, it would use space that might be better used for another type of business. This is why I would oppose a plan for a new restaurant.

11

> **Some people think that they can learn better by themselves than with a teacher. Others think that it is always better to have a teacher. Which do you prefer? Use specific reasons to develop your essay.**

Most people can learn to do something simple on their own with just a set of instructions. However, to learn something more complex, it's always best to have a teacher. Teachers help you find the way that you learn best. They help you stay focused on what you're learning. They provide you with a wider range of information than you might find on your own. In short, teachers provide you with a lot more support and knowledge than you can usually get by yourself.

Teachers can help students learn in the way that is best for each student because teachers understand that different people have different learning styles. For example, some students learn better by discussing a topic. Others learn more by writing about it. A teacher can help you follow your learning style, while a book can give you only one way of learning something.

Teachers help you focus on what you are learning. They can help you keep from becoming distracted. They can show you which are the most important points in a lesson to understand. If you have to study on your own, on the other hand, it might be difficult to keep your attention on the material or know which points are most important.

Teachers bring their own knowledge and understanding of the topic to the lesson. A book presents you with certain information, and the teacher can add more. The teacher might also have a different point of view from the book and can provide other sources of information and ideas, as well.

There is nothing wrong with studying on your own. For the best possible learning, though, a teacher is the biggest help you can have.

12

> **It is better for children to grow up in the countryside than in a big city. Do you agree or disagree? Use specific reasons and examples to develop your essay.**

I have to disagree that it is better for children to grow up in the countryside. In the countryside, children have limited opportunities to see and learn about things. In the city, on the other hand, they are exposed to many different things. They see all kinds of different people every day. They have opportunities to attend many cultural events. They see people working in different kinds of jobs and therefore can make better choices for their own future. Growing up in the city is definitely better.

All different kinds of people live in the city, while in a small town in the countryside people are often all the same. City people come from other parts of the country or even from other countries. They are of different races and religions. When children grow up in this situation, they have the opportunity to learn about and understand different kinds of people. This is an important part of their education.

In the city, there are many opportunities to attend cultural events, whereas such opportunities are usually limited in the countryside. In the city there are movies and theaters, museums, zoos, and concerts. In the city children can attend cultural events every weekend, or even more often. This is also an important part of their education.

People in the city work in different kinds of jobs, while in the countryside there often isn't a variety of job opportunities. People in the city work at all different types and levels of professions, as well as in factories, in service jobs, and more. Children growing up in the city learn that there is a wide variety of jobs they can choose from when they grow up. They have a greater possibility of choosing a career that they will enjoy and do well in. This is perhaps the most important part of their education.

People usually move to the city because there are more opportunities there. Children who grow up in the city have these opportunities from the time they are small. The city is definitely a better place for children to grow up.

13

> **In general, people are living longer now. Discuss the causes of this phenomenon. Use specific reasons and details to develop your essay.**

People are living to be much older these days than ever before. The main reasons for this are greater access to health care, improved health care, and better nutrition.

Basic health care is available to many more people now than it was in the past. When someone is ill nowadays, he or she can go to a public hospital instead of having to pay for private care. There are also more clinics and more trained doctors and nurses than there used to be. Years ago, health care was not available to everyone. People who didn't live in big cities often did not have easy access to doctors or hospitals, and many people couldn't afford to pay for the medical care they needed.

In addition to increased access to health care, the quality of that health care has greatly improved over the years. Doctors know now much more about diseases and how to cure them. In the past, people died young because of simple things such as an infection or a virus. Now we have antibiotics and other medicines to cure these diseases. Furthermore, advances in medical science have made it possible to cure certain types of cancer and to treat heart disease. This has prolonged the lives of many, many people.

The quality of nutrition has also improved over time. Because of this, people tend to be healthier than they used to be. Now we know how to eat more healthfully. We know that eating low fat food can prevent heart disease. We know that eating certain fruits and vegetables can prevent cancer. We have information about nutrition that can help us live longer, healthier lives.

Improved health care and healthy eating habits are allowing us to live longer. Now we need to make sure that everyone in the world has these benefits.

14

> We all work or will work in jobs with many different kinds of people. In your opinion, what are some important characteristics of a good co-worker (someone you work closely with)? Use reasons and specific examples to explain why these characteristics are important.

I've worked in several offices, and I've found there are certain characteristics that all good co-workers have in common. They tend to be cooperative people, they adapt well to changes, and they are helpful to others in the office. People who have these characteristics are easy to work with.

A good co-worker is very cooperative. She does her best to get along with others. She tries to do her work well because she knows that if one person doesn't get her work done, it affects everyone else. She also has a positive attitude that creates a pleasant working environment.

A good co-worker is adaptable. She is not stubborn about changes in schedules or routines. She doesn't object to having her job description revised. She has no problem with new procedures. In fact, she welcomes changes when they come.

A good co-worker is helpful. For instance, she lends a hand when someone falls behind in his or her work. She is willing to change her schedule to accommodate another worker's emergency. She doesn't keep track of how often she has to take on extra work.

We spend more time with our co-workers during the week than we do with our family. Thus, it's important for our co-workers to be people we can get along with. When co-workers are cooperative, adaptable, and helpful, everyone gets along better and can get their jobs done well.

15

> **It has recently been announced that a large shopping center may be built in your neighborhood. Do you support or oppose this plan? Why? Use specific reasons and details to support your answer.**

There would be both advantages and disadvantages to having a shopping center built in my neighborhood. Overall, however, I think the advantages are greater. The most important advantage would be convenience. In addition, a shopping center would give local residents more choices for shopping and entertainment. Finally, it would provide employment opportunities.

It would be very convenient to have a shopping center in the neighborhood. Now there are very few stores near my house, and we have to drive long distances to buy groceries and other necessities. Shopping would be much easier and faster if we had a shopping center in our own neighborhood. Also, in a shopping center all the stores are together in one place, so that would make shopping even more convenient for us.

In addition to convenience, a shopping center would give us more choices. There would be a variety of stores selling different kinds of products. There would probably also be restaurants and food courts, so we would have a greater variety of places to eat. There would likely be a movie theater, too. So, the shopping center would provide us with a range of options for both shopping and entertainment.

Having a shopping center built in the neighborhood would also bring more jobs to the community. Initially, these jobs would be in the construction of the center. In the long term, there would be jobs in the stores, theaters, and food establishments. The shopping center would provide a variety of employment opportunities, from maintenance and janitorial work to retail jobs to managerial positions.

On the whole, though, I think my neighborhood should support having a shopping center built here. It would bring more variety to our shopping, give us the opportunity to amuse ourselves at movie theaters and restaurants, and create more jobs in the area.

16

> **It has recently been announced that a new movie theater may be built in your neighborhood. Do you support or oppose this plan? Why? Use specific reasons and details to support your answer.**

Some people will say that a new movie theater in our neighborhood would be a bad thing. However, I fully support the plan to build one. I feel that a movie theater would provide more opportunities for entertainment, reduce teenage delinquency, and bring more business to our town.

A movie theater would provide a much needed source of entertainment to our area. Right now, there is little to do in my town. There is almost nowhere to go in the evenings, and the nearest place that has movie theaters and restaurants is thirty minutes away. If we build a movie theater here, we can enjoy evenings right in our own neighborhood.

A movie theater would reduce juvenile delinquency. Like everywhere else, teenagers here are bored. They need activities to keep them busy and out of trouble. A movie theater would not only provide them with entertainment, it would also be a source of jobs for them. We need more businesses that want to employ young people, and a movie theater is the perfect sort of business for that.

A movie theater would attract more business to our town. People who come from other towns to use our movie theater would also shop in our stores. New stores and restaurants might open because there would be more customers for them. Our town could become more prosperous, and more interesting, too.

I believe our town would benefit greatly from a new movie theater. It would make life here more interesting and could make us more prosperous. I fully support the plan and hope that others in the neighborhood will join me to convince residents and local governments.

17

> **Do you agree or disagree with the following statement? People should sometimes do things that they do not enjoy doing. Use specific reasons and examples to support your answer.**

I agree that people should sometimes do things that they don't enjoy doing. This is a basic part of life. There are many small things we have to do in both our personal and professional lives that we may not enjoy, but that are part of our responsibilities. In addition, sometimes by doing things we don't enjoy, we actually learn to like them.

Most people's personal lives are filled with tasks that they don't enjoy doing, but they do them anyway. Who likes going to the doctor or dentist, for example? But we do this because we know that it is important to take care of our health. I don't know many people who like changing the oil in their cars or mowing the lawn. We do these things, however, because we understand that we need to maintain our personal property.

Similarly, our professional lives are filled with tasks that are not fun, but that are necessary parts of our jobs. No one likes to do boring assignments or to work with someone who no one else likes. If we're in management, we may sometimes have to fire someone. No one likes to do things like these, but if they are part of our professional responsibilities, we have to do them.

On the other hand, sometimes doing something we don't enjoy can lead to enjoyment. Simply by trying it again, we may decide we like doing it. For instance, we may think we hate to dance. We agree to go to a club only to please someone else. Yet, for some reason, this time we enjoy dancing. The same can be true of trying new foods or going to a new type of museum.

Not everything in life is fun. Unpleasant or boring tasks are a necessary part of life. We don't like them, but we do them anyway. And sometimes they surprise us and turn into something enjoyable.

18

Some people spend their entire lives in one place. Others move a number of times throughout their lives, looking for a better job, house, community, or even climate. Which do you prefer: staying in one place or moving in search of another place? Use reasons and specific examples to support your opinion.

Even though I have lived in the same house, in the same neighborhood, in the same city my entire life, I know I would be happy living in a variety of places. Moving would expose me to new people, new weather, and new housing.

Even if I moved to another part of my own city, I would encounter new people. Each neighborhood has a distinct personality. If I moved to a new neighborhood, I would meet the shopkeepers and residents that shape that neighborhood's personality. It would be a new experience for me and I could become part of a new community.

If I want to experience a different kind of climate, I would have to move far from my city. Where I live now, it is the same temperature all year. I would like to go to a place where there are four seasons so I can experience really cold weather. I would like to walk in the snow and learn winter sports such as skiing.

Now I live with my parents in their house. It is a one-story house built around a court-yard where we spend a lot of time. If I could move to a different kind of house, I would like to live in an apartment on a very high floor so I could see all around me. I could also meet my neighbors on the elevator and we could get together for coffee in my apartment.

The more I moved the more I would experience change. I would meet new people in every place I lived; I could move to sample countries with four seasons or even a conti-nent like Antarctica, which only has two. Wherever I lived, I would experience living in housing particular to that area. I would then be a citizen of the world, wouldn't I? Could you call me a foreigner if I called everyplace my home?

19

You have received a gift of money. The money is enough to buy either a piece of jewelry you like or tickets to a concert you want to attend. Which would you buy? Use specific reasons and details to support your answer.

The choice between spending money on tickets to a concert or spending money on jewelry is an easy one. Given this choice, I would definitely buy jewelry. To me, the reasons are obvious. Jewelry is a good financial investment, it lasts a long time, and it is beautiful.

Buying jewelry is a good way to invest money. In fact, I believe that everyone should own some gold jewelry because its value always goes up. Then, if one day you have a financial problem, you can sell your jewelry to get the money you need. You would not be able to sell a used concert ticket, however. After the concert is over, the ticket has no value at all.

Jewelry also lasts a long time. You can wear it as often as you like, and it will give you pleasure for years and years. Each time you put it on, you can remember the day you bought it. Your jewelry may need a little cleaning from time to time or an occasional minor repair, but it never wears out. Your concert ticket, on the other hand, is no longer useful once you've attended the concert.

Jewelry is beautiful to look at. I would feel very attractive wearing a shiny gold bracelet or a sparkly diamond pin. I could use my jewelry to dress up for a fancy party, to make my business outfits look better, or just to make a boring day a little nicer. Other people would enjoy the beauty of my jewelry, too, when they saw me wearing it.

I would feel very rich with my jewelry. I would have a good investment that was long lasting and beautiful, as well. Then, when someone invited me to a concert (and paid for my ticket), I would have something nice to wear.

20

> The expression "Never, never give up" means keep trying and never stop working for your goals. Do you agree or disagree with this statement? Use specific reasons and examples to support your answer.

As the old saying goes, "If at first you don't succeed, try, try again." I think there is great wisdom in these words. If you give up, you lose your chance to try again for what you want. But if you keep working for your goals, you will find that there is always another opportunity, another goal, or another option.

Once I ran for president of my class. Unfortunately, I lost the election because I did little to promote myself. I looked at my mistakes and saw how I could correct them. The following year, I ran for class president again. This time I did the things I hadn't done before. I gave speeches, called voters on the phone, and handed out brochures, and this time I won the election. Instead of giving up, I waited for another opportunity to try, and I was successful the second time.

Once I thought I wanted to study medicine. Unfortunately, I found that I didn't like science, and I failed all my science courses at school. After thinking about it for a while, I realized that what attracted me to a career in medicine was the chance to help people. So, I changed my goal from healing people to helping people, and now I am studying psychology. Instead of giving up, I adjusted my goal to one where I was more likely to be successful.

Once I was going through a difficult time and I really needed to talk to my best friend. My computer was down, so I couldn't email him. I tried calling him several times, but he didn't answer the phone. Finally, I decided to get on the bus and go to his house so we could talk in person. I didn't give up when I found that I couldn't reach my friend by email or phone. I looked for another option, and I successfully reached my goal.

If you give up, you might as well die. My advice is always look for another opportunity, another goal, or another option. There is always something else. Don't give up.

21

> Some people like to travel with a companion. Other people prefer to travel alone. Which do you prefer? Use specific reasons and examples to support your choice.

Traveling alone is the only way to travel. If you take someone with you, you take your home with you. When you travel alone, you meet new people, have new experiences, and learn more about yourself.

When you travel with a friend, you spend all your time with that friend and do everything together. Since you have a companion, you don't make an effort to reach out to other people. When you travel alone, on the other hand, you are more motivated to look for new friends. You seek out opportunities to talk with other tourists or with local people. You might share a meal or go on an excursion with them, and then you become friends. It's much easier to meet new people when you travel alone.

When you travel with a friend, your routine is predictable. You probably act the same way that you do at home. When you travel alone, however, you have to adapt yourself to the customs of the place. You might take a nap in the afternoon and then eat dinner late at night, for example, even if that is not how you behave at home. You might be adventurous and go dancing at a club all night instead of going to bed at your usual time. You will be more open to new experiences like these when you travel alone.

When you travel with a friend, you have someone to take care of you, but when you travel alone, you have to learn to take care of yourself. If you encounter a difficult situation, you have to find a solution on your own. If you don't speak the local language, you have to figure out how to make yourself understood. If the food is unfamiliar, you have to make your own decisions about what to eat. When you travel alone, you have many opportunities to learn about how you handle yourself in new or strange situations.

I think it is always important to do things on your own. You can find new friends, have new experiences, and learn a lot about yourself, too. Isn't that the point of travel?

22

> **Do you agree or disagree with the following statement? Businesses should do anything they can to make a profit. Use specific reasons and examples to support your position.**

After I get my degree, I plan to start my own business. Like any business owner, my goal is to make as much money as I can. However, I can't forget that there are more important things in life than earning a profit. I must always keep in mind that the success of my business depends on the people I work with, the customers I serve, and the community I live in.

My employees are a very important part of my business. Without them, my company would not be able to function. I depend on my employees to carry out the day-to-day operations of the business, and I rely on them for their advice on what to sell and how to sell it. Naturally, I have to compensate them for their contributions to the company. I can't take a large profit without sharing it with the people who made it possible.

Similarly, I would not have a business without my customers. I can never forget that they could take their business somewhere else. Therefore, I have to give them good value for their money and not overcharge them just because I want to make a few more pennies. I want my customers to trust me and keep coming back.

My employees and I are part of the social life of our community. We have an obligation to be active community members. I feel it is important that some of the profits my business earns from the community be returned to the community. We need to support local programs to support our neighbors, for example, summer jobs for high school students, campaigns to clean up city parks, and efforts to make the shopping area more attractive.

A business must make profits, of course, but we all—workers, customers, community members—must profit from a successful business, as well.

23

Many teachers assign homework to students every day. Do you think that daily homework is necessary for students? Use specific reasons and details to support your answer.

I believe that daily homework is not necessary. Students already spend most of the day in school. They need their time outside of school to do other things. They need time to spend with their families, to work, and to just relax. They can learn their lessons with homework two or three times a week, but every day isn't necessary.

All students need to spend time with their families. They are still young and they need the guidance and support their parents can give them. They need the companionship of their brothers and sisters. In addition, many families rely on their older children to help out at home. They take care of the younger children and help with the cooking and cleaning. If students have too much homework, they won't have time for their families.

Many high school students have jobs. They go to their jobs after school and on weekends. Some work in order to help their families. Others work to save money for college. Students' jobs are important to them. If they have too much homework, they won't have time and energy to go to work.

Students need time to relax. They study hard in school all day and many work at jobs after school. But they are still young. They need to spend time with their friends and have fun. When students relax with friends, they then have more energy for school and work. They have a chance to develop social skills or to pursue their own interests. Having free time is important for a child's development. If students have too much homework, they won't have time for relaxation.

Homework is important for students, but other things are important, too. Some homework is good, but daily homework can take time away from a student's family, job, and relaxation. There needs to be a balance.

24

If you could study a subject that you have never had the opportunity to study, what would you choose? Explain your choice, using specific reasons and details.

I have always been interested in art and literature, so people will think my choice is strange. If I could study something I have never had the opportunity to study, I would choose calculus. If I could actually learn something as difficult as that, it would give me a lot of confidence. Besides that, I think I would like it and it could help me learn some useful skills.

The only mathematics I have studied are the required courses in high school. I finished those requirements early and since then I have chosen to study other subjects. I never liked my math classes and I didn't do well in them. I have always thought that I couldn't learn math. But now I would like to try it. I think if I made the effort, I could learn calculus. If I learned calculus, I would feel very smart.

I like art and literature because I like beauty and creativity. I never liked math because I didn't think it was beautiful and creative. I like solving problems, however. And I might actually discover something beautiful and creative about math. I think if I tried studying calculus, I would actually like it.

There are some new skills I would like to develop. There are some electrical problems in my house and I would like to learn how to fix them myself. I would like to learn how to do repair work on my CD player or even on my computer. If I learned calculus, it would help me develop the skills I need to do these things.

I think it would be really interesting to try learning something completely new. For me, calculus would be a big challenge. If I learned it, I would feel smart, I would enjoy myself, and I could develop new skills. It would be a big accomplishment for me.

25

> Some people think that the automobile has improved modern life. Others think that the automobile has caused serious problems. What is your opinion? Use specific reasons and examples to support your answer.

There is no question that the automobile has improved modern life. It has opened up job opportunities to people, allowed families to stay connected, and given people the chance to travel to new places. The automobile is one of the best modern inventions.

With an automobile, a person has more choices of places to work. He can work close to his home if he finds a suitable job nearby, but he can also pursue job opportunities farther away. An automobile makes it possible to take a job in another town or city without having to go there to live. Without an automobile, however, a person can only look for jobs near the place where he lives. This puts a big limit on his choices.

With an automobile, it is much easier for a person to visit his family. Many people these days live far away from their relatives. Young adults pursuing their careers often find jobs in other cities. If they have cars, it is easy for them to visit their parents and other relatives whenever they want to. They can stay connected with their families even though they live at a distance. But without an automobile, they have to spend time and money taking a bus or train. It is not easy to visit relatives as often and family ties start to loosen.

With an automobile, a person can explore new places. He can just get in the car and drive wherever he wants to go, whenever he wants to. He has many opportunities to see new places, meet new people and learn more about the world. Without an automobile, a person can only go where the bus, train, or plane takes him. It is not very convenient.

The automobile has greatly improved modern life. It has opened up new worlds and new opportunities to people. It has made many things possible. Where would we be without it?

> Some people say that computers have made life easier and more convenient. Other people say that computers have made life more complex and stressful. What is your opinion? Use specific reasons and examples to support your answer.

Almost everything these days is done with the help of a computer. Computers make communication much more convenient. They make many tasks of daily life easier. They help many people do their jobs better. Overall, computers have made life easier and more convenient for everybody.

Through the Internet, computers make communication much more convenient. Email makes it possible to communicate with people instantly at any time of day. This is important for both our work and our personal lives. The Internet makes it possible to find out the latest news right away—even if it is news that happens someplace far away. The Internet makes it possible to get almost any kind of information from anyplace quickly, right in your own home or office.

Although we may not realize it, computers make many daily tasks easier. Check-out lines at stores move faster because a computer scans the prices. The bank manages your account more easily because of computers. The weatherman reports the weather more accurately with the help of computers. A computer is involved in almost everything we do, or that is done for us.

Most people these days do their jobs with the help of a computer. Architects use computer programs to help them design buildings. Teachers use computers to write their lessons and get information for their classes. Pilots use computers to help them fly planes. With the help of computers, people can do complicated jobs more easily.

We are living in the computer age. We can now do more things and do them more easily than we could before. Our personal and professional lives have improved because of computers.

> Do you agree or disagree with the following statement? Boys and girls should attend separate schools. Use specific reasons and examples to support your answer.

I don't think it is a good idea for boys and girls to attend separate schools. They will not be separated when they finish school and start their careers, so why should they be separated in school? When boys and girls study together, they are assured of getting equal quality of education, they learn how to work together, and they learn how to become friends. It is a much better preparation for life than studying in separate schools.

When boys and girls attend the same school, they get equal education. They are in the same classrooms with the same teachers studying from the same books. If they attend separate schools, the quality of the schools might be different. One school might be better than the other. By studying together, girls get the same education as boys. This helps them work toward having equality in society.

By attending the same schools, boys and girls learn how to work together. Some people say they should study separately because they have different learning styles. I think it's better to study together, however. It gives them the chance to learn to work together despite their differences. This will help them in the future when they have to work together professionally.

When boys and girls see each other in school every day, they have the chance to become friends. They see each other as normal people, not as strangers. If they attend separate schools, they don't know each other. It's easy to misunderstand, or even fear, each other. When boys and girls have the chance to become friends, their lives are much richer. They will have better relationships in the future.

By studying together, boys and girls get equal education, they learn to work together, and they become friends. This prepares them for adult life where men and women live and work together every day.

28

> **Is it more important to be able to work with a group of people on a team or to work independently? Use reasons and specific examples to support your answer.**

The ability to work on a team is one of the most important job skills to have. It is usually necessary because most jobs involve teamwork. It is usually the best way to work because a team can get more work done than an individual. In addition, a worker on a team has a lot of support from his coworkers.

Most work is done in groups or teams. Professionals work with their professional colleagues, and they also usually have assistants and support staff. Construction workers work with other construction workers, auto mechanics work with other auto mechanics; they all have assistants, and almost nobody works alone. It is necessary for all coworkers to get along and work well together.

More work can be done by a team than by individuals working alone. On a team, each member is responsible for one part of the job. Each member has to concentrate only on her part and do it as well as possible. Then all the parts are put together and the job is done. An individual working alone has to worry about every aspect of the job. He might not do such a good job because he has to think about everything at once.

A worker on a team has the advantage of support from his coworkers. If a worker can't finish a job on time or doesn't understand a task or needs help planning, he has a group of people to help him. The team supports him and he can get the job done. An individual working alone has to solve all her problems herself. She has to stop work while she finds a solution, or do a poor job.

Most jobs involve teamwork. Teams can usually do a better job than an individual working alone. A person who cannot work well on a team will have a hard time in today's workplace.

29

> **A foreign visitor has only one day to spend in your country. Where should this visitor go on that day? Why? Use specific reasons and details to support your choice.**

A foreign visitor with only one day to spend in my country should definitely spend that day in the capital. Spending time in the capital is the easiest way to see many aspects of our country in one place. In this city, the visitor can learn about our history, see examples of our culture, and buy our best products.

Our country's history is represented in several ways throughout the city. In the Government Palace, a visitor can learn about the history of our independence. In our National Museum, a visitor can see exhibits that show all the different stages of our history, from ancient times to the present. In parks all around the city, a visitor can see monuments to famous historical people and events.

It is also possible to see different representations of our culture throughout the city. Our art museums and galleries show paintings and sculptures by our artists. Plays written by national playwrights are performed in the theaters. Folk ballet performances show examples of our traditional dances. Many restaurants in the capital serve our native dishes.

The best products of our country are sold in the capital city. The large department stores sell clothes, furniture, and household items manufactured in our country. The Central Market sells fruit and vegetables from the surrounding agricultural region. Tourist and craft shops sell native handicrafts made in the countryside.

The capital city is the best place to learn a lot about our country in one place. Of course, it is difficult to see all of the city's attractions in one day. With some planning, though, it is possible to see at least a few examples of our country's history, culture, and products in one day.

30

> **Some people prefer to live in places that have the same weather or climate all year long. Others like to live in areas where the weather changes several times a year. Which do you prefer? Use specific reasons and examples to support your choice.**

If I could choose a place to live according to climate alone, I would definitely live in a place that has warm weather all year. It would make my life much easier and more comfortable. I would be healthier, have more fun, and save money if I lived in a warm climate.

I would always be healthy if I lived in a warm climate. Where I live now the winters are long and cold, so I get sick every winter. I often miss days of school because I get bad colds. I wouldn't have this problem in a warm climate. Also, in a warm climate I would be able to be outside all year long. I would play sports and get exercise everyday. That would make me healthier, too.

I would have more fun if I lived in a warm climate. I really enjoy outdoor activities such as going to the beach, playing soccer, and riding my bicycle. I can't do these things when the weather is cold, which means I can't do them at all during the winter in a cold climate. In a warm climate, I would be able to enjoy my favorite activities all year.

I would save money if I lived in a warm climate. It costs money to heat the house during cold winters, and this can get very expensive. In a warm climate I would not have to worry about this expense. It also costs money to buy new clothes every time the season changes. This is another expense I wouldn't have to worry about in a warm climate because I could wear the same clothes all year.

My life would be better if I lived in a warm climate. My health, my free time activities, and my bank account would all improve. In fact, I plan to move to a warm climate as soon as I finish school.

31

> Many students have to live with a roommate while going to school or university. What are some of the important qualities of a good roommate? Use specific reasons and examples to explain why these qualities are important.

You want to feel comfortable in the place where you live, so it is very important to have a good roommate. A bad roommate can become your worst enemy, but a good roommate can end up being your best friend. In my opinion, a good roommate is one who is considerate, flexible, and fun.

A good roommate is considerate of your needs and thinks about the effects her actions might have on you. For example, she tries to be quiet when you want to sleep or study. She doesn't plan a party or use your things without asking you first. A good roommate doesn't think only about herself; she thinks about you, too.

A good roommate is flexible. She is willing to bend a little in order to make things easier for both of you. If, for example, you are neat and your roommate is messy, you can each try to change a little bit so that you will both be happy. Your roommate can try to be a little neater, and you can try to live with a little mess.

Finally, a good roommate is fun. If she is planning to go to a party or a concert, she invites you to go with her. She introduces you to her friends and includes you when she plans activities with them. She is also open to planning free time activities with you. A good roommate may be serious about her studies, but she knows that it is important to have fun, too. She also knows that when you enjoy fun activities together, your friendship is strengthened.

The best situation is to have a roommate who is also your friend. If your roommate is considerate, flexible, and fun, you are sure to get along well and have a good experience living together.

32

> Some people think governments should spend as much money as possible exploring outer space (for example, traveling to the moon and other planets). Other people disagree and think governments should spend this money for our basic needs on Earth. Which of these two opinions do you agree with? Use specific reasons and details to support your answer.

I believe that we should spend whatever money is required to explore outer space. It is true that we have many needs here on Earth, and many problems to solve. Exploring outer space, however, has invaluable benefits for people on Earth. It helps medical research, it leads to useful inventions, and it can help solve our overpopulation problem. I think space exploration is worth the cost.

Research carried out in space contributes a great deal to medical science. There is some research that can be conducted only in space. The research on the effects of gravity on bone marrow is one example. Research such as this will continue to contribute to advances in medicine. It benefits everybody on Earth.

Many useful inventions have happened because of space exploration. Different kinds of plastics that were developed for space travel are also now used on Earth. Things we use in our daily lives are made from "space age" materials. This is another aspect of space exploration that benefits everyone.

The search for other planets can help solve our overpopulation problem. People are living longer and healthier lives these days. That's a good thing, but it means more people on Earth. The Earth will not get bigger. Through space exploration, we may be able to find other planets where people can live. This is one more thing that will have a benefit for all people.

Space exploration results in benefits for people everywhere on Earth. It contributes to medical science, to inventions, and to a solution to overpopulation. It is expensive, but the benefits are worth the price. Space exploration is one of the best ways governments can spend our money.

33

> **You have been told that dormitory rooms at your university must be shared by two students. Would you rather have the university assign a student to share a room with you, or would you rather choose your own roommate? Use specific reasons and details to explain your answer.**

I'd rather have the university assign a roommate to share a room with me. I don't know many people at the university I plan to attend. I'm sure the university will choose a roommate who is compatible with me, and this will give me the chance to make new friends.

None of my close friends will attend the university with me. We all plan to attend different schools. I have a few acquaintances at my university, but I don't know them well. I don't think they are people I would choose to live with. At this time, I really can't choose my own roommate. I am glad the university can do it for me.

The university has a very good system for assigning roommates. All the students have to fill out information sheets. We write about our majors, our interests, our study habits, and our goals. The university uses this information to match roommates. They can match people who have similar habits and interests. I think it is a good system.

When the university assigns me a roommate, I have a chance to make new friends. For one, my roommate will be a new friend. We already know that we will have similar habits and interests, so we will probably enjoy spending time together. In addition, my roommate's friends could become my friends, too. My roommate can introduce me to new people, and I can do the same for him.

I think it's a good idea for a university to choose roommates for the students. They can match people who are compatible and give everyone a chance to make new friends. Meeting new people is an important part of a university education, and this is one way to make that happen.

34

> **Some people like doing work by hand. Others prefer using machines. Which do you prefer? Use specific reasons and examples to support your answer.**

I prefer using machines to doing work by hand. Machines can work faster than I can. They can also work more neatly. Most of all, machines never get tired.

Machines are fast. If I want to make a dress, it would take me hours and hours working with a needle and thread to make each stitch by hand. If I use a sewing machine, however, I can make a dress in an hour or less. If I want to build something out of wood, I could cut each piece with a handsaw. That would take a very long time. But a power saw cuts much more quickly. When I bake a cake, I can stir in each ingredient by hand, or I can use an electric mixer, which makes the work go so much faster.

Machines are neat. They never make mistakes. Every line or cut is neat, straight and in the right place. Machines don't get distracted and spill coffee all over the work or cut something the wrong size or add the wrong ingredients. Machines can do the same job over and over again, each time as neatly as the time before. I could never be as neat as a machine.

Machines never get tired. I can sew one seam with my sewing machine, or ten. The machine never gets tired of pushing the needle and thread through the fabric. The power saw doesn't slow down because it has cut too many pieces of wood. A machine keeps working with the same amount of energy until the job is done, and doesn't even need to stop for a rest break.

I can depend on machines to do the job right each time, but I can't always depend on myself to be fast, neat, and tireless.

35

> **You need to travel from your home to a place 40 miles (64 kilometers) away. Compare the different kinds of transportation you could use. Describe which method of travel you would choose. Give specific reasons for your choice.**

When I think about the different methods of transportation I could choose to travel 40 miles from my home, I have three options: bicycle, car, or public transportation. In order to pick the best way to travel, I have to consider how much it will cost, how long it will take, and why I need to make the trip. Then I can decide on the best method for the circumstances.

Bicycle is the least expensive alternative. The only cost is the physical energy I need to pedal for 40 miles. This method, however, is extremely time consuming. I imagine it would take me all day to make the trip. On the other hand, biking is excellent exercise, so if my only goal is to burn calories and get stronger, then bicycle is my best choice.

Public transportation is another method that is inexpensive, since the fares in my area are low. On the other hand, you cannot depend on buses and trains where I live. The schedules are inconvenient, and it might take me all day to make my 40-mile trip if I include waiting time. Mass transit is good for the environment since it causes less pollution than cars. But, I can't rely on it to get me to my destination on time, so I don't like to use it.

Private car is the most costly way to travel. Since I don't own an automobile, I would need to borrow one from my parents. I would have to pay for the gasoline, which costs a lot, and I would also have to pay for parking at my destination. A private vehicle is the most dependable way to go if you need to get somewhere fast. If convenience is my goal, I should choose to make a trip by this type of transportation.

When I consider these points, I must confess that I am spoiled. I prefer the convenience of the car over the exercise of a bicycle and the virtues of public transportation. I like to come and go as I please without waiting, even if it costs me more.

36

> **Some people prefer to spend most of their time alone. Others like to be with friends most of the time. Do you prefer to spend your time alone or with friends? Use specific reasons to support your answer.**

There are people who say they prefer to be alone, but I cannot understand this. I always choose to spend time with friends whenever possible because friends bring so much to my life. They keep me company, are enjoyable to talk with, and teach me new things. I cannot imagine my life without them.

There is nothing better than to be in the company of my friends. They keep me from feeling lonely. If I feel like doing anything, I call a friend or friends to do it with me. Whether it's going shopping, seeing a movie, or even studying at the library, it's always fun to do things with friends. It isn't fun, on the other hand, to do anything alone.

One of my greatest pleasures is talking with my friends. If I have a problem, the first thing I do is talk it over with my friends. By discussing something together, we can find the solution to just about any kind of problem. Additionally, if something good or interesting happens to me, I share that with my friends, too. My friends share their problems and experiences with me, as well, and I always enjoy hearing about them. Our lives are so much richer because we share important things with each other.

I learn a lot when I spend time with my friends. A friend might invite me to a movie that I haven't ever heard of. A friend might tell me about a trip she took or a book she read. A friend might have a different point of view about a political issue. I learn a lot of new and interesting things when I am with my friends.

Friends make our lives fuller. They keep us company, share their problems and experiences with us, and teach us many things. Life would be sad and lonely without friends.

37

> **Some people prefer to spend time with one or two close friends. Others choose to spend time with a large number of friends. Compare the advantages of each choice. Which of these two ways of spending time do you prefer? Use specific reasons to support your answer.**

We all need to have friends, and I think the more friends we have the better. When you have a lot of friends, you are never alone. You always have people who will entertain you, people you can trust, and people who teach you about life.

I want to have a lot of people I can have fun with. If I have a lot of friends, I always have people to laugh and joke with me. I have people to go to the movies or the mall with me. I have people to go to parties with me. If I have only a few friends, they might be busy when I want to do these things, or they might not enjoy some of the things I enjoy.

I need to have a lot of people I can trust. If I have a problem, I want to share it with several friends. If I make a mistake or fail a test or have a fight with my parents, I need my friends to help me. I want to be able to pick up the phone and know I can easily find some friends to talk with. If I have only a few friends, they might not be available when I need them.

I like to have a lot of people who teach me about life. If I have a lot of friends, I have a lot of different people to learn from. Each person has different experiences and a different point of view. I can learn a lot of things from a lot of different people. If I have only a few friends, I will see only a few points of view.

I like to have a lot of friends around me. I like to have fun with them and to learn from them and to know that I can rely on them. My life is better because of all the friends I have.

38

> **Some people think that family is the most important influence on young adults. Other people think that friends are the most important influence on young adults. Which view do you agree with? Use examples to support your opinion.**

Although friends make an impression on your life, they do not have the same influence that your family has. Nothing is as important to me as my family. From them I learned everything that is important. I learned about trust, ambition, and love.

Your family is with you forever. They are not going to leave you because they find another son or daughter they like better. They are not going to leave you because they think you cause too many problems. They stick by you no matter what happens because they are your family. Friends come and go, but a family is permanent. I know that my family will always be there for me. I have learned that I can always trust them.

Your parents know that they are responsible for preparing you for the future, and they want you to have the best future possible. They encourage you to do your best, to push yourself, and to improve yourself. Friends, on the other hand, may care about you, but they aren't concerned about your future. Often, they don't want you to change because they don't want to lose the friendship. My family, not my friends, have taught me to have ambitions.

A family's love is not judgmental. They love you just the way you are. Friends, on the other hand, may love you because of circumstances. They may want to spend time with you because you have a new car or know how to play soccer well. They may be interested in you because you go to the same school or share a similar interest. Then, when the circumstances change, the friendship changes, too. But your family always loves you independent of the circumstances. From my family I have learned what love really is.

I wouldn't know what to do without my family. I wouldn't feel as secure. I might not have the ambition to go to school. I probably would be afraid to love. My family is my greatest influence.

39

> **Some people choose friends who are different from themselves. Others choose friends who are similar to themselves. Compare the advantages of having friends who are different from you with the advantages of having friends who are similar to you. Which kind of friend do you prefer for yourself? Why?**

There are a lot of advantages to having friends who are different from you. They can introduce you to new food, books, and music. They can present you with a different way of looking at the world. However, there are times when you need a friend who really understands you. That is why I enjoy having all kinds of friends—both those who are different from me and those who are similar.

Someone who is different from you can show different ways of looking at things. If you tend to be a spontaneous person, a scheduled person can help you be more organized. And you can help that person loosen up a bit at times, too. If you are impatient, a patient friend can help you calm down. If you are a little bit timid, an assertive friend can help you develop more self-confidence.

Someone who has different tastes from you can introduce you to new things. A friend might persuade you to read a book that you thought you wouldn't like. A friend might get you to try new kinds of food. You can share your different tastes and interests with your friend, too. Together you can dare to try new things.

There are times, however, when you really need a friend who is similar to you. Sometimes you get tired of compromising on what you want to do. You want to be with someone who has the same tastes as you. A friend who is similar to you probably has the same reactions to situations as you do. Therefore, if you feel unhappy, a friend who is similar to you can understand just why you feel that way.

Friends who are different from you have a lot to offer. Friends who are similar offer something else. That is why it is important to know all kinds of people.

40

> **Do you agree or disagree with the following statement? People behave differently when they wear different clothes. Do you agree that different clothes influence the way people behave? Use specific examples to support your answer.**

People behave differently depending on what they are wearing. The reason is not because they have changed, but because people's reactions to them have changed. Strangers react to your appearance because it is all they know about you. A friend may be influenced by your dress also, if it is inappropriate for a situation. In addition, appearance is almost always important at work.

Strangers can judge you only by the clothes you wear. Once I was wearing an old army coat. I went into a fancy candy shop to buy some chocolates. The woman saw my coat and was very suspicious of me. Because of the woman's negative reaction to me, I acted more politely than usual. The woman reacted to my clothes and that made me behave differently.

With friends clothes are less important because friends know more about you. However, friends can also react to you because of your clothes. Imagine you arrive at a friend's party. Everyone is wearing formal clothes and you are wearing casual clothes. You might have a good reason for this mistake, but your friend will still be disappointed. You will probably feel uncomfortable all evening because you disappointed your friend and because you are dressed differently from everyone else.

Certain clothes are appropriate for certain jobs. For example, business clothes are appropriate for some jobs; uniforms are appropriate for others. If you are not dressed appropriately for your job, clients and coworkers take you less seriously. You might begin to take yourself less seriously also, and your work could suffer. On the other hand, if you are wearing the right clothes, people will have confidence that you are the right person for the job, and you will feel this way, too.

Clothes don't change you into a different person, but they can make you behave differently. If you are dressed inappropriately for a situation, people will react to you in a different way. This reaction can, in turn, change your behavior. If you want good reactions from people, make sure to dress appropriately for every situation.

41

> Some people trust their first impressions about a person's character because they believe these judgments are generally correct. Other people do not judge a person's character quickly because they believe first impressions are often wrong. Compare these two attitudes. Which attitude do you agree with? Support your choice with specific examples.

Some people think it is unfair to judge others based on first impressions, but I disagree. People can show us who they really are in just a few minutes. Even if someone is having an unusually bad day, it is still easy to see their true character. If I don't like someone at first, I don't want to waste time being friendly just because he or she might change later. First impressions give us valuable information.

It doesn't take long for people to show their true character. Some people think you have to see how people act in different situations and talk to them a lot to get to know them. I don't believe this is true. When you meet someone, pay attention to how the person greets you. You can see right away if the person is friendly or shy, polite or rude. See how the person tries to make conversation and you will know what topics are interesting to him or her. All of this gives us a lot of information about a person.

Even on a bad day, you can see what a person is really like. Some people think that it isn't fair to judge people quickly because they might be having a bad day. I disagree. A bad day tells you a lot about people. You can see how they react to bad situations. Do they get very angry or take it all in stride? Do they get depressed and cry or just try to forget the problem? These are important parts of a person's character.

I feel I can learn a lot about a person in a few minutes, so I don't want to waste my time if the first impression isn't good. If I don't like the way a person greets me, or if I am uncomfortable with the way a person responds to a bad situation, will my impression change later on? Probably not. If I spend more time with the person, I'll probably just see more of the same. I would prefer to spend that time looking for people who I like.

If we all based our final opinion of others on first impressions, we would save ourselves a lot of time. We would probably have more opportunities to meet other people we have more in common with. First impressions provide us with enough insight to a person's character to indicate if a further friendship is possible.

42

> Do you agree or disagree with the following statement? It is more important for students to study history and literature than it is for them to study science and mathematics. Use specific reasons and examples to support your opinion.

In my opinion, it is much more important for students to study science and mathematics than it is for them to study history and literature. Science and mathematics are much more practical. It is easier to get a job with science and math skills. Scientists and mathematicians have more social prestige, and they can earn higher salaries.

People who study science and mathematics get jobs more easily than people who study history and literature. There are always jobs in fields such as medicine, computer science, engineering, and other professions that require a science or math background. People who study history or literature can only become writers or college professors. It is difficult to get well-paying jobs in those fields.

Scientists and mathematicians have a lot of social prestige. Let's face it—our society values science and math. If you go to a party and say, "I am a rocket scientist," people will be interested in you. They will want to talk to you and be your friend. If you say, "I am an historian," no one will pay any attention to you.

Scientists and mathematicians also earn more money than people in other fields because society values them more. A doctor, a chemist, a medical researcher,—a person in any one of these professions usually earns a far higher salary than a literature professor, for example, or a history expert.

Our society values science and math, so it is important to develop skills in these areas. If you have a science or math background, you are sure to get a good job, have lots of social prestige, and earn a good salary. Faced with this fact, who would want to study anything else?

43

> Some people say that physical exercise should be a required part of every school day. Other people believe that students should spend the whole school day on academic studies. Which opinion do you agree with? Give specific reasons and details to support your answer.

While physical exercise is important, I do not believe that it is a school's responsibility to provide physical training for its students. If physical exercise is part of the school program, that means that students have to receive grades for it and that the school has to pay for the necessary space and equipment. This seems a waste of effort and resources when students can usually get enough physical exercise on their own.

If a school offers physical education classes, then students will have to be graded in them. It is not always easy to do this fairly. Some schools, especially smaller ones, may not be able to offer activities that interest everyone. Then some students might get poor grades simply because the school couldn't offer an activity they enjoy or do well in. In addition, research suggests that participation, not excellence, in physical activities is what benefits the body.

Another issue is economic. Physical education costs money and many schools do not have the money to provide gym facilities, playing fields, and athletic equipment for their students. Other schools are located in cities where that kind of space just isn't available. A few schools would rather keep money for academic purposes.

Many students get plenty of physical exercise as part of their daily life or recreation. Some students walk or ride their bicycles to schools. Some participate in soccer teams or tennis leagues outside of schools. Young people are usually active and have plenty of chances to get exercise outside of school, whether in organized activities or not.

It is important to get plenty of physical exercise, and young people usually do this. They don't need the school to focus effort and money on their physical education. It is much better to direct the school's resources toward academic achievement.

44

> If you could invent something *new*, what product would you develop? Use specific details to explain why this invention is needed.

If I could invent something new, I'd invent a device or pill that could put people to sleep immediately and would have no side effects. The proper amount of sleep is important for our concentration, mental health, and physical health.

When we don't get enough sleep, our concentration is strongly affected. We're easily distracted, we can't remember things, and we don't notice what's happening around us. For example, a lot of car accidents are caused by tired drivers. When we get enough sleep, our powers of concentration are sharper. We're more focused on what we're doing. We perform better.

Mental health is also affected by lack of sleep. When we don't get enough sleep we're irritable. We lose our tempers easily and overreact to situations. In fact, experiments have shown that lack of sleep over a long period of time can cause a complete mental breakdown. When we get our proper rest, we're more alert and responsive. Our outlook is positive, and we're much easier to get along with.

Sleeplessness also affects our physical health. We have less energy, and everything seems like a major effort. Over a long period of time, we become slow and unresponsive. The wear and tear on the body from lack of sleep can be a very serious health problem. Every doctor will tell you that getting enough sleep is important for your health.

Wouldn't it be great to go to bed every night knowing you'd have no problem getting to sleep? Getting enough sleep is always going to be an important part of how you respond to your situation. I think this device would be very helpful to all of us.

45

> **Do you agree or disagree with the following statement? Children should be required to help with household tasks as soon as they are able to do so. Use specific reasons and examples to support your answer.**

I believe that children should be required to help with household tasks because it facilitates their development in important ways. It helps them learn skills, develop a sense of responsibility, and contribute to family life. Sharing in household tasks benefits children of all ages.

First of all, doing household tasks builds skills. When very young children do a simple task such as picking up their toys and putting them away, they develop motor and classification skills. Older children learn skills that they will need when they grow up and have homes of their own. They learn to cook, clean, and do laundry. They learn to carry out the tasks that they will need to do in order to take care of themselves and their own families when they are adults.

Secondly, children learn about responsibility when they help with household tasks. They learn to organize their time so that they can do everything that needs to be done. They learn that duties come first and that they have to complete their chores before they can play. Children who understand that effort pays off will be more successful later in life.

When children help with household tasks, the entire family benefits. When parents come home tired from their jobs, they're faced with all the housework. But if their children help with the household chores, then everything is easier for everyone. The work gets done more quickly, and the family has more time to relax together afterwards. The children are helpers, and the parents don't feel like servants to them.

Children should not work all the time. A happy life needs balance. If children can successfully handle tasks at home, they will handle life better, too. They will know the satisfaction of doing a good job, be involved in family life, and become more confident and responsible adults.

46

> **Do you agree or disagree with the following statement? Playing a game is fun only when you win. Use specific reasons and examples to support your answer.**

I agree with the old saying, "It's not whether you win or lose, it's how you play the game." I have fun playing all games because they give me time to be with my friends, learn new things, and work as a team.

Tennis is one game that I enjoy. It's a great opportunity to socialize. First, I have to talk to my partner in order to arrange a time to play a game. We also talk about other things at the same time. We have another opportunity to talk while we are waiting for the tennis court to be free. After the game, we almost always go out for coffee and talk some more. We often don't even talk about tennis. The game is just an excuse for us to get together.

The board game Scrabble provides a good opportunity to build my language skills. It's a challenge to try to form words from the letters that are in front of me. I always learn new words from my opponents, too. Often we don't even keep score when we play the game. We just enjoy being together and improving our English.

The game of soccer gives me the chance to be on a team. I like traveling with the group when we go to other schools to play games. I like learning how to play as a team. Our coach tells us that the most important thing is to play well together. It's also important to have fun. Winning is secondary.

I play games because they are fun. Playing games gives me the opportunity to do things that I enjoy and be with people that I like. You can't win every time, but you can always have fun.

47

> **If you could make one important change in a school that you attended, what change would you make? Use reasons and specific examples to support your answer.**

A big problem at my high school is the foreign language program. The math and science programs receive a lot of attention, but foreign language instruction has been neglected. This is unfortunate because I believe that foreign languages are as important as other school subjects. The school can improve the foreign language program by offering more classes, hiring well-trained instructors, and incorporating the use of technology.

The first thing the school should do is add more levels to the foreign language program. Right now we don't have any classes above the second-year level. Two years just isn't enough time to develop skills in a foreign language. This situation is especially frustrating for those of us who want to continue language study in college because we won't be well prepared.

Next, the foreign language program should be staffed with well-trained instructors. The current teachers in the program don't speak the languages well enough. In our classes, teachers make errors that the students repeat. If the teachers were well trained, they would be good models for the students.

Finally, we need to use current technology in our language classes. Our school has a well-equipped computer laboratory, and many classrooms have computers in them. Strangely enough, however, we don't use computers in our language classes. The school needs to provide us with computer software that is made for learning languages. We also need to be able to spend class time using the Internet to search for current, real-life materials in the languages we study.

In the modern world, foreign language skills are just as important as math, science, and other skills we learn in school. Our school needs to make an investment in the foreign language program so that we can develop the language skills we will need for our future.

48

> **Do you agree or disagree with the following statement? Playing games teaches us about life. Use specific reasons and examples to support your answer.**

Almost everyone, whether child or adult, loves games. The types of games we like may change as we grow up, but our enjoyment of them never does. I believe that playing games is both fun and useful because it teaches us the skills we need in life. Games teach us about cause and effect relationships, teamwork, and following rules.

First of all, games teach us about cause and effect. If we hit a ball, for example, it will land somewhere or someone will catch it. If we hit the ball harder, it will land farther away or be more difficult to catch. If we are able to make certain combinations of cards because we have followed the action of the game, then we win points. We learn how our actions lead to certain results.

Playing games also teaches us how to deal with other people. When we play team games, for instance, we learn about teamwork. We learn how to work with others to reach a goal and how to use the strengths of each individual. When we play other sorts of games, we can still learn about interacting with other people. We learn how to negotiate rules and how to get along with others.

Finally, playing games teaches us about rules. We learn about the importance of rules and how to follow them. We find out that if we want to reach a particular goal, we need to know what the rules are for getting there. We learn how to develop strategies for working within the rules to reach our desired ends.

Games are fun to play, but they are more than just a pleasant pastime. Games provide us with important experiences, and by playing them, we develop skills that are useful in all aspects of our lives.

49

> **Imagine that you have received some land to use as you wish. How would you use this land? Use specific details to explain your answer.**

I would like to use my land for something that everyone can enjoy. Therefore, I would build a campground on it. Right now we don't have any good places for outdoor recreation in my town. A campground would be an inexpensive place for outdoor recreation and would provide activities that everybody would enjoy.

There aren't many opportunities for outdoor recreation in my town. We have only one small park and a playing field behind the high school. That really isn't enough space for our needs. In addition, the park is not well maintained so people don't like to use it. A well maintained campground would give our town a nice place to enjoy outdoor activities.

We have many opportunities for indoor recreation, but they are all expensive. We have a brand new movie theater, but the ticket prices go up every day. It is especially hard to pay for tickets if you have several children. We have a museum of local history, but that, too, is expensive. Young people like to go to the mall, but of course that just encourages more spending. A campground, on the other hand, is an inexpensive place to spend time, even for large families.

At a campground, everybody can find activities that they enjoy. People can play different kinds of games outdoors, they can go hiking or study nature, or just sit and relax. At night they can enjoy talking around a campfire. It is a nice place for families to enjoy some free time together.

A campground would provide an inexpensive and enjoyable place for families and friends to spend time together. It would be a great asset to our town. I think it would be a very good way to use land.

50

In some countries people are no longer allowed to smoke in many public places and office buildings. Do you think this is a good rule or a bad rule? Use specific reasons and details to support your opinion.

I strongly believe that it is not fair to ban smoking in public places. It is not fair to take away smokers' rights, and it is not fair to impose on their ability to relax. Since it is possible to protect nonsmokers by designating special smoking and nonsmoking areas, there is no reason to ban smoking in public.

Smokers have rights just like everyone else. Just because some people don't like to be around smoking, that doesn't mean it should be banned. Some people don't like motorcycles, either. Some people don't like being around dogs. Some people don't like seeing action movies. However, there are no laws against having these things in public. People who don't like smoking have to learn to tolerate it just as they tolerate anything else they may not like.

People smoke to relax. They don't smoke to harm other people. Many people like to unwind by enjoying a cigarette after a meal, for example, but if they have to leave a restaurant to go home and smoke, then it isn't relaxing. Other relaxing activities are allowed in public, so smoking should be allowed, too.

It is easy to designate special smoking areas in public places. Smokers can sit in their own section of a restaurant, airport, bus, or any other place. Nonsmokers can sit in their own section, too, and then they won't be bothered by the smoke. In this way, both smokers and nonsmokers can enjoy their use of the public space equally.

It is true that smoking is bothersome to many people, and some people are even allergic to it. It isn't fair, however, to take away smokers' rights just because some people don't like it. It is possible for smokers and nonsmokers to share public space. It is the only fair thing to do.

51

> In the future, students may have the choice of studying at home by using technology such as computers or television or of studying at traditional schools. Which would you prefer? Use reasons and specific details to explain your choice.

I believe that it is better to study at school than at home. I can learn a lot if I study alone at home, but I can learn more if I study at school with other people. I can gain a lot of information from other people. I also learn a lot by interacting with them. I am motivated to study more if I don't work alone. Therefore, I believe I can learn a lot more at school.

Information comes from technology, but it also comes from people. If I study at home, I can get a lot of information from my computer, DVD player, and television. If I study at school, I can get all this information, and I can also get information from my teachers and classmates. So, I learn more.

Interaction with other people increases my knowledge. At home I have nobody to talk to. Nobody can hear my ideas. At school I have the opportunity to interact with other people. We can explain our ideas to each other. We can agree and disagree. Together we can develop our ideas and learn to understand new things.

Competition motivates me. When I am at home, nobody can see my work. Nobody can tell me that I did a good job or a bad job. When I am at school, my teacher and my classmates see my work, and I can see my classmates' work. I want to do a good job like my classmates, or even a better job. So, I want to study harder.

Some people can study very well when they are alone at home, but I can't. I need to have other people near me. When I am with other people, I have the possibility to learn more information. I have the opportunity to develop my ideas more completely. I have the motivation to do a better job. Therefore, school is the best place for me.

52

> The twentieth century saw great change. In your opinion, what is one change that should be remembered about the twentieth century? Use specific reasons and details to explain your choice.

There were many important changes, both technological and cultural, during the twentieth century. In my opinion, the most important of these is the advances that were made in medical science. The development of vaccines and antibiotics, increased access to health care, and improvements in surgical techniques are all things that improved, and saved, the lives of people all around the world.

Vaccines and antibiotics have saved the lives of many people. Fifty years ago, many people became crippled or died from polio. Now the polio vaccine is available everywhere. In the past, people could die from even simple infections. Now penicillin and other antibiotics make it easy to cure infections.

Increased access to health care has also improved the lives of millions of people. In the past, many people lived far from hospitals or clinics. Now hospitals, clinics, and health centers have been built in many parts of the world. More people have the opportunity to visit a doctor or nurse before they become very sick. They can be treated more easily. They are sick less and this leads to a better quality of life.

Improved surgical techniques make it easier to treat many medical problems. Microscopic and laser surgery techniques are more efficient than older methods. It is easier for the doctor to perform them, and easier for the patient to recover. Surgery patients can return to their normal life more quickly now than they could in the past.

Everybody needs good health in order to have a good quality of life. Advances in medical science have improved the lives of people all around the world. They are improvements that are important to everyone.

53

> **People remember special gifts or presents they have received. Why? Use specific reasons and examples to support your answer.**

I think we remember special gifts we've received because these gifts often hold special memories for us. They may be memories of special people, of special events, or even of ourselves as we once were in the past.

Gifts can remind us of special people in our lives. When we look at gifts, we remember the good times we have enjoyed with the giver. We think of the good feelings we have about that person. The giver may be someone we see frequently or infrequently. Either way, the gift is a special reminder of him or her.

Gifts may also bring back memories of special events in our lives. Some gifts mark special turning points in our lives such as school graduations. Some gifts may hold memories of special birthdays or anniversaries. They help us remember the special times in our lives.

Gifts can also be a symbol of our past. A gift received in childhood may remind us of games we enjoyed then. A gift received in high school makes us think of the music or clothes we loved when we were young.

Gifts are important to us because they remind us of the special people, events, and interests of our lives. They are a way of surrounding ourselves with our past.

54

> **Some famous athletes and entertainers earn millions of dollars every year. Do you think these people deserve such high salaries? Use specific reasons and examples to support your opinion.**

Famous athletes and entertainers earn a lot of money and they deserve it. They work hard to achieve fame, they provide us with good entertainment, and they give up their privacy in order to do this. I think they deserve every cent they get.

Fame doesn't just appear overnight; people have to work hard to achieve it. If someone has a lot of fame now, it means he has spent years working hard to develop his talent. He has spent a lot of time at low-paying jobs in order to get experience and recognition. He continues to work hard now in order to maintain his talent and fame. Just like anybody else, famous people deserve to be rewarded for their hard work.

Athletes, actors, and musicians provide us with entertainment. On weekends, most of us attend at least one sporting event or movie or concert. After watching a famous person perform, we might even be inspired to learn to play a sport or a musical instrument ourselves. Famous athletes and entertainers help us make good use of our free time. They deserve to be paid for this.

Famous people suffer a loss of privacy. Since we admire them, we want to feel as if we know them. We want to know how they live and what happens in their daily lives. Therefore, journalists follow them all the time in order to find out the details of their private lives. These details, true or not, are published in magazines all around the world. This is a big disadvantage to being famous. Earning a lot of money can, in part, compensate for this.

Famous people work hard to entertain us, and then they lose their privacy. They contribute a lot to our lives. They deserve to earn a lot of money.

55

> **Every generation of people is different in important ways. How is your generation different from your parents' generation? Use specific reasons and examples to explain your answer.**

The one thing that makes the difference between my parents' generation and my own is modern technology. When my parents were growing up, they had TV, radio, and cars, but they didn't have the amount of technology we have now. They didn't have personal computers, they didn't have satellite TV, and they didn't have cell phones.

My parents didn't grow up with computers, but I did. They have a computer now, but they don't use it as I do. I write all my schoolwork and keep all my files on the computer. My parents still like to use paper. I do all my research and get all my news off the Internet. My parents still use newspapers and TV. Because of computers, I am accustomed to having more access to information than my parents are. I am used to doing more work more efficiently. It is a completely different way of living.

My parents had only local TV when they were young, but I have satellite TV. I grew up seeing programs from all over the world. I am used to seeing foreign movies and cartoons. I have some ideas about things in foreign countries and a lot of interest in them. Satellite TV exposes me to things that have opened up my mind. My parents didn't have the same opportunity when they were young.

Cell phones are common now, but they didn't exist when my parents were young. They didn't even have answering machines or voice mail. They couldn't talk to people at any time or leave messages easily. I can do this. Right now it is a fun part of my social life. When I have a job it will be more important. I will be able to contact people easily and that will make my work more efficient. Cell phones have made a big difference in the way we work.

Modern technology has made a big difference in the way we work, in our understanding of the world, and in the expectations we have of friends and colleagues. It has completely changed the way we live. The world of my generation is a different place than it was for my parents' generation.

56

> Many people have a close relationship with their pets. These people treat their birds, cats, or other animals as members of their family. In your opinion, are such relationships good? Why or why not? Use specific reasons and examples to support your answer.

Pets are important because they provide us with companionship and even with love. It is not good, however, to have too close a relationship with a pet, or to treat it like a human being. Devoting too much attention to pets can prevent you from focusing on other activities and on relationships with people. It can also be a waste of money.

Sometimes people who love their pets don't want to become involved in other activities. If you invite such a friend out for coffee, for example, the friend might say, "I don't have time. I have to walk the dog." Sometimes people don't want to take a weekend trip because they don't want to leave their pets alone. They put their pets' interests before their own. Then they live life for their pets and not for themselves.

Loving a pet too much can interfere with good relationships with people. Sometimes people neglect their spouses and children in favor of their pets. A person who lives alone might devote all his attention to his pet. He might lose interest in making friends and being with people. A relationship with a pet is less complicated than a relationship with a person. Sometimes it seems easier to choose pets over people.

People spend thousands of dollars on their pets, but this money could have other uses. It seems strange to buy special food for a pet or take it to the doctor, when some people don't have these things. Children all around the world grow up without enough food, or never get medical care. It would be better to give a pet simple things and send the extra money to charity.

Pets give us a lot and they deserve our care and attention. It is never a good idea to go to extremes, however. It is important to balance your pet's needs with your own.

57

> Nowadays food has become easier to prepare. Has this change improved the way people live? Use specific reasons and examples to support your answer.

Food is a basic part of life, so it follows that improved methods of food preparation have made our lives better. Nowadays we can prepare meals much faster than we could in the past. We can also enjoy a greater variety of food and eat more healthfully, all because of modern methods of food preparation.

Microwave ovens have made it possible to prepare delicious food quickly. People these days rarely have time to shop and prepare meals the old-fashioned way. We live very fast lives. We are busy working, caring for our families, traveling, playing sports, and many other things. Because of microwave ovens, we have time to enjoy a good meal with our family and then play soccer, go to a movie, study, or do anything else we want to afterwards.

Modern methods of preserving food have made it possible to enjoy a wide variety of food. Because of refrigerators, freezers, canning, and freeze-drying, we can eat fruits and vegetables that come from far away places. We can prepare a meal one day and save the leftovers in the refrigerator or freezer to eat at another time. We can keep different kinds of food in the refrigerator or on the shelf. It's easy to always have food available and to be able to eat completely different meals every day.

Healthful eating is easier now than it ever was. Because of modern transportation methods, fresh fruits and vegetables are available all year round. Modern kitchen appliances make it easy to prepare fruits and vegetables for cooking. Bread machines make it possible to enjoy healthful, home-baked bread whenever we like. We can eat fresh and healthful food every day because modern methods have made preparation easy.

Our lifestyle is fast, but people still like good food. New food preparation methods have given us more choices. Today we can prepare food that is more convenient, healthier, and of greater variety than ever before in history.

58

> It has been said, "Not everything that is learned is contained in books." Compare and contrast knowledge gained from experience with knowledge gained from books. In your opinion, which source is more important? Why?

"Experience is the best teacher" is an old cliché, but I agree with it. We can learn a lot of important things from books, but the most important lessons in life come from our own experiences. Throughout the different stages of life, from primary school to university to adulthood, experience teaches us many skills we need for life.

As children in primary school, we learn facts and information from books, but that is not all we learn in school. On the playground we learn how to make friends. In our class work, we learn how it feels to succeed and what we do when we fail. We start to learn about the things we like to do and the things we don't. We don't learn these things from books, but from our experiences with our friends and classmates.

In our university classes, we learn a lot of information and skills we will need for our future careers, but we also learn a lot that is not in our textbooks. In our daily lives both in class and out of class, we learn to make decisions for ourselves. We learn to take on responsibilities. We learn to get along with our classmates, our roommates, and our workmates. Our successes and failures help us develop skills we will need in our adult lives. They are skills that no book can teach us.

Throughout our adulthood, experience remains a constant teacher. We may continue to read or take classes for professional development. However, our experiences at work, at home, and with our friends teach us more. The triumphs and disasters of our lives teach us how to improve our careers and also how to improve our relationships and how to be the person each one of us wants to be.

Books teach us a lot, but there is a limit to what they teach. They can give us information or show us another person's experiences. These are valuable things, but the lessons we learn from our own experiences, from childhood through adulthood, are the most important ones we learn.

59

> Do you agree or disagree with the following statement? Television has destroyed communication among friends and family. Use specific reasons and examples to support your opinions.

Some people believe that television has destroyed communication among friends and family. In my opinion, however, the opposite is true. Television can increase communication. News and other information we see on TV gives us things to discuss with our friends and family. TV also helps us understand each other better because we all have access to the same TV programs. Finally, TV can help us share our interests with other people.

Television programs give us things to think and talk about. These days it is always possible to hear up-to-the minute news every time we turn on the television. We hear about things happening all around the world that directly affect our lives. Everybody has opinions about these things and everybody wants to discuss their opinions with other people. So, TV news and information programs encourage us to discuss our ideas with our friends and family.

No matter what city you live in, you have access to the same TV programs as people in other parts of the country. When you go to a new city to work, study, or take a vacation, you will already have something in common with the people there. When you meet new people, you will probably be familiar with at least some of the same TV programs. This gives you something to talk about and a way to begin new friendships.

Most people use TV as a way to pursue their interests. People who play sports usually like to watch sports on TV. People who like to cook watch cooking shows. If your friends and family watch some of the same programs as you do, they can learn more about the things that interest you. This is an excellent form of communication that helps people understand each other better.

TV is a tool that gives us access to information, entertainment, and education. When we watch programs that interest us, we want to share this interest with other people. That is why I believe TV encourages communication among people.

60

> "When people succeed, it is because of hard work. Luck has nothing to do with success." Do you agree or disagree with the quotation above? Use specific reasons and examples to explain your position.

When people succeed, it is because of hard work, but luck has a lot to do with it, too. Luck is often the final factor that turns years of working hard into success. Luck has helped people invent and discover things, it has helped people become famous, and it has helped people get jobs.

Many people have discovered or invented things with the help of luck. Columbus worked hard for years to prepare for his trip around the world. Many thought he was crazy, but still he was able to get support for his endeavor. He worked hard to be able to make his trip to India, but it was because of luck that he actually found the Americas.

Luck can help people become famous. Consider movie stars. Many work hard to learn how to act. They take acting classes. They work at small, low-paying jobs in order to gain experience. Then one day a lucky actor may be given a certain part in a movie, and he gets noticed for it. Or he meets a movie director at the right time and place. Years of hard work bring him close to success, but that one lucky chance finally helps him succeed.

Because of luck, many people find jobs. A person may spend weeks writing and sending off résumés, looking at help wanted ads, and going on job interviews. But often it is because of luck that a job hunter meets the person who will give him or her a job, or hears of an opportunity that isn't advertised in the newspaper. Being in the right place at the right time is often what gets a person a job, and that is all about luck.

It is certainly difficult to be successful without hard work, but hard work also needs to be helped by a little luck. Luck has helped many people, both famous and ordinary, become successful. I think that luck and hard work go hand in hand.

61

> **Some people believe that university students should be required to attend classes. Others believe that going to classes should be optional for students. Which point of view do you agree with? Use specific reasons and details to support your answer.**

Some people believe that going to classes should be optional for university students, but I disagree with this point of view. Students learn a lot more in classes than they can from books alone. In class, they have the advantages of learning from the teacher, interacting with their classmates, and developing the responsibility it takes to be a good student.

When students attend class, they receive the benefit of the teacher's knowledge. The best teachers do more than just go over the material in the class textbook. They present their own interpretations and opinions of the material. They draw their students into discussions so that the students can develop and present their own interpretations, too. Teachers also provide supplementary information by inviting guest speakers or showing films. None of these experiences are available by reading alone.

Going to class also teaches students how to work with other people. In class, students have to present their ideas to their classmates. They have to defend their ideas if their classmates disagree with them but still remain friendly when the discussion is over. In addition, they may have to work in groups to complete class projects, so they have the opportunity to learn to work with others in order to reach a goal.

Attending classes teaches students responsibility. They have to be in class on time and ready to participate. They have to hand in their assignments by the due date. These are all skills they will need if they want to be successful in their future careers.

Anyone can get information from books, but students receive many more advantages when they attend class. They get the benefit of the teacher's knowledge and experience, and even more than that, they learn how to work with others and how to develop a sense of responsibility. These are not optional skills in life, so attending classes should not be optional at a university.

62

> Neighbors are the people who live near us. In your opinion, what are the qualities of a good neighbor? Use specific details and examples in your answer.

A good neighbor is always appreciated, but it takes certain qualities to be one. If you have a good neighbor, you are a lucky person. You live near someone who is respectful of your property, is helpful when those little everyday problems arise, and is supportive in times of crisis.

A good neighbor is someone who respects your property. That means she thinks about how her actions might affect you. She doesn't plant a huge tree between your houses, for instance, without first asking you how you feel about it. Or, if she wants to put up a fence that abuts your yard, she talks it over with you before finalizing her plans. In other words, when she wants to make changes to her property, she takes her neighbors' feelings into consideration.

A good neighbor is someone who is willing to lend a hand when you need a little help. She gladly lends you some butter if you run out in the middle of cooking dinner. She doesn't mind giving you a ride if your car breaks down. She watches your children for you if you have to stay late at work. She pitches in when you need a little help, and you do the same for her. Both of you help make each other's lives easier.

A good neighbor is someone who offers her support when you are going through a crisis. If there is a death or illness in your family, for example, your neighbor might offer to cook some meals for you or clean your house. She might stay by your side during the sadness of a funeral. She looks for ways, big or small, to help you get through the challenging times of life.

A neighbor might be a close friend or a more distant acquaintance. Either way, she is someone who respects you and supports you when she can. We should all be lucky enough to have good neighbors.

63

> What are some important qualities of a good supervisor (boss)? Use specific details and examples to explain why these qualities are important.

Whether working in a large company or a small one, a factory or an office or another setting, all good supervisors have certain qualities in common. A good supervisor treats her employees fairly, gives them clear directions and, most important of all, acts as a good role model.

A good supervisor is fair. She treats all of her employees with equal respect and doesn't have favorites. When it's time for performance evaluations, she uses the same set of criteria to assess each person. She doesn't let her personal feelings about an individual influence her treatment or evaluation of him. Instead, she is careful to conduct herself professionally in all situations.

A good supervisor gives clear and understandable directions. She doesn't get angry when an employee is confused and needs more explanation. Rather, she looks for ways to help that person understand what is required of him. She is also consistent with her instructions. She doesn't constantly change her mind about what she wants done. Therefore, her employees can feel confident that they are doing what they are supposed to be doing.

Finally, a good supervisor sets the standards for her employees by her own behavior. She works hard, acts responsibly, and gets her work done on time. She follows the company's rules and guidelines, dresses appropriately for the job, and treats everyone with respect. In short, she does what is expected of her and does it the best she can. She can only expect her employees to act professionally if she acts professionally too.

Employees are more likely to do a good job when they are treated fairly, given good directions, and have a good example to follow. This is why good supervisors are so important to the success of any type of business.

64

> **Should governments spend more money on improving roads and highways, or should governments spend more money on improving public transportation (buses, trains, subways)? Why? Use specific reasons and details to develop your essay.**

Governments should definitely spend more money on improving all forms of public transportation. The widespread use of private cars has contributed to some serious problems in society, including depletion of natural resources, increased pollution, and the loss of a sense of community. By encouraging the use of public transportation, governments can do a lot to counteract these problems.

Cars depend on oil and gasoline, which are nonrenewable resources. Once we have used them up, they are gone forever. Every time a person gets into a private car to go to work, to the store, or anywhere, gasoline is used up just to take one person to one place. The more people drive their cars, the more resources are used up. When people use public transportation, on the other hand, less oil and gasoline are used up per person.

Cars cause pollution. Every time a person drives his car somewhere, more pollution is put into the air. In many big cities, the high amount of air pollution causes health problems for the residents. Public transportation means fewer cars on the road, and that means less pollution.

Cars tend to isolate people from each other. When a person uses a private car, he is alone or only with people that he already knows. He doesn't have the opportunity to see other people or talk to them or feel that he is part of a larger community. When he uses public transportation, however, he is surrounded by neighbors and other fellow city residents. He has a chance to be with people he might not otherwise see, and maybe even to get to know them a little.

Environmental problems and increased isolation are some of the most serious problems of modern society. Encouraging the use of public transportation is one way governments can work against these problems and start creating a better world.

65

> **In some countries, teenagers have jobs while they are still students. Do you think this is a good idea? Support your opinion by using specific reasons and details.**

I don't think it is a good idea for teenagers to have jobs while they are still students. It can interfere with their studies, it can disrupt their home life, and it takes away part of their childhood that they can never replace.

A job can interfere with a teenager's schoolwork. Education today is very complex and difficult. In order to learn and get good grades, a student must work very hard and concentrate. This means attending classes for most of the day, then doing research for projects, then going home and doing homework. It is very difficult to do all this and have a job, too.

Having a job can also disrupt a teenager's home life. If a teenager has a job to go to after school, he won't be home for dinner. He won't be home after dinner either, and may not get home until late at night. This means he doesn't have much time to spend with his family. Teenagers may be almost grown up, but they still need the companionship and support they get from their families.

The main drawback of a teenager having a job is that he misses out on the fun of being young. He has a whole lifetime ahead of him in which he'll have to earn a living. This is the last free time he'll have. It's the last chance he'll have to hang out with friends and just enjoy himself. Soon enough he'll have to start worrying about paying the rent and buying food.

Jobs bring money, but money isn't everything. For a teenager it is important to concentrate on his studies, spend time with his family, and enjoy being young. A teenager with a job gives up too much.

66

> **A person you know is planning to move to your town or city. What do you think that person would like and dislike about living in your town or city? Why? Use specific reasons and details to develop your essay.**

A friend of mine from college is moving to my city. I think there are things she will like about living here, but there are also things she might dislike. I like living here because there are a lot of things to do, there are a lot of nice neighborhoods to live in, and we have beautiful parks. On the other hand, my friend might not like it because it's very crowded and expensive and we're far from beautiful places like the mountains and the beach.

Living in this city is very exciting because there are so many interesting things to do, although you pay a price for it. We have museums, art galleries, and lots of movie theaters. We have restaurants with food from all over the world. However, when you go to these places they are always very crowded. Also, there is almost always heavy traffic on the way and it is difficult to find parking once you arrive. I know my friend likes peace and quiet, so she may not enjoy the crowds in my city.

In this city we have many beautiful neighborhoods, although some of them are very expensive. We have neighborhoods of old houses with interesting architecture. We have more modern neighborhoods with new apartment buildings. We have lots of nice places to live, but it isn't always easy to find a place that you can afford. I know my friend doesn't earn a big salary, so she might not like this aspect of living here.

Even though we are far from the countryside, we have many beautiful, natural areas right here in the city. We have a big park where people go hiking and biking, and in the winter they go ice skating. We also have many small parks throughout the city and lots of trees and gardens. It is a pretty city and I know my friend will like that. However, we are far from the mountains and far from the beach. I know my friend likes to spend time in the countryside, so she might not like living far away from those places.

All in all, there are both advantages and disadvantages to living here. My friend will have to decide if she prefers excitement and crowds or quiet and nature before she makes her final decision about moving here.

67

> Do you agree or disagree with the following statement? Television, newspapers, magazines, and other media pay too much attention to the personal lives of famous people such as public figures and celebrities. Use specific reasons and details to explain your opinion.

I think the media pay too much attention to the private lives of famous people. They discover things that happened years ago and report them as if they still mattered. They publicize things about famous people's lives that are really private, personal matters. They put out information that could end up having a bad effect on a person's family and personal life. They do this just to entertain the public, but I don't find it entertaining at all.

The media like to dig up bad information about the past actions of famous people. They find out that a person took drugs when he was young, or that someone was a reckless driver and caused a bad accident. Then a person in her forties has to explain something that she did when she was fifteen. I don't understand how something that happened so long ago could have any interest or importance now.

The media says that the public has the right to know about the private actions of famous people. They say it is our right to know if someone had an extramarital affair or didn't pay back some money that he owed. I say these are personal matters. We respect the privacy of ordinary people and we should do the same for famous people.

The media seem to report these things without considering what might happen as a result. Reporting on a celebrity's personal affairs could have an effect on that person's family, especially the children. A celebrity's good name and credibility could be ruined before he or she can prove that the rumors are false. A person's entire career could be ruined by something that is reported in the media.

Having details of one's personal life reported in public can have all sorts of negative consequences on a person's life. Ordinary people don't have to suffer this sort of attention, and I see no reason why celebrities should either.

68

> Some people believe that the Earth is being harmed (damaged) by human activity. Others feel that human activity makes the Earth a better place to live. What is your opinion? Use specific reasons and examples to support your answer.

The quality of human life has improved greatly over the past few centuries, but Earth is being harmed more and more by human activity. As we develop our technology, we use more and more natural resources and cause more and more pollution. As our population grows, we destroy more and more natural areas in order to expand towns and cities. The Earth is being harmed, and this harms people as well.

We often act as if we have unlimited natural resources, but this isn't true. If we cut down too many trees to build houses and make paper, not all the trees will grow back. If we catch too many fish, the fish population will get smaller and smaller. If we aren't careful about how we use our natural resources, we will lose many of them. We are already losing some.

We don't seem to pay attention to the amount of pollution human activity can cause. Our cars pollute the air. Our factories pollute both the air and the water. We throw our waste into rivers and streams. We act as if the air and water can clean themselves up, but they can't.

As urban populations grow, the cities grow too, taking over more and more land. New houses, stores, and office buildings are built all the time. Land that was once forest or farms is now parking lots and apartment buildings. We seem to act as if we have unlimited land, but we don't. We need to plan more carefully so that we use our limited land in the best way possible.

People need to respect the Earth and try to preserve it. If we don't, we will lose all the natural resources that we depend on for life. Then what will happen?

69

> **It has recently been announced that a new high school may be built in your neighborhood. Do you support or oppose this plan? Why? Use specific reasons and details in your answer.**

I oppose having a new high school built in my neighborhood. I don't think there is a real need for one. I think it would cause traffic problems in our area, and it would mean that we would lose the use of our beautiful neighborhood park. I don't think a high school would be of any benefit to us at all.

First of all, there are very few teenagers in our neighborhood. Most of the residents here are either retired or are young couples with babies and small children. This means that most of the high school students would come from other parts of town, but that the majority of the people who live here would not benefit.

Second, a high school would cause a lot of traffic. Most of the students would live too far away to walk to school, so they would come by car or school bus. In addition to the traffic on regular school days, there would be even more traffic after school and on weekends for sports events, school drama productions, and other school activities. This would disrupt the quiet life style of our neighborhood.

Finally, everyone in the neighborhood would be upset by the loss of the park, which is the site that has been selected for the high school. Parents take their small children to the park every day to play. Older people like to walk there in the evenings after dinner. On weekends, people enjoy having picnics and playing games in the park. We would be sorry to lose our neighborhood park.

Our town may need a new high school, but our neighborhood is not the right place for it. We don't want our quiet lifestyle disrupted, and most people in this area have no need for a high school, anyway.

70

> Is it better to enjoy your money when you earn it, or is it better to save your money for some time in the future? Use specific reasons and examples to support your opinion.

When I have a choice between spending money and putting it in my savings account at the bank, I always choose to put it in the bank. I know I will have a lot of expenses in the near future. I need to finish my education, I would like to travel, and then there are always unforeseen emergencies. I need to set money aside so that I will be able to pay for these things.

Education is expensive. My parents aren't able to pay all my bills. My tuition, room and board, books, and incidental expenses all have to be paid for. My parents help me, but I am still responsible for paying part of it. If I spend all the money I earn now, I won't have enough to meet my expenses next semester. So, saving money now will enable me to finish my education.

Another thing that is important to me is travel. Right now I am trying to save money so that I can take a big trip as soon as I graduate. I would like to travel around the world and visit as many countries as I can. If I save money now, there's a good chance that this dream will come true. But If I spend all my money now, I doubt I will ever have enough to make such a trip.

Finally, we should always remember that emergencies can happen at any time. I might have an unexpected illness and need to pay for doctors and medicines. Or, one of my family members may need help, and I will have to send some money. We can't predict emergencies such as these, but we can be prepared. If I save money now, then I will have what I need if the unforeseen occurs.

It is better to plan ahead rather than spend money carelessly. I know I will need money for my schooling, and I would like to have some for travel. I know that I will also have unexpected expenses from time to time. I need to save money for all these things.

71

> Businesses should hire employees for their entire lives. Do you agree or disagree? Use specific reasons and examples to support your answer.

In some places, the common practice is to hire workers when they are young and keep them employed for the rest of their working lives. In other places, companies commonly hire people to do a particular job and then fire them when they are no longer needed. I agree with the latter position. In the modern economy, companies need to consider an employee's performance, speed, and ability to change. Loyalty is not important.

In today's competitive business climate, we need to hire workers who can help us keep up with the competition. This means we need to employ people who have the skills needed for the modern workplace and who can do the job without the need for a lot of extra training. We require employees who are suited to the job we need done, and if the job changes, we change the worker.

Because of the competitive climate, we also need to be able to produce goods and services quickly. We need young people who will push themselves to do the job faster and who are willing to work long hours when necessary. We can't accommodate workers who are unable to keep pace with the pressures of the modern workplace.

The competitive climate also means that we have to be ready to meet changing demands. If we change our workforce regularly, we can bring in new and contemporary ideas. By hiring new workers, we get fresh points of views, We don't stagnate and lose our position in the market because of sticking with outdated approaches.

Although a feeing of loyalty between a company and its workers is a noble idea, it is not practical today. A company needs to keep up with the changing forces of the economy. In order to be able to do this, it needs to be able to change its workforce as necessary.

72

> **Do you agree or disagree with the following statement? Attending a live performance (for example, a play, concert, or sporting event) is more enjoyable than watching the same event on television. Use specific reasons and examples to support your opinion.**

Some people think that attending a live performance is preferable to watching it on television. I say, however, that if you have a good TV, it is much better to watch a performance that way. It is much more convenient and comfortable, and it is cheaper, too. I almost never attend a live performance of anything.

It is much more convenient to stay home and watch a performance on TV. I don't have to go anywhere. I don't have to worry about leaving the house on time. I don't have to worry about traffic or parking. I don't have to stand on line for a ticket. I just turn on the television at the time the event begins, sit back, and enjoy myself.

It is much more comfortable to watch a performance at home. I can wear any clothes that I want to. I know I will have a good seat with a good view. I can get up and get a snack at any time. I can relax and enjoy myself in the comfort of my own home.

It is much cheaper to watch a performance on TV. I don't have to buy a ticket. I don't have to pay for parking or for dinner at a restaurant before the performance. I already own a TV, so watching a performance on it doesn't cost me anything. If it turns out I don't like the performance, I can just turn off the TV and go do something else. I haven't lost any money, or much time either.

Watching a performance on TV is so comfortable and convenient, I don't know why people attend live performances. It's much better to enjoy them at home.

73

> **Choose one of the following transportation vehicles and explain why you think it has changed people's lives.**
>
> ■ **automobiles**
> ■ **bicycles**
> ■ **airplanes**
>
> **Use specific reasons and examples to support your answer.**

Ever since the discovery of the wheel, innovations in transportation have had profound effects on the way people live. In the modern era, the airplane is a form of transportation that has changed our lives in a number of ways. Thanks to the airplane, our lives are now faster, more exciting, and more convenient than before.

It cannot be denied that airplanes are fast. A business person can leave London in the morning and arrive in New York just a few hours later, in time to begin a full day's work. The speed of airplane travel makes it possible for friends and relatives to visit each other more frequently. In both our business and personal lives, airplanes make it possible for us to travel to more places more quickly.

Trips by airplane are also exciting. When you travel by plane, you might cross time zones, oceans, and many countries. When you get off the plane, you could be in a completely different part of the world. You could be in a place where the language, food, and climate are entirely new to you. Because of airplanes, we have the possibility to experience new and exotic places.

Nothing can beat the convenience of an airplane. You can go anywhere at any time you want. You don't have to spend long hours sitting in traffic on the highway. You don't have to wait months before you can get a reservation on a boat. Airplanes leave for destinations around the world at all times of the day. You can choose the schedule that suits you best and arrive at a distant place after just a few, short, comfortable hours of travel.

No form of transportation has changed the way we work and live more than the airplane. Thanks to the speed, excitement, and convenience of the airplane, our lives are filled with more possibilities.

74

> Do you agree or disagree that progress is always good? Use specific reasons and examples to support your answer.

Who could disagree with the statement, "Progress is good?" Progress is a fact of life. Without it, there would be no change. We would still be living the harsh lives our ancient ancestors did. Without progress, there would be no improvements in our economy, our standard of living, or our health.

We can't keep the economy moving forward without progress. Progress means growth. It means the development of new products and the creation of new services. If we didn't have progress, the economy would stagnate. Eventually, there wouldn't be enough jobs to keep people employed or enough industries and businesses to provide us with what we need. We need progress for our economic well-being.

Progress is required to raise our standard of living. Today we live in homes that are more comfortable and have more amenities thanks to developments in home construction technology. We drive better cars and have safer highways thanks to innovations in the transportation industry. Our educational system is greatly improved thanks to the use of computers and the Internet. Progress means that our daily lives are better now than they were in the past.

We need progress to improve the health of the world's population. Without progress, there would be no vaccines against terrible diseases such as smallpox or polio. We wouldn't have treatments for conditions such as heart disease and cancer. We would have high infant mortality rates and a shorter life expectancy. Because of progress, our lives are now longer and healthier than they used to be.

Progress is a natural state. Without it, we wouldn't evolve. Without it, our economy, our standard of living, and our health would deteriorate. Who could deny the necessity of progress?

75

> **Learning about the past has no value for those of us living in the present. Do you agree or disagree? Use specific reasons and examples to support your answer.**

People often say, "Those who don't understand history will repeat the mistakes of the past." I totally disagree. I don't see any evidence that people have made smart decisions based on their knowledge of the past. To me, the present is what is important. I think that people, weather, and politics determine what happens, not the past.

People can change. People may have hated each other for years, but that doesn't mean they will continue to hate each other. Look at Turkey and Greece. When Turkey had an earthquake, Greece sent aid. When Greece had an earthquake, Turkey sent aid. These two countries are cooperating now. No doubt, if we had looked at the past, we would have believed this to be impossible. But people change.

The weather can change. Farmers plant certain crops because these crops have always grown well in their fields. But there can be a long drought. The crops that grew well in the past will die. The farmers need to try a drought-resistant crop. If we had looked at the past, we wouldn't have changed our crop. Weather changes.

Politics can change. If politicians looked only at the past, they would always do the same thing. If we looked at the past in the United States, we would see a lot of discrimination against races, women, and sexual orientation. On the whole, people now are interested in human rights, and the government protects these rights. Politics change.

As a rule, it is important to follow the mood of today. It doesn't help us to think about the past. People, the weather, and politics can change in any direction. The direction of this change, in my opinion, cannot be predicted by studying the past.

76

> **Do you agree or disagree with the following statement? With the help of technology, students nowadays can learn more information and learn it more quickly. Use specific reasons and examples to support your answer.**

It cannot be denied that technology has greatly improved the way we get information, and this has certainly had effects on the lives of students. Recent innovations in technology have made it possible for students to get more information more quickly and more conveniently than they did in the past.

An amazing amount of information is available through the Internet. It is like having all the world's libraries at your fingertips. Students can research any topic they need to learn about or answer just about any question that occurs to them. They can look up information about past events or follow current events as they unfold. Technology has made it possible to access just about any sort of information a student may need through the Internet.

Information comes through the Internet almost instantly. A student just types a few words into a search engine, and in a matter of seconds sources from all over the Internet appear on the screen. It is no longer necessary to take the time to go to the library and search the shelves there, or wait for newspapers and magazines to arrive at the store. Information is available the minute a student needs it.

A variety of electronic devices have made access to information more convenient than ever. A student can use a desktop or laptop computer to access the Internet from home or school any time of night or day. In addition, smart phones and tablet computers make it possible for students to carry around their Internet access with them. They can go online while sitting in a café or waiting for a bus. They can look for information at any time and in any place they choose.

Technology has improved the way students get information. The Internet and the devices students can use to access it have made more information available more quickly and conveniently.

77

> **Some people think that human needs for farmland, housing, and industry are more important than saving land for endangered animals. Do you agree or disagree with this point of view? Why or why not? Use specific reasons and examples to support your answer.**

Many animals are now extinct and many more are in danger of extinction. This is because their habitat is destroyed when people use land to build houses, factories, and farms. Does it matter? It certainly does. Our basic human needs, our quality of life, and the way we live are all affected when animals' habitats are destroyed.

Many animals affect our basic human needs even though we may not realize it. There is a delicate balance of nature. If one small part is removed, it will affect all the other parts. For example, if certain trees are cut down, bats will have no place to live. If there are no bats, there will be no animal to eat certain insects that destroy our crops. This will affect our basic need for food.

The loss of certain animals affects the quality of our lives. Certain flowers are pollinated by butterflies that migrate from Canada to Mexico. Some of the breeding grounds of these butterflies was destroyed. Now, these flowers are disappearing. We will no longer be able to enjoy their beauty, and we will no longer be able to enjoy the beauty of the butterflies. This is just one small example.

When animals' habitats are destroyed we may think that it only affects the animals, but it affects our way of life, too. Large parts of the Amazon rain forest have been cut down to make room for farms. This rain forest is an important part of the weather system all around the world. Weather patterns have been changing because of this. This will have a huge effect on how we live.

When animals' lives are endangered, our way of life is endangered, too. I would encourage humans to look for other alternatives for our farmlands, housing, and industries. We have alternatives; the animals do not.

78

What is a very important skill a person should learn in order to be successful in the world today? Choose one skill and use specific reasons and examples to support your choice.

Although success is often defined economically, I define it socially. Therefore, a skill I would identify as being important for success is tolerance. To succeed in society, in my opinion, we need to be tolerant of one another's background, opinions, and lifestyle.

The world is filled with people from all different backgrounds. These days, the world is also becoming increasingly mobile. In the past, we tended to work only with people who grew up in the same place we did or who went to the same schools we went to. Now we often find ourselves working with people whose backgrounds are completely different from ours. This is why it is important to be tolerant of one another's differences, not only so we can work together amiably but also so we can learn from each other.

Different people have different opinions, but we cannot stop speaking to one another just because of this. We shouldn't start a fight just because someone has a different point of view. Instead, we need to look for common ground, something we can agree on. We need to respect the people we live and work with and be tolerant of their opinions. We need to look for ways to get along with everyone in our lives.

There are people living different lifestyles all around us. A woman might be living on her own, working at an important job, and supporting her family by herself. A man might choose to stay at home and raise the children while his wife earns money at a job. Social roles can change and people choose the lifestyles that suit them best. We must be tolerant of these different choices.

To succeed socially, it is important to be able to adapt to differences. It is important to be tolerant of all people regardless of their background, opinions, or lifestyle.

79

Why do you think some people are attracted to dangerous sports or other dangerous activities? Use specific reasons and examples to support your answer.

Many people enjoy watching or reading about dangerous sports. Few, however, are attracted to actually participating in such sports themselves. These are usually people who love risks, seek a feeling of power, or need a way to deal with personal problems. Dangerous sports give them a way to meet these kinds of needs.

Dangerous sports are attractive to risk takers. Most people take risks in their daily lives such as risks with their money, their jobs, or their love lives. These are only ordinary risks, however, and are generally not life threatening. Risks takers, on the other hand, are people who seek the excitement of a different kind of risk—that of putting their lives in danger. Dangerous sports have that special kind of thrill that risk takers seek.

People who want a feeling of power are also attracted to dangerous sports. Climbing to the top of a remote mountain peak or learning how to sky dive successfully can give a great feeling of accomplishment. When people perform such amazing feats and survive them, they feel as though they have conquered the forces of nature. They feel more powerful than fate.

Finally, I think dangerous sports may sometimes attract unhappy people. When people are dissatisfied at work or when they have difficulties at home, they may turn to dangerous sports as a way of dealing with their problems. At the very least, this type of activity can distract them from the things that are bothering them. But even more, learning how to do something difficult can increase a person's self esteem. It can help a person feel good about himself despite any personal problems he may have.

Dangerous sports can be attractive for several reasons. They appeal to people who seek thrills, power, or a way to forget their problems. I, however, do not count myself among these people and in my opinion, dangerous sports are never worth the risk.

80

Some people prefer to get up early in the morning and start the day's work. Others prefer to get up later in the day and work until late at night. Which do you prefer? Use specific reasons and examples to support your choice.

Some people have lots of energy early in the day, but I am not one of them. No one could ever accuse me of being a "morning person." I definitely prefer to get up later in the day and stay up until late at night. This routine fits my body's rhythm, my work schedule, and my social life.

I believe in following my body's natural rhythm. For me, it is natural to feel wide awake at night and sleepy in the morning. Therefore, I prefer to stay in bed until 10:00 or 11:00 every morning. When I do this, I wake up feeling energetic and ready to start the day. If I get up earlier, I feel grumpy and foggy and unable to do anything properly.

Sleeping late also suits my work schedule. I work best in the afternoon. Fortunately, I don't usually have a lot of work to do and don't need to spend all day at it. If I work from after lunch until just before dinner, that is enough time to get my work done.

My active social life is another reason I prefer to sleep late. Who gets up early in the morning to have fun? No one. If I want to go out and have a good time with my friends, I have to do it in the evening. Anything entertaining, such as parties, concerts, dances, or dinners, happens then. If I got up early in the morning, I would be too tired to enjoy myself later.

Getting up and going to bed late is the sort of schedule that suits me best. It allows me to follow my natural rhythms, get my work done, and have fun with my friends. I will probably follow this pattern for the rest of my life.

81

What are the important qualities of a good son or daughter? Have these qualities changed or remained the same over time in your culture? Use specific reasons and examples to support your answer.

Most parents will tell you that they wish their children will have certain qualities. They want them to be obedient, loyal, and respectful. These are expectations that parents have had of their children for generations. These days, however, parents often find that their children demonstrate these qualities less and less.

All parents expect their children to obey them. Even when their sons and daughters grow up and have children of their own, parents still expect obedience from them. At least, that's the way it was traditionally. Nowadays, children still obey their parents when they are young. When they reach age 18 or 20, however, they start wanting to make their own decisions. They want to follow their own ideas even if these ideas are contrary to their parents' wishes.

Parents also expect their children to be loyal. They expect them to put their family first, before other relationships they may have. Also, if a dispute arises between families, parents expect their children to side with their own family. This is a quality that is still commonly valued among the younger generation. Most children today will support their family against others.

Finally, parents, quite naturally, demand respect of their children. As children become accustomed to nontraditional ways of doing things, however, this quality starts to lose strength. The world is changing rapidly, making it easy for children to view their parents as old-fashioned. They think their parents are too old to understand them and the world they live in, and they start losing respect.

The traditional virtues of obedience, loyalty, and respect are being challenged today. Children nowadays tend to show these qualities to their parents less and less.

82

Some people prefer to work for a large company. Others prefer to work for a small company. Which would you prefer? Use specific reasons and details to support your choice.

While small companies and large companies each have their advantages, I am sure I would prefer to work for a large company. A large company has more to offer its employees in terms of advancement, training, and prestige.

As the employee of a large company, I could start at an entry level position and work my way up to the top. I might start working in the mailroom, for example, and get to know the company that way. Then, when there was an opening for a better position, I could apply for that. Eventually I could work my way up to a managerial job. In a small company, on the other hand, I would have fewer opportunities to advance.

If I worked for a large company, I would also have the chance to learn a variety of jobs. For instance, I might work in shipping for a while and then move on to sales. I could be trained in a variety of positions and gain valuable experience. In addition to on-the-job training, I would also probably have opportunities to take professional development classes through my company. A small company can't provide the same advantages.

In a large company, there would be more prestige. In the first place, the name of a large company would look very good on my resume. Additionally, my friends and acquaintances would be impressed when I told them where I worked. If I worked for a small company, on the other hand, few people would recognize its name and I would always have to explain what the company did.

Working for a small company would not give me the same opportunities for advancement or training as a large company would, and it would not have the same prestige. I would benefit in many ways by choosing to work for a large company over a small one.

83

> **People work because they need money to live. What are some other reasons that people work? Discuss one or more of these reasons. Use specific examples and details to support your answer.**

Although the main reason most people work is to earn a living, it is not the only reason they stay at their jobs. Working also fulfills other human needs. It provides people with the opportunity to be with other people, to contribute something to society, and to feel a sense of accomplishment.

Many people enjoy going to work because it gives them the chance to be with other people. They like interacting with their coworkers and clients. They like working with others to find ways to get a job done, and they like the chance to socialize, as well. Work provides opportunities to develop both professional and personal relationships.

People also enjoy their jobs because it gives them the chance to contribute something to society. Teachers, for example, educate our future generations. Doctors and nurses help us stay healthy. Manufacturers produce things that we need to carry out our daily lives. Through work, each individual is able to do his or her part in the world.

A lot of people like to work because it gives them a sense of accomplishment. People who work in factories, for example, can take pride in the cars they produce or the televisions they assemble. A business owner gets a sense of achievement when he sees the business he built from scratch become successful and profitable. Anybody who develops professional skills through training and experience knows the feeling of accomplishment that comes from having achieved certain levels of expertise.

Money is nice to have, but it is not the only reason people get up and go to work every day. I believe that people also value work because it allows them chances to interact with others, to make a contribution to society, and to feel that they have accomplished something. These needs may not be as fundamental as the need to have money to pay for food and shelter, but they are important needs nevertheless.

84

> **Do you agree or disagree with the following statement? Face-to-face communication is better than other types of communication, such as letters, email, or telephone calls. Use specific reasons and details to support your answer.**

I would have to agree that face-to-face communication is the best type of communication. It can eliminate misunderstandings immediately, cement relationships, and encourage continued interaction.

When you talk to someone directly, you can see right away if they don't understand you. A person's body language will tell you if they disagree or if they don't follow your line of thought. Then you can repeat yourself or paraphrase your argument. When you send an email, the receiver may misinterpret what you want to say. He or she could even be insulted. Then you have to waste time explaining yourself in another email.

When you talk face to face, you communicate with more than words. You communicate with your eyes and your hands. You communicate with your whole body. People can sense that you really want to communicate with them. This energy bonds people together. Your relationship with a person can grow much stronger when you communicate in person.

When you meet someone face to face, the interaction tends to last longer than other forms of communication. An email lasts a second; a telephone call, a few minutes. When you meet someone face to face, however, you've both made an effort to be there. You will probably spend longer talking. The longer you talk, the more you say. The more you say, the stronger your relationship will be.

In summary, if you want to establish a relationship with another human being, the best way is talking face to face. When you communicate directly, you can avoid misunderstandings that may occur in writing. You can communicate on levels other than just words and you can spend more time doing it.

85

> Some people like to do only what they already do well. Other people prefer to try new things and take risks. Which do you prefer? Use specific reasons and examples to support your choice.

I am not a risk taker. I like to do just those things that I am proficient at. I don't want to waste my time doing things that I don't do well. I always feel better when I do something well, and other people have a better impression of me. I don't see a good reason to try something new that I don't know how to do at all.

I don't have time to waste doing things that I don't really know how to do. For example, I don't know how to sew. I could spend a whole day trying to make a dress, and at the end of the day I still wouldn't have a dress to wear. It would be better to spend an hour buying a dress at the store. Then I could spend the rest of the day doing other things that I know I can do.

I feel good when I do a good job, but I feel terrible when I do something poorly. Once, I decided to figure my income taxes myself. But I am not an accountant and I made many mistakes. I felt very bad about it. Finally, I realized I could pay a professional accountant to do it for me. Then I could spend my time feeling good about other things that I know how to do.

When I do something well, I make a better impression on other people. If I tried to cook a meal for you, you would not have a good impression of me at all. I am a terrible cook. But I can change the oil in your car for you and I can tune up the engine. When you see me do a good job at that, you see me as a competent, accomplished mechanic instead of as a sorry cook.

Some people like to take risks and try doing new things, but I am not one of those people. When I do something that I really don't know how to do, I just end up feeling bad and I give other people a bad impression. I don't see the point of wasting my time this way.

86

> Some people believe that success in life comes from taking risks or chances. Others believe that success results from careful planning. In your opinion, what does success come from? Use specific reasons and examples to support your answer.

I think we must all take risks if we want to get anywhere in life, but they must be calculated risks. If we look at the great explorers and scientists of history, we see that their successes were usually a combination of both planning and risk taking. Like the great thinkers, we must plan carefully, take the risk, then be ready to change direction when necessary.

It is hard to be successful without careful planning. In his search for a new route to India, Columbus drew maps, planned his route carefully, and spent time gathering the necessary support and supplies. Madame Curie worked long hours in her laboratory setting up her experiments, then carefully recording each step she took and the results she got. Neither of these two legendary figures would have achieved what they did without this planning.

The willingness to take risks is the other important ingredient of success. Despite all his careful planning, Columbus couldn't know what would happen on his trip. He couldn't be sure he would be successful in finding a new route to India or know what he might encounter instead. Madame Curie could not be certain about the results of her experiments, of course, and the only way to find out was to actually carry the experiments out.

When things don't go according to plan, success can still be achieved if you are ready to change direction. Columbus planned to bring back spices from Asia. When he landed in America instead, he didn't just give up and go home. He didn't find spices, but he did find gold. You can reach success if you are able to make your mistakes work for you and change your plans when necessary.

You will never succeed in life if you don't take chances. But before you start, you must plan carefully so that you are ready to take advantage of every opportunity and change your plans as required.

87

> What change would make your hometown more appealing to people your age? Use specific reasons and examples to support your opinion.

There is almost no place in my town where young people can go to spend time with their friends after school. Therefore, I think it would be a good idea to have a teahouse that would be only for young people. We could go there to socialize, have meetings, and relax in a quiet place.

The young people in my town need a place to socialize. There are already several teahouses, but they are reserved for our fathers and their friends. Teenagers are not allowed to spend time in them. If we had a teahouse of our own, we would have a place to get together with our friends and talk about school and other things that interest us.

A teahouse of our own would also mean that we would have a place to hold meetings. Several of my friends would like to start a poetry club, but they have no place to meet. I would be interested in starting a debating society, and I know a number of young people who are interested in politics. If we had a place to hold meetings, we could form clubs to pursue these and similar interests with our friends.

Finally, it would be nice to have a place to relax away from our families. Most people in my town come from large families. This means that our homes are usually noisy and busy. Many of us have younger brothers and sisters whom we love but who can be annoying at times. Sometimes we need to get away from our hectic home lives. We need to have a quiet place where we can go to study, read, or just sit quietly.

If our town had a teahouse reserved for teenagers, it would be good for our parents. They would always know where we were. They could rest assured knowing that if we aren't at home, we are at the teahouse socializing, having a meeting, or just relaxing with our friends.

88

> Do you agree or disagree with the following statement? **The most important aspect of a job is the money a person earns.** Use specific reasons and examples to support your answer.

I strongly agree that the most important aspect of a job is the amount of money I can earn from it. When I was thinking about what kind of profession I wanted to have, I only considered professions that have a high earning potential. What is the point of working, after all, if not to make as much money as possible? If I earn a lot of money, people will know I am successful, smart, and a good marriage candidate.

Money equals success. If I earn a lot of money, I can afford to buy nice things such as fashionable clothes and a luxury car. I can also help my family and friends. I can buy a nice apartment for my parents, for instance, and lend money to my friends whenever they need it. Everyone will see that I am rich and, therefore, successful.

Earning a lot of money will show people how smart I am. Everyone knows that you need to be smart to make money. You can't move up to high positions in a company without intelligence and knowledge. No one will pay you a high salary if you are stupid.

When I earn a lot of money, my mother will be able to find a good wife for me. She will be able to tell everyone that I have a good job and a high salary. It will make it easy for her to find someone for me since all girls want to marry a rich man. They want someone who can easily take care of their material needs.

When I start working, it would be nice to get a job that is interesting to do. More important than that, however, is the amount of money I earn. Having a high-paying job will show everyone that I am successful, smart, and a good catch.

89

> Do you agree or disagree with the following statement? **One should never judge a person by external appearances.** Use specific reasons and details to support your answer.

In most cases, you shouldn't judge a person by external appearances. It is better to reserve judgment until you have had a chance to get to know the person. Judgments based on external appearances prevent you from really getting to know a person, reinforce stereotypes, and can lead you to conclusions that aren't true.

When you judge people by their external appearance, you lose the chance to get to know them. In high school I stayed away from students who were called "bad students" because they dressed a certain way. I wanted nothing to do with them. Later, I had a chance to meet a "bad student" because his mother was a friend of my mother. Then I realized that we actually had a lot in common. My impression of him was very different once I got to know him.

Judging people based on external appearances just reinforces stereotypes. You might think that a person with a tattoo, for example, is not a nice person. It's easy to start thinking that all people with tattoos are not nice people. Then you will never make friends with people who have tattoos or want to work with them or like to live near them. You will feel uncomfortable around them because all you will see about them is their tattoos.

Judgments based on external appearances can often lead you to conclusions that aren't true. Maybe you know someone who dresses in old, unfashionable clothes. If all you see are the clothes, it is easy to think that the person has bad taste or bad habits. But maybe the truth is different. Maybe that person comes from a less fortunate family than you and doesn't have money. Maybe the person is working hard to save money for school. You will never know if all you do is look at external appearance.

You should always take time to get to know new people before making judgments about them. External appearance often does not tell us anything about a person. Judging someone by their appearance is misleading, reinforces stereotypes, and doesn't lead to the truth. It can prevent you from making a true friend.

90

> **Do you agree or disagree with the following statement? A person should never make an important decision alone. Use specific reasons and examples to support your answer.**

You should never make an important decision alone. You should think out your important decisions carefully, and you need other people to help you do this. People close to you can give you good advice, give you a different perspective, and share their own experiences. It is hard to make big decisions without this kind of help.

It is very important to have advice when making decisions. When I had to decide which courses to take in high school, I talked to the school counselor. He had the knowledge and expertise to help me determine which classes were best for my goals. Without his advice, I might have chosen unsuitable courses.

Getting a friend's perspective on a situation is also usually helpful. I have always loved drama, but I thought I wasn't good enough to act in the school play. When a friend of mine found this out, she was shocked. She was able to provide me with another perspective on myself and my talents. I changed my mind and decided to audition for the school play. Imagine my surprise when I got an important part.

When other people share their experiences with you, that can help you in making your decisions. When I was trying to decide if I should study overseas, I talked with a friend. She had studied overseas the year before. She really helped me because I was very unsure about my decision. After hearing about her experiences, I decided it would be a good experience for me too. I went and it was amazing.

Whenever I am faced with an important decision, I seek advice from others so that I am well-informed and have the benefit of their experience and perspective.

91

> A company is going to give some money either to support the arts or to protect the environment. Which do you think the company should choose? Use specific reasons and examples to support your answer.

Deciding between supporting the arts and protecting the environment is a difficult choice to make, but I think I would choose protecting the environment. We need a healthy environment in order to survive, so we must protect it. We need to protect the environment now to help prevent health problems, to maintain the ecosystem, and to preserve the Earth for our children.

Pollution from factories and cars can cause damage to the environment. It makes the air dirty. Breathing this dirty air causes health problems, particularly for children and the elderly. We need to control the amount of pollution we produce in order to prevent health problems.

We also need to pay attention to the ecosystem. Plant life, animal life, and people all depend on each other. An unhealthy environment disturbs this ecosystem. For example, changes in the environment might cause a certain kind of plant to die. If that plant is food for a certain kind of animal, the animal will die too. If people use that animal as a food source, there could be big problems.

If we do not protect our environment now, it will continue to get worse and our children will suffer the consequences. The air and water will get dirtier, and more plants and animals will die. Our children won't have as much natural beauty to admire. Even worse, their well-being will be threatened.

Without clean air to breathe, a healthy ecosystem, and a future for our children, the human race will not survive. That's why protecting our environment is important. If we have a healthy environment, we have healthy children who can participate in and appreciate the arts.

92

> Some movies are serious, designed to make the audience think. Other movies are designed primarily to amuse and entertain. Which type of movie do you prefer? Use specific reasons and examples to support your answer.

Some movies make you think deeply about important issues, while others distract you from your problems. Although I sometimes enjoy watching movies that are serious, I generally prefer to see movies that amuse and entertain. These movies help me relax, laugh, and keep my perspective.

At the end of a long day, what I need to do most is relax. My classes and my job keep my mind working all day, so I am usually too tired mentally to enjoy a serious movie. An entertaining movie, however, gives my mind the rest it needs. I don't have to think while watching such a movie. I just sit back and relax. Then my mind feels renewed and I feel ready to get back to work and study.

Entertaining movies make me laugh. Laughing is important in many ways. It is good for both one's soul and one's physical health. So, laughing helps me keep feeling good. It also helps connect me with other people. When I see an amusing movie with my friends and we laugh together, it helps strengthen our friendship.

When I watch an amusing movie, it helps put my problems in perspective. Sometimes the troubles of the day can seem overwhelming. I can't stop thinking about them and they push all other thoughts out of my mind. An amusing movie can help me forget about my problems for a while. Then, when I think about them again, they don't seem so big, and solutions may be easier to find.

While I can appreciate serious movies that make you think, I prefer to be amused and entertained at the end of a hard day. Such movies allow me to take a break from the rigors of daily life by helping me relax, making me laugh, and putting my problems into perspective.

93

> **Some people are always in a hurry to go places and get things done. Other people prefer to take their time and live life at a slower pace. Which do you prefer? Use specific reasons and examples to support your answer.**

Life is short. Haste makes waste. What's your hurry? I feel there is a lot of wisdom in these words. These three sayings characterize the way I manage my daily life. I would rather take my time than rush through things just to get them done.

Life is short. You never know what may happen tomorrow, so it is important to appreciate today. By doing just a few things slowly and doing them well, you can savor the experience. You can truly enjoy what you are doing and make each minute count.

Haste makes waste. You can't just rush through your chores as if you were a machine. If you did, you might miss some steps and end up doing a poor job. Then you would have to start from the beginning and do the job all over again. It would take twice as long to get things done. But by going more slowly, you can do a chore carefully, completely, and correctly the first time around.

What's your hurry? I don't see the point of rushing through something just to get to the next experience. If you did, you would miss a lot along the way. If you are taking care of your younger brother for example, you could just keep him by your side while you work on other chores. Or, you could devote your whole attention to him, interact with him, and get to know him. There is a lot to be gained by focusing your entire attention on the task at hand rather than thinking the whole time about what you are going to do next.

I believe it is important to appreciate life by savoring each moment we have, not wasting any bit of precious time, and always slowing down enough to appreciate what is right in front of us.

94

> Do you agree or disagree with the following statement? Games are as important for children as they are for adults. Use specific reasons and examples to support your answers.

We usually think of games as being a significant part of childhood, but adults enjoy them, as well. In my opinion, games are important at all stages of life. They help you keep your mind sharp, they challenge you to learn new things, and they allow you to maintain social skills. These are things that are important for people of all ages.

Playing games exercises the mind. For children, this helps them develop their thinking skills. For adults, this helps them stay sharp even as they grow older. Doing things such as learning the rules of a game, working out a winning strategy, and keeping track of opponents' moves, helps both children and adults keep their brains growing and functioning. It helps them stay mentally active.

People can learn a lot from playing games. Certain types of games, for example, test the players' knowledge of geography, history, science, or current events facts. Other games require an understanding of vocabulary. Both children and adults enjoy learning and showing off the knowledge needed to play these sorts of games, so playing games can make learning fun for everyone.

Games provide an opportunity to develop and use social skills. Playing games means interacting with other people. It means learning to follow rules, playing fairly, and being considerate of others, even if they are your opponents. These are skills that are important for children to develop and for adults to maintain. Playing games also allows people to develop and maintain personal contacts. This is important for everybody because we all need friends, no matter what age we are.

Playing games is important for everyone, regardless of age. Games help you keep your mind alert, learn new things, and build friendships. These are things that matter in all phases of life.

95

> Do you agree or disagree with the following statement? Parents or other adult relatives should make important decisions for their older (15–18 year old) teenaged children. Use specific reasons and examples to support your opinion.

No one knows me as well as my parents, and no one cares about me like they do. It is natural that I should allow my parents to make important decisions for me. I think all older teenagers should take their parents advice on decisions that concern their education, their social life, and their future careers.

My parents are the ones who can make the best decisions about my education. They have always chosen the best schools for me to attend. They have hired tutors to make sure I understood my classes well. They have sent me to special prep classes to help me prepare for exams. When it is time to choose a college, I know they will choose the right college for me.

My parents make good decisions about my social life. When I was young, they invited children over to play with me. I became very close to these children and we are still friends. Even though I am older now, my parents still guide me in my social life. I know they don't want me to hang out with the wrong crowd. I know they want me to marry a good person who is right for me. They have more experience than I have and they can help me make decisions about my social life.

I need my parents to help me make decisions about my future career. Both my parents have successful careers of their own. My father runs a business and my mother is a well-known politician. I want to be as successful as they are, so of course I will listen to their advice about my career.

If all children follow their parents' wishes, they will be happier. They will be more successful in school, in work, and in their social life. After all, parents want only the best for their children.

96

> **What do you want most in a friend—someone who is intelligent, or someone who has a sense of humor, or someone who is reliable? Which one of these characteristics is most important to you? Use reasons and specific examples to explain your choice.**

I like people who are intelligent and I always enjoy someone with a good sense of humor. What I look for first, however, is a friend who is reliable. I need to be able to rely on my friends to provide me with companionship, to support me, and to encourage me.

I depend on my friends for companionship. If I want to see a movie or go to a concert, of course I ask some friends to accompany me. If I feel sad or lonely, I can count on my friends to spend some time with me. If I feel happy, I can invite all my friends to a party. I know they will come over to have a good time with me.

When I am having troubles, I turn to my friends for support. If I fail an exam, or have a fight with someone, I call up a friend. I rely on my friends to be willing to talk to me and help me solve my problems. I expect my friends to be there when I need them, and I do the same for them.

I need my friends to encourage me. If I am afraid to do something such as enroll in a difficult course or apply for a job to earn some extra money, my friends help me. They talk to me and give me the confidence I need to try new and difficult things. I know I can count on them to give me encouragement when I need it.

We all like to spend time with smart and entertaining people. I think the people who make the best friends, though, are people who are reliable. If someone is reliable, you know he or she will always be ready to give you companionship, support, and encouragement when you need it. That's what friends are for, isn't it?

97

> **Do you agree or disagree with the following statement? Most experiences in our lives that seemed difficult at the time become valuable lessons for the future. Use reasons and specific examples to support your answer.**

People say that experience is the best teacher, and I believe this is true. Difficult experiences, especially, can teach us valuable lessons. They can help us overcome fears, they can teach us better ways to do things, and they can show us that we have friends who are ready to help us.

Difficult experiences can help us overcome fears. I remember the first time I had to give a presentation to my classmates. I was very shy and afraid to speak in front of the whole class. I spent a long time preparing for my presentation. I was nervous and didn't sleep well the night before. I was surprised when I gave my presentation and everyone listened. No one laughed at me. They asked questions and I could answer them. Now I know I can talk in front of the class and do a good job.

Difficult experiences can teach us better ways to do things. I had a very embarrassing experience when I took the test to get my driver's license. I didn't practice for the test because I thought I was such a good driver. But I failed. I didn't really know what to expect so I got nervous and made mistakes. I was embarrassed about my failure and my parents were disappointed. Now I know that it is always better to prepare myself for something, no matter how ready I think I am.

Difficult experiences can show us that we have friends. Once I was very sick and I missed several months of school. I thought I would have to repeat the year. I didn't have to because there were a lot of people who helped me. My teachers gave me extra time to do my work. My classmates explained the homework to me. People who I didn't even know well helped me make up the work I lost. I learned that I had friends where I hadn't expected any.

Nobody looks for difficult experiences, but we all have to go through them from time to time. They help us overcome fears, learn better ways of doing things, and show us who our friends are. These are all valuable lessons for our future.

98

> **Some people prefer to work for themselves or own a business. Others prefer to work for an employer. Would you rather be self-employed, work for someone else, or own a business? Use specific reasons to explain your choice.**

Many people have dreams of becoming self-employed or starting their own business, but I don't understand this. I think it is much better to work for someone else. When I work for someone else, I don't have to take risks or make difficult decisions alone. I have someone to tell me what to do, someone to evaluate my work, and most important of all, someone to give me a regular paycheck.

As an employee, I don't have to decide what to do every day. My employer gives me work to do and she gives me deadlines for it. I don't have to worry about what needs to be done next on a project. That's my employer's job. Without this worry, I can just focus on getting the job done right.

When I have an employer, I never have to wonder if my work is good or bad. My employer tells me if I did a good job, or if I need to do something over again. I don't have to worry if a client will like my work or if a product is good enough to sell. That is my employer's concern. My employer lets me know how my work is and if necessary, I will do it again or do it better the next time.

I know I will get a paycheck every two weeks when I work for someone else. I don't have to worry if the clients have paid or if we have sold enough merchandise. If I go to work every day, I get my paycheck on a regular basis. I work so I can get paid and I want to be able to be sure of receiving my money.

Many people want to feel independent and that is why they want their own business. For me, however, it is more important to feel secure. I feel secure knowing that I have an employer to give me directions, evaluate my work, and pay me regularly. That is why I prefer to work for someone else.

99

Should a city try to preserve its old, historic buildings or destroy them and replace them with modern buildings? Use specific reasons and examples to support your opinion.

Of course a city should preserve its old, historic buildings. New buildings can always be built, but old ones can never be replaced. They are usually more beautiful than modern buildings, they represent the city's history, and they can even help the city by attracting tourists. Historic buildings should always be preserved.

Old buildings are usually very beautiful. Depending on when they were built, they show different periods of architecture. They have a lot of character. They were made by hand, the old-fashioned way. You can feel the personalities of the people who built them and of the people who have lived and worked in them. Modern buildings, on the other hand, are usually not so beautiful. They seem like impersonal giants that have no character.

Old buildings represent a city's history. Important things may have taken place in an old building. Maybe a peace treaty was signed there or an important meeting took place. A famous person may have lived there. Maybe it was a former president or a famous writer. When we have historic buildings around us, we learn more about our history and we appreciate it.

Old buildings attract tourists to a city. People want to see old buildings because they are beautiful or because important things happened in them. If a city has a lot of old, interesting buildings, many tourists will visit the city. That is good for the city's economy. People usually don't visit a city in order to see its modern buildings.

A city's old, historic buildings are among its greatest treasures. They are a source of beauty and a representation of history. It would be a crime to try to replace them.

100

Do you agree or disagree with the following statement? Classmates are a more important influence than parents on a child's success in school. Use specific reasons and examples to support your answer.

I believe that parents have more influence on a child's school success than classmates do. Classmates have an important social influence on each other, especially as they get older, but the influence of parents is stronger than this. Parents are the most important model a child has, parents love their children, and they have expectations of them. All of these things are important influences on a child's success in school.

Parents are important role models for their children. Young children like to copy other children, but they like to copy adults more. When children see their parents read, they read too. When children hear their parents talk about books or news or politics, they will think these are interesting subjects, too. Children may learn other things from their classmates, but the examples they get from their parents are stronger.

Parents are the most important people who love and care for a child. Children know how important this is, and they love their parents, too. They may have close friends in school, but their feelings for their parents are more important. If they feel loved and cared for at home, they will have the necessary confidence to do well in school.

Parents have expectations for their children. They expect them to behave well and be good people and be successful in school. Children want to please their parents so they try to fulfill their parents' expectations. They want to be nice to their classmates and get along with them, but this is not the same as fulfilling their parents' expectations.

Many people have influence on children while they are growing up, but parents are the ones who have the strongest influence. They are the most important role models their children have, they love them the most, and they have the greatest expectations of them. Nobody can influence a child more than a parent can.

101

> If you were an employer, which kind of worker would you prefer to hire: an inexperienced worker at a lower salary or an experienced worker at a higher salary? Use specific reasons and details to support your answer.

If I were an employer, I would prefer to hire an inexperienced worker at a lower salary. There would be several advantages to doing this. First of all, it would save me money, at least initially. I would also be able to train an inexperienced person exactly as I want, and he or she might be willing to work longer hours, as well.

As an employer, my first concern is money. In order to make a profit, I have to make sure the business brings in more money than it spends. I can save a lot of money if I spend less on salaries. I don't mean that I would pay my employees unfairly. Of course, I wouldn't want to pay them less than they expect, but I want to save on salaries when I can. Hiring inexperienced workers is one way to do this.

I like to train my employees to work according to my company's methods. Experienced people are used to doing things a certain way. If they get their experience at another company first, it is hard to change their work habits when they come to my company. It is much easier to train inexperienced people to follow my company's methods. Then I can be sure that the work is done in the way that I want it done.

I don't like to ask my employees to work overtime, but sometimes I have to. Sometimes the pressures of the market make this necessary. Inexperienced workers are usually eager to gain experience, so they more often volunteer to work extra hours. This makes the situation easier for everyone.

People may think it is not good for a company to hire inexperienced workers, but I disagree. I think everyone benefits this way. The company saves money and the workers get training and experience. I think it is the best plan all around.

102

> **Which would you choose—a high-paying job with long hours that would give you little time with family and friends or a lower-paying job with shorter hours that would give you more time with family and friends? Explain your choice, using specific reasons and details.**

At this time in my life I would definitely choose a higher-paying job even if I had to work long hours. If I want a good future, first I have to gain experience, move up in my company, and save a lot of money. I will have plenty of time for friends and family later, after I get a good start on my career.

When I finish school, I will have a lot of knowledge. I won't have any experience, however. I can get experience only by working. I want a lot of experience so that I can be among the best in my career. The only way to get experience is to work a lot of hours.

I want to have a high position in my company. I don't want to be just an employee, I want to be a supervisor, and someday, director or president. I can't do this if I work only forty hours a week. The only way to move up is to work long hours.

Living a comfortable life is important to me. I want to have a nice house, fashionable clothes, and a couple of cars. When I get married, I want my family to have nice things too. This takes money. The best time to save money is now, before I have a family. The only way to save a lot of money is to work hard and earn a high salary.

A high-paying job with long hours will give me the experience, opportunities, and money that I want. After I reach a high position in my company and have a big bank account, I can take all the free time I want to relax with friends and family.

103

> **Do you agree or diagree with the following statement? Grades (marks) encourage students to learn. Use specific reasons and examples to support your opinion.**

I believe that grades are an essential part of education. They are important for several reasons. Grades measure a student's progress in class. They give students a goal to work towards. They are something that a student can show her parents. In short, grades help students become motivated to learn.

Grades show students their progress in class. Students have a lot of required work. They have to read, work on group projects, do homework, write reports, and take tests. Without grades, students have no way of knowing how well they are doing on all this work. They have no way of knowing where they are improving and where their weak points are. Grades show students what they have learned and what they need to keep working on.

Grades also provide students with a goal. A good grade is a type of reward, and students want to work hard to receive this reward. A good grade on a test makes the student feel that his hard work was worthwhile. A bad grade motivates him to study harder so he can do better next time.

Finally, grades are something students can take home to show their parents. Students want to please their parents. They want to work hard to earn good grades so their parents will be proud of them. Conversely, parents are happy when their children bring home good grades because they know this means that their children are studying and learning. If their children bring home bad grades, then the parents know they have to give their children extra help and support.

Grades are important for students. All students want to get good grades, so they will study hard to earn them. Grades show students their progress, present them with a goal, and give them something to show their parents. They encourage students to learn.

104

> **Do you agree or disagree with the following statement? The best way to travel is in a group led by a tour guide. Use specific reasons and examples to support your answer.**

When I travel, I always prefer to go with a group led by a tour guide. The tour guide makes all the necessary arrangements for the trip. The tour guide knows the best places to visit. The tour guide is familiar with the local language and customs. When I travel with a tour guide, the only thing I have to do is relax and enjoy myself.

If I travel in a group with a tour guide, I don't have to worry about arranging the trip. I just look for a group that is going to a place I like, and I let the tour guide take care of the rest. The tour guide makes the hotel reservations and chooses the restaurants and plans the activities for each day. I don't have to worry about anything because the guide does everything for me.

If I travel in a group with a tour guide, I don't have to figure out which places to visit. The tour guide knows which are the best museums. The tour guide knows where the good beaches are and which stores have the best prices. If I had to figure this out myself, I might make the wrong choices. With a tour guide, I am sure of having the best possible experience on my trip.

If I travel in a group with a tour guide, I don't have to know the local language and customs. The tour guide knows the language and can speak for the group when necessary. The tour guide knows when the local holidays are, or how to dress appropriately for each situation. I don't have to worry about confusions with the language or customs because the tour guide can help me.

When I go on vacation, I want to relax. I don't want to worry about making hotel reservations, or learning the museum schedules, or speaking the local language. A tour guide can take care of all these things for me, and I can have a good time.

105

> **Some universities require students to take classes in many subjects. Other universities require students to specialize in one subject. Which is better? Use specific reasons and examples to support your answer.**

Universities offer opportunities to study many different subjects and university students should take advantage of this. Studying many subjects can help students better prepare for their careers. It can also help them become responsible members of society and can add to their personal enjoyment, as well.

Studying many subjects can help students be better prepared for their careers. A doctor doesn't need to know only about medicine, for example. She also needs to know how to respond to patients' emotional needs. She might need to know about accounting and legal contracts so she can run her own office. Each profession requires certain specialized skills, but all professionals also need other, more general skills in order to do their jobs well.

Studying many subjects can help students become more responsible members of society. They need to understand the economic and social issues of their communities so that they can vote responsibly. They might want to do volunteer work at a community organization. They will need to be able to educate their children, no matter what their children's abilities and interests are. They will need to know about more than just their profession in order to do these things.

Studying many subjects can add a great deal of enjoyment to a student's life. If students understand art and music, they will get a lot of enjoyment from museums and concerts. If they study literature, they will continue to read good books. Life is about more than just career. If students know about a lot of subjects, they will get a lot out of life.

Some university students think only about their careers. If the choice is left to them, they might only study courses for their future profession. They will have a much better future, however, if they study subjects in addition to their career. Therefore, universities should require students to take classes in many subjects.

106

> **Do you agree or disagree with the following statement? Children should begin studying a foreign language as soon as they start school.**

I agree with the statement that children should begin foreign language study as soon as they start school. Childhood is the best time to learn a foreign language, so it is important not to miss the opportunity. Foreign language learning is easier for younger children. It contributes to their development, and it helps them expand their knowledge.

Everybody knows that it is much easier to learn foreign languages when you are younger. Young children's minds are ready to learn many new things, including languages. When children start learning foreign languages at an early age, they learn to speak them as well as they speak their native language. If they put off language learning until they are older, it is much harder to become fluent.

Many studies have shown that learning a language helps a child's mind develop. It helps expand the intellect. Children who learn at least one foreign language tend to do better in their other school subjects as compared to children who don't study foreign languages. This effect is less apparent in children who begin foreign language study at a later age.

Learning foreign languages can help children expand their knowledge of the world. If they learn a foreign language, they will become interested in the people who speak that language. They will want to know about their country and customs. They will want to understand them instead of being afraid of them because they are different.

Learning foreign languages has benefits for all of us, no matter what our age. It contributes to our intellectual development and our understanding of the world. However, the younger a person is, the more benefits he gets from foreign language study. Therefore, it is best for children to begin learning foreign languages as soon as they start school.

107

> **Your city has decided to build a statue or monument to honor a famous person in your country. Who would you choose? Use reasons and specific examples to support your choice.**

The person I would choose to honor is not one specific famous person, but a famous type of person. I come from a small rural town. Most people here are farmers, so I would choose a farmer as the subject for a statue. The farmers of my town deserve the honor. They work hard so the rest of the country can eat, but they are not rich. They deserve to be appreciated.

The farmers in my town make an important contribution to our country. They grow the food that the rest of the country eats. Our major products are corn and milk. These things are a basic part of everyone's diet. Without our farmers, it would be harder and more expensive for people to have these things to eat.

The farmers in my town are not rich even though they work hard. A farmer's job begins at sunrise and doesn't stop until dark. A farmer rarely has a chance to take a vacation because there are always things to do on a farm. Farming is not a profitable business. If the weather is bad one year, there might be no profits at all. Still, farmers do their work because people need to eat.

The farmers in my town work hard, but they are not appreciated. People in other parts of the country don't pay much attention to my town. Nobody comes to visit because there are no tourist attractions. Nobody wants to work here because there aren't many professional jobs. Nobody thinks about the contributions our farmers make. They just buy our products in the stores without thinking about the work it takes to put them there.

Nobody thinks about the farmers in my town, but they deserve to be honored. They work hard to grow food for everyone in the country. I think we should put a big, shiny statue of a farmer in the middle of our town park. It would make everyone in town feel proud.

108

> **Describe a custom from your country that you would like people in other countries to adopt. Explain your choice using specific reasons and examples.**

In my country, many people in the towns still follow an old custom that people in the cities no longer practice. This is the custom of taking a big break at noon. In the towns, all stores and businesses close from noon until 2:00 P.M. This not only gives people a needed rest in the middle of the day, it also allows them time with their families and contributes to a slower pace of life.

In the towns, all workers get a good rest in the middle of the day. They go home, enjoy a nice meal, take a nap, and then they return to work for the rest of the afternoon. They have energy and enthusiasm for the rest of the day's work. Their afternoons can be as productive as their mornings. Without this rest, they might be tired all afternoon and not get much work done.

In the towns, most families eat their noon meal together. They have time to enjoy their food, talk about their morning activities with each other, and just be together. It is good for families to have this time together. Parents hear about their children's activities. Husbands and wives learn about each other's daily concerns. Without this opportunity, families might not be together until evening. They are usually tired then and just want to rest.

In the towns, there is a slower pace of life. Nobody can do any business at lunchtime. They have to wait until the afternoon. Because of this, people don't expect things to be done in a hurry. They have more patience. If something doesn't get done today, it doesn't matter. This is a much healthier way to live.

A big rest at noon contributes to a better quality of life. In the towns, people don't worry about getting a lot of work done fast. They are more interested in spending time with their families and enjoying their lives. I think that in the long run this actually improves work. In any case, it is a better way to live. I think everyone everywhere should follow the custom of taking a big break at noon.

109

Do you agree or disagree with the following statement? Technology has made the world a better place to live. Use specific reasons and examples to support your statement.

Technology has made our lives better in many ways, but it has also made them more complicated. Technology is often expensive to buy and run, it can be difficult to use, and it often isn't easy to repair.

Technology isn't cheap. The more technology we depend on in our daily lives, the more money we have to spend. Everybody wants a modern TV, a digital camera, a DVD player, etc. Even though these things might be considered luxuries, people want them. In addition, some technology is more than a luxury. For example, teachers nowadays expect their students to have computers at home for their schoolwork. Parents have to buy the latest computers so their children can keep up with their classmates. This can be a real hardship for some families.

Technology isn't always easy to use. In fact, it is getting more and more complicated. The computers of today do many more things than the computers of even just five or ten years ago. That means a lot more things that computer users have to learn how to do. Even a simple thing like using a VCR to record a movie takes some practice and learning.

Technology isn't easy to repair. If the average person has a problem with his computer or DVD player, he probably doesn't know how to fix it himself. He'll have to spend time and money taking it to a place to get fixed. In the past, a lot of people enjoyed doing routine maintenance work on their cars. Modern technology has made today's cars more complicated. It is harder to learn how to repair and maintain them.

People think modern technology has made our lives easier. In a way this is true, but in other ways it has made our lives much less convenient. Modern technology costs us money and time and can add complications to our lives.

110

> **Do you agree or disagree with the following statement? Advertising can tell you a lot about a country. Use specific reasons and examples to support your answer.**

Advertising is like a window onto the life of a country. It tells a lot about the people there. Advertisements show what kinds of things the people in a country like to buy. It shows what kinds of situations are attractive to them. It even shows whether or not the people tend to be affluent. You can learn a lot by looking at advertisements.

By looking at advertisements, you can see what kinds of things people like to buy. Are there more advertisements for soda or for juice? For movies or for music? For vacations or for furniture? You can see what kinds of food people prefer, how they like to spend their free time, or what they save their money for. You can learn just about anything about the average lifestyle in a country.

By looking at advertisements, you can see what kinds of situations are attractive to people. If an ad shows someone driving a car freely down an open highway in beautiful scenery, you can see that people value feeling free. If an ad shows a professional-looking person in an expensive car in front of an elegant house or office building, you will know that people value success.

By looking at advertisements, you can know whether or not a country is affluent. If ads are usually about food, clothes, and other necessities of life, the people in the country may not have a lot of money. If more ads are for luxury items and expensive, high-quality products, then you know that more people in that country have money.

Advertisements can tell you a lot about a country. They show how the people there live. They show what the people want to buy and can buy. Ads give a picture of a country's daily life.

111

> **Do you agree or disagree with the following statement? Modern technology is creating a single world culture. Use specific reasons and examples to support your answer.**

Modern technology is creating a single world culture. This is because it is now much easier to communicate with people who are far away. Satellite TV, modern transportation, and the Internet have all brought people closer together. People the world over share the same sources of information and this leads to the creation of a single world culture.

Because TV is broadcast by satellite, TV programs can be received anywhere in the world. Now people in every part of the world can have access to all the same TV programs. Everybody knows that TV is one of the biggest cultural influences there is. When people everywhere see the same news, educational, and entertainment programs, they move toward the development of a single world culture.

Because modern methods of transportation are fast, a trip to a faraway place becomes easy. People from all different places are together more now than they ever were before. They can see how people in other countries dress, eat, and spend their time. People have more exposure to customs from other countries and might start to adopt some of those customs. This also contributes to the development of a single world culture.

Because of the Internet, people have access to information and news from all over the world. They can communicate easily with people far away and share sources of information. This can do a lot toward international understanding but it can also have another result. When people share sources of information on the Internet, they come more and more under the same cultural influence. They move toward the creation of a single world culture.

Modern communications technology has brought people from all around the world closer together. People these days have more and more opportunities to share ideas and information. In this way they are coming more and more under the same cultural influence. A single world culture is being created.

112

> **Some people think the Internet provides people with a lot of valuable information. Others think access to so much information creates problems. Which view do you agree with? Use specific reasons and examples to support your opinion.**

The Internet provides us with a lot of valuable information. This is important because it keeps us informed about the world today, contributes to children's education, and even helps us shop better. It helps improve our lives in many ways.

When we want to know the latest news, we can just go to the Internet and get it right away. We don't have to wait for a news program on TV or the radio. We also don't have to listen to just one source of news. On the Internet we can get news from different newspapers and different countries. We can get information from different points of view. This greatly contributes to our understanding of current events.

When children need information for their schoolwork, they can find it on the Internet. Most schoolchildren these days do their research online. They have access to more information than they could probably find in their school libraries, and they can get the information more easily. In addition, any time a child wants to know something or needs the answer to a question, he can probably find it online.

When we want to buy something, we can usually get the information we need for our purchase online. Of course you can order almost anything you want on the Internet, but this isn't the most important part. On the Internet it is easy to find information about the quality of different products and to compare prices. This really matters if you plan to buy something expensive.

The ability to get information from the Internet has improved our lives in many ways. We can learn more about the news, improve our children's education, and become more informed shoppers. The Internet is one of the most important tools we have in modern society.

113

> **If you could go back to some time and place in the past, when and where would you go? Why? Use specific reasons and details to support your choice.**

If I could go back to a time and place in the past, I would go back to ancient Egypt. The reason is that I would like to find out how the pyramids were built. This is a great mystery to us today. We in the modern world cannot understand how the ancient Egyptians cut the stones so precisely, moved them to the building site, and lifted the heavy blocks to build the pyramid walls, all without the aid of the type of technology we have today. I would like to solve this mystery.

The stones that were used to build the pyramids were cut very precisely. All of them fit together exactly, without any space between them. How were the ancient Egyptians able to cut the stones so well without the aid of modern equipment? Nobody knows.

The stones are also very heavy, weighing several tons each. The ancient Egyptians didn't have any kind of motorized machinery to move the stones around. Yet they found those heavy stones in one place and moved them to another place to build the pyramids. How did they do this? Nobody today can figure it out.

The pyramids are very tall. They were built by placing stone blocks on top of each other. The ancient Egyptians didn't have any cranes or other type of lifting equipment such as the ones we have today. Yet they built huge pyramids out of heavy stone blocks. How did they do this? We still aren't able to understand.

The Egyptian pyramids are among the great mysteries of the ancient world. Nobody knows how the stones were cut, transported, and lifted to build the great pyramids. If I could go back in time to visit ancient Egypt, I could find this out. Then I would return to the modern world and tell everyone the answer.

114

What discovery in the last 100 years has been most beneficial for people in your country? Use specific reasons and examples to support your choice.

A discovery that has been beneficial to people in my country and everywhere is the use of electricity. Electricity has made the development of modern technology possible. Without electricity we wouldn't have modern communications technology, we wouldn't have computers, we wouldn't even have electric light. Almost everything about modern life depends on electricity.

Electricity has made modern communications technology possible. Telephones, television, and radio all depend on electricity. Because we have these things, we can communicate with friends and business associates instantly. We can hear the latest news almost as soon as it happens. We can follow the newest developments in music. Both our personal and professional lives are completely different now from what they were 100 years ago.

If we didn't have electricity, we wouldn't have computers. We use computers in almost every aspect of our lives. We use them to get information in school. We use them to make our jobs easier. Computers help people fly airplanes and design buildings. We couldn't do many of the things we do today without computers. And we couldn't use computers without electricity.

Because of electricity, it is easier to light up buildings and streets at night. This seems so simple that sometimes we forget it. Before electricity, people used candles. It was hard to read at night, to go anywhere, or to do any work. Now we can live our lives as fully at night as we do during the day. We can work or play at any hour we choose. It really is an amazing thing.

Electricity has made many things possible in modern life. We wouldn't have any modern technology without it. It is the most important discovery of the modern world.

115

Do you agree or disagree with the following statement? Telephone and email have made communications between people less personal. Use specific reasons and examples to support your opinion.

Some people think that telephone and email have made communication between people less personal, but I disagree. If anything, they have made communication more personal. This is because these types of communication are easy, informal, and inexpensive.

It is easy to communicate with someone by phone or email. You just pick up the phone or turn on the computer, and that's it. Email is especially easy because you can send your message at any time. If the receiver isn't available when you send the message, it doesn't matter. The message will be there when she's ready to answer. Because this sort of communication is so easy, people communicate more frequently. This brings them closer together, so it becomes a more personal form of communication.

Communication by phone or by email is informal. On the phone you converse with someone as informally as you do in person. When you write email messages, you usually use less formal styles of writing. Traditional letters, on the other hand, have formal conventions that the writer must follow. Even friendly letters have certain rules to follow. Communication that is informal is more personal than formal communication.

Telephones and email are inexpensive to use. Nowadays even long distance phone calls are cheap, and local ones are free. Email costs nothing if you already own a computer. Letters are cheap, but seeing someone in person isn't always. Even if the person lives nearby, it still costs something for the bus or gasoline to go meet them somewhere, and it takes time, too. Since email and telephone are cheap, people communicate more frequently and, therefore, more personally.

Some people think you have to meet face to face in order to have personal communication, but this isn't so. Telephones and email make frequent communication convenient. They help maintain personal relationships.

116

If you could travel back in time to meet a famous person from history, what person would you like to meet? Use specific reasons and examples to support your choice.

If I could travel back in time to meet a famous person from history, I would go to Renaissance Italy to see Leonardo da Vinci. There has probably been no other person like him in all of history. I would like to meet someone who was so talented an artist and so imaginative an inventor. He was a rare genius, and I would like to know what it felt like to be so unique a person.

Da Vinci's artistic talents are well known. The Mona Lisa is, of course, his most famous painting. Its exquisite beauty has been admired all around the world. Da Vinci drew and painted many other beautiful works of art, as well. I like to draw and paint, too. Of course, my talent will never approach Da Vinci's, but because of my interest in art, it would be inspiring to meet him.

Da Vinci invented many things that were well ahead of his time. For example, he made drawings of a flying machine centuries before anyone else ever thought of building an airplane. Perhaps his inventions never got beyond the drawing board during his lifetime, but he was still able to imagine them. He came up with ideas that no one around him was thinking about. It would be amazing and inspiring to talk with a person with such a creative mind.

Da Vinci was unusually smart and talented. There was no one else like him around. In fact, throughout history there have been few others like him. I wonder what it felt like to be so different from his friends and neighbors. It must have been difficult at least some of the time. If I could meet him, I could ask him about this.

To tell the truth, I don't know a great deal about Da Vinci. I would like to learn more about him, however, because of his unique talents and ideas. It would be an inspiring experience to meet him.

117

> If you could meet a famous entertainer or athlete, who would that be, and why? Use specific reasons and examples to support your choice.

There are many famous entertainers that would be interesting to meet. If I could choose only one, however, I would choose Paul Newman. I realize I've missed my chance since he died several years ago, but I still think it would be interesting to know him. On top of being famous for his good looks, he was a talented actor, and a generous businessman as well. I'm sure it would be fun to spend a little time talking with him.

Paul Newman was legendary for his good looks. His most famous feature was his piercing blue eyes. He attracted a lot of attention because he was so handsome, and he could have gotten by on his good looks alone. He didn't do this, however, and that is one thing that makes him interesting.

Newman was also a talented actor. He played many different kinds of characters, and he did all of them well. He didn't just walk on screen and stand there looking handsome. He portrayed each character believably. I would enjoy talking with him about his work in movies because I really admire his talent.

Newman didn't just sit around living off the money and fame from his acting career. He and a friend started a food business. It became very successful, but Newman didn't use that as an opportunity to become wealthier than he already was. He donated one hundred percent of his profits to charitable causes. He supported educational programs, conservation projects, and other work that he believed in. He lived according to his values, and I think that is an inspiration to us all.

Paul Newman is a Hollywood legend because of his looks and acting talents. He is also a good role model for business people. I think I could learn a lot from talking with him, if only I had ever had the chance.

118

> If you could ask a famous person one question, what would you ask? Why? Use specific reasons and details to support your answer.

If I could ask a famous person one question, I would ask Neil Armstrong what it felt like to walk on the moon. Sometimes I think it would be scary; sometimes I think it would be fun. On the other hand, maybe Neil Armstrong was too busy to feel scared or have fun while he was walking on the moon.

I think it could be very scary to go to walk on the moon. Neil Armstrong was the first person to do it. He was well prepared for the event, but he still couldn't be sure what he would find. Also, maybe he worried that something might happen. What if he had a problem with his oxygen or couldn't get back to the spaceship on time? I wonder if he thought about these things, or if he just did his job.

On the other hand, maybe Neil Armstrong had fun walking on the moon. The gravity is different so just taking steps would feel different. I think that would be fun. If I went to the moon, I would want to run and jump and shout, "Hurray! I am on the moon!" I wonder if Armstrong felt that way.

Maybe Armstrong didn't have time to feel scared or happy or anything else. He had a very important job to do. The whole world was watching him. He had to be serious and focus on his work. His time was short. He probably didn't have time for anything except to get his job done.

It can be a scary thing or a fun adventure to do something for the first time. Being the first person to walk on the moon is one of the most incredible adventures of all time. I would like to meet Neil Armstrong so I could ask him how it felt.

119

> Do you agree or disagree with the following statement? Dancing plays an important role in a culture. Use specific reasons and examples to support your answer.

I agree with the statement that dancing plays an important role in a culture. Dancing meets several human needs. It keeps us connected with our traditions, brings people together, and helps us release energy. These are all things that help keep a culture alive and strong.

Folk dances keep us connected with our traditions. Folk dances were developed hundreds, if not thousands, of years ago. In the past, whole villages used to dance together to celebrate important events such as harvests or weddings. Even though our lives are different now, people still enjoy folk dances. When we dance them, we feel connected to our ancestors. We do the same dances they did and remember the things that were important to them.

Dancing brings people together. When we dance at an event such as a birthday or graduation party, we celebrate a happy occasion together. Sometimes we enjoy going out dancing with friends on weekends. It is a way of spending time and enjoying life together. Whether at a formal or spontaneous occasion, dancing helps us enjoy good times with each other.

When we dance, we release energy. After working hard all week at school or at our jobs, we feel tired and stressed. We need a change of activity and a chance to relax. Dancing is a good way to do this. When we dance, we release all our built up energy and any anger or frustrations we've been carrying around. We relax and have fun. Then we can feel ready to start a new week of school and work.

Dancing keeps us connected to our traditions and to each other. Furthermore, it helps us release energy so we can perform our daily responsibilities. These are important roles that dancing plays in our culture.

120

> **People have different ways of escaping the stress of modern life. Some read, some exercise, others work in their gardens. What do you think are the best ways of reducing stress? Use specific details and examples in your answer.**

Stress is one of our biggest enemies. It affects all aspects of our lives. I find that in order to manage stress in my life, first I have to identify the cause. Then I can decide the best way to deal with it. The most common causes of stress in my life are work, friends, and myself.

Stress at work is the easiest to combat. If I feel tense or pressured, I simply stop working for a while. I might get up from my desk and go down the hall to talk with a colleague (about topics unrelated to work, of course). Or I might go outside and take a short walk around the block to give my mind a rest. Work-related stress can be cured just by getting away from work.

Stress caused by my friends is a little more difficult to manage. It feels very stressful when a friend is angry with me. Or, if a friend is feeling anxious about something, that usually makes me anxious, too. The best way to deal with this kind of stress is to talk about the problem with my friends and to spend some time with them. Unlike work, you can't walk away from friends.

Stress I cause myself is the most difficult to deal with. If I feel anxious about an upcoming exam or worried about my future, there isn't much I can do. I just have to tell myself that I can only do my best and leave the rest up to fate.

It is important to try to lead a life with as little stress as possible. If you can reduce stress by walking away from it (as at work), talking about it (as with friends), or facing it head on (as with yourself), you will benefit in all aspects of your life.

121

> **Do you agree or disagree with the following statement? Teachers should be paid according to how much their students learn. Give specific reasons and examples to support your opinion.**

It is a bad idea to pay teachers according to how much their students learn. It just encourages teachers to teach only the material on a test. It discourages them from paying attention to slow students. It is unfair because teachers can't decide which students will be in their class. Instead of improving teaching, it keeps teachers from doing the best job they can.

If a teacher is paid according to how well his students do on a test, then he will teach only what is on the test. He will spend time teaching his students to memorize facts. He won't be able to teach them other things. The students will miss the opportunity to gain a wider variety of knowledge. They won't have the chance to develop skills besides memorization. They will learn less, not more, in this way.

Another problem is that teachers may ignore the slower students. Some students learn more quickly and easily than others. The teacher won't want to spend time with the few slowest students. She will prefer to focus on the average and fast students to make sure they get high scores on tests. She can't waste time with the students who can get only mediocre scores. These students, who need the most help in school, will get very little help at all.

Finally, a teacher has no control over which students are placed in his class. One teacher may get all the best students in a school. Another may get several of the worst. If the teacher has some average students, a few below average, and no students who are above average, then of course the class will get lower test scores on their tests. People will think those students didn't learn much. It is not fair to base a teacher's salary on something over which he has no control.

Most teachers, like other professionals, want to do the best job possible. They want to teach their students useful skills and knowledge and they want to help the students who need help. Teachers need encouragement and support, but basing their salary on their students' performance is not a good way to provide this.

122

> **If you were asked to send one thing representing your country to an international exhibition, what would you choose? Why? Use specific reasons and details to explain your choice.**

When asked to send something representative of their country to an international exhibition, most people tend to think of specific objects. I would send something completely different, however: one week's worth of television programming. I feel that TV programs are a good representation of my country because they show how we live, what we value, and what we teach our children.

TV programs show how we live in my country. For example, they show the different ways we make our livings, the different kinds of houses we live in, the different types of relationships we have, and the different sorts of activities that fill our days. In short, they give a broad representation of daily life in my country.

TV programs also show what we value in my country. Comedy programs, for instance, demonstrate what we think is funny, while documentaries show what issues we are concerned about and how we want to resolve them. Sports programs show which sports are more and less popular as well as how we approach competition. In general, the range of programs that appear on TV demonstrate what we think is important and interesting and worth our while to spend time on.

Children's programs show what we think is important to teach our children. Some programs are designed to specifically teach reading and math skills. Others expose children to classic stories from literature or to traditional folktales. And some programs, such as cartoons, are simply meant to be enjoyed, which is also something we teach our children to do.

You can learn a good deal about a country by watching its television programs. You can learn about daily life, values, and education. That is why I would send a week's worth of TV programs from my country to an international exhibition.

123

> Some people think that governments should spend as much money as possible on developing or buying computer technology. Other people disagree and think that this money should be spent on more basic needs. Which one of these opinions do you agree with? Use specific reasons and details to support your answer.

Developing computer technology is important for the development of the country as a whole. However, we have some basic needs and issues in our country that are even more important than technology. Our children need to get a good education. Our transportation system needs to be improved. We need to develop new sources of energy. We need to work on these issues before we put a lot of money into computers.

Our children need to get a good education. We need to make sure that every child in the country has the opportunity to learn to read and write. In addition, they all need to learn skills for the modern world. They need to learn how to use computers. It costs money to buy computers for schools and train teachers to use them. If children don't learn basic computer skills in school, who will be able to use modern computer technology?

We need to improve our transportation system. In big cities, the roads are very crowded and it is hard to get around. It takes a long time for people just to get to work every day. We need to spend money developing a good public transportation system. We need to get cars off the road and have more buses and trains. Computer technology helps people at work. If it is difficult for people just to get to work, computer technology won't help them much.

We need to develop new sources of energy. Our current methods of generating energy cause a lot of pollution. We need to develop the use of solar energy and other nonpolluting energy technology. Energy research and development costs a lot of money, but it is necessary. If we don't have clean, cheap sources of energy, what will we use to run our computers?

Computer technology is important. However, we can't take advantage of it if we don't solve some problems first. We need well-educated children, good public transportation, and clean sources of energy before we can spend money on computers.

124

> Schools should ask students to evaluate their teachers. Do you agree or disagree? Use specific reasons and examples to support your answer.

I think it is a good idea for schools to ask students to evaluate their teachers. It is good for the teachers, good for the school administrators, and good for the students themselves.

Teachers can get a lot of useful information from student evaluations. They can find out what the students like about the class and what they don't like. They can learn what the students think is easy or difficult. They can discover which kinds of activities the students prefer. Generally, they can find out the ways they reach the students and the ways they don't. All of these things can help teachers improve their classes.

Student evaluations are also helpful for school administrators. Student evaluations help administrators learn which teachers are most effective. They give an idea of how students are satisfied or dissatisfied with their school program. With this kind of information, administrators can work better with the teachers. They can work together to improve the school program where necessary.

Evaluating teachers is a good exercise for students. They have to organize their thoughts about their teacher. They have to think about how they themselves learn best and what kind of help they need. This can help them do better in class. Evaluations also give students a chance to develop honesty and responsibility. Evaluations with real and useful information are valuable to the school. Evaluations that are used as a way of being mean or getting favors aren't worthwhile.

Student evaluations can provide a lot of useful information to a school. They help the teachers, the school administrators, and the students. I think they are a very good idea.

125

In your opinion, what is the most important characteristic (for example, honesty, intelligence, a sense of humor) that a person can have to be successful in life? Use specific reasons and examples from your experience to explain your answer. When you write your answer, you are not limited to the examples listed in the question.

Although honesty, intelligence, and a sense of humor are all worthwhile characteristics, I feel the most important one to have is sensitivity. A sensitive person is aware of the way his or her actions affect others. A sensitive person knows the place of honesty, intelligence, and a sense of humor.

Honesty is not always the best policy. There is such a thing as a white lie. You don't want to tell someone that her expensive new dress doesn't look good on her. You wouldn't tell your friends that you don't like their house. Sensitive people know when it is necessary to tell the truth and when it is better to tell a white lie.

Intelligence is a wonderful thing to have, but not all intelligent people use their intelligence sensitively. It isn't good to show off your intelligence and make other people feel dumb. Sometimes you might have to say, "My answer might be wrong. We should check it." Sensitive people know when to use their intelligence and when to step back and let others answer.

A sense of humor is always valued. Different people, however, laugh at different things. A joke that is funny to you might be offensive to someone else. Some people can laugh at their mistakes but others are uncomfortable about them. A sensitive person knows when it's o.k. to laugh or tease, and when it's better to be sympathetic or just quiet.

A sensitive person can make everyone feel comfortable. A sensitive person knows that people are different and that honesty, intelligence, and humor need to be applied to each situation differently.

126

> It is generally agreed that society benefits from the work of its members. Compare the contributions of artists to society with the contributions of scientists to society. Which type of contribution do you think is more valued by your society? Give specific reasons to support your answer.

Artists and scientists make very different types of contributions to our society, and the contributions of both are valuable. Although the contributions of both are important, however, our society seems to value the contributions of scientists more.

Artists lift our spirits and show us who we are. A painter or writer shows us in pictures and words what we're like as a people. Performing artists entertain us. Artists take our minds off our troubles and remind us of the beauty of life. Artists also help keep society mentally and emotionally healthy, because they provide us with a means of expression. Art of all types is necessary to the human spirit.

Scientists make contributions to our material lives. The cars we drive, the computers we use at school and work, the appliances we use to clean our houses, are all results of the hard work of scientists. We can grow more food, and cure more diseases, and live healthier lives thanks to scientific research. Scientists have helped improve our material lives in many ways.

Artists make valuable contributions to society, but society seems to value scientists more. Scientists are more often rewarded with money than artists are. They generally earn higher salaries, and it is easier for them to get government funding for their work. They have more social prestige and are generally considered to be smarter people than artists. There are always exceptions, of course. Some scientists struggle to earn money. Some artists are very rich and have a great deal of prestige, but they are few. Overall, scientists have a better position in society.

The contributions of both artists and scientists are valuable to our society. They each contribute to different aspects of our lives. Unfortunately, artists don't always get the recognition they deserve.

127

> Students at universities often have a choice of places to live. They may choose to live in university dormitories, or they may choose to live in apartments in the community. Compare the advantages of living in university housing with the advantages of living in an apartment in the community. Where would you prefer to live? Give reasons for your preference.

I think it is better for university students to live in a dormitory. It makes their lives much easier, it gives them more opportunities to make friends, and it helps them become more involved in the university community.

Dormitory life is much easier than apartment life for a university student. If a student rents an apartment, that means she has to buy furniture and kitchen utensils. She has to shop and cook for herself every day. She has to spend time keeping the apartment clean. A dormitory room, on the other hand, already has furniture, and meals are served in the dormitory dining room. The student doesn't have to spend time taking care of household things and can just concentrate on her studies.

A student living in a dormitory has potential friends living all around her. First she'll make friends with her roommate, then with the other students living on her floor. She can make friends in the dormitory dining room and the lounge. If she feels lonely, if she needs help with her classwork, if she misses her family, there is always someone to turn to. If she lives in an apartment, she won't have all this support. She might have a roommate, but otherwise she will be alone. She'll have to put more effort into making friends in her classes.

By living in a dormitory a student is right in the middle of the university community. She is close to all the university activities and it is easy to participate in them. She can become involved in clubs, sports, or the student government. If she lives in an apartment, she is farther from all these activities. It takes more time to get to club meetings. It is harder to find out what activities are going on. It's more difficult to be part of the community.

Living in an apartment has advantages for some people, but for me dormitory life is much better. It makes daily tasks, meeting new friends, and being involved in university activities much easier. It is a convenient and fun way to live.

128

> Some people believe that a college or university education should be available to all students. Others believe that higher education should be available to only good students. Discuss these views. Which view do you agree with? Explain why.

Some people believe that only the best students should go to a college or university, but I don't. Academics are not the only purpose of a university education. Another important goal is to learn about yourself. When you are separated from your parents, you have to learn to be independent and make decisions about your future. I believe every student should have the opportunity to have this kind of experience.

I can understand why some people think that a college or university education should be available to only good students. Higher education is very expensive. It might seem like a waste of money to send a mediocre student to college. If a better student will learn more, why not send only the better student to college? Higher education is also a big investment of time. Maybe a mediocre student could spend his or her time in a better way, by getting a job or going to trade school.

I don't agree with this position. I think higher education should be available to all students. It is true that it is expensive and takes a lot of time, but I think every student deserves the opportunity to try it. People change. A student who didn't like school as a teenager may start to like it as a young adult. Also, having the opportunity to make independent decisions is part of a good education. A student may try college for a while and then decide that trade school is a better place for him or her. Or a student may decide, "I will work hard now because I want a good future." At a college or university students have the opportunity to make changes and decisions for themselves.

All students who want to should be given the chance to go to a college or university. In college they will have the opportunity to learn independence and to make adult decisions about their future. This is a basic part of education and an experience every student should have.

129

> Some people believe that the best way of learning about life is by listening to the advice of family and friends. Other people believe that the best way of learning about life is through personal experience. Compare the advantages of these two different ways of learning about life. Which do you think is preferable? Use specific examples to support your preference.

Both learning through personal experience and learning through the advice of others can help you a lot in life. I think learning through personal experience comes first, however. No one can teach you how to get along with other people, how to judge your own abilities, or how to understand who you are. You can learn this only through experience.

When we are small children, adults tell us, "Play nicely with the other children. Don't fight. Don't hit." In this way, we learn that it is important to get along with others. Only through our own experience, however, can we learn how to do this. If another child hits us, we learn that hitting isn't a nice thing. If we fight with other children, we learn that fighting doesn't always get us what we want and maybe there are other solutions. Through our own experiences, we begin to learn about ourselves and we carry this learning into our adult lives.

Friends and relatives might say to us, "You are good at science. You should become a doctor." Or, "You are a talented artist. You should study painting." Our friends and relatives can observe our abilities and point them out to us. But they can't know everything about us. Maybe you get good grades in science but you think its boring. Maybe you are a talented artist, but you like sports better. Through our daily experiences we have the chance to learn about our abilities and our tastes. If we value these experiences, we pay attention to them and use them to make decisions for our future.

The people who know us might say, "You are so hardworking." Or, "You are too shy and quiet." They can point out our good qualities to us and that is good. We need our own experience, however, to tell us who we really are. Maybe you really are shy, or maybe it just looks that way to another person. Your own experience will tell you if this is true and if it is important to you or not. When we pay attention to our own experiences, we learn a lot about who we are and who we want to be.

The advice of other people can be very helpful. It isn't much good, however, if we don't have our own experiences to compare it to. I like to ask other people for advice, but I always pay attention to my own experience first.

130

> When people move to another country, some of them decide to follow the customs of the new country. Others prefer to keep their own customs. Compare these two choices. Which one do you prefer? Support your answer with specific details.

When you move to another country, you have to change some of your customs of daily living. For example, you will have to make some changes in your language, your food, and your work habits. It is also important, however, to maintain some of your old customs because they are part of your identity.

The most important thing to do in a new country is learn the language. Daily life will be very difficult without it. You will need the language to find things in stores, to understand TV programs, to go to school, and for many other things. You don't have to stop speaking your own language, though. You can continue to speak it with family and friends. You need your language to maintain your connection with your own country and origins.

It is a good idea to learn to eat the food in a new country. It will make your life easier. You can't always find stores and restaurants that sell your country's food. Eating the new country's food also helps you get to know something about the country and the people. If you shop and eat only in places that sell your country's food, you will get to know only people from your country. You should also eat your country's food sometimes. You will probably prefer it on holidays, for example. It is also a good thing to share with new friends from your new country.

When you get a job, it is important to learn your new country's work habits. If the custom in the country is to arrive at work on time, you must do it. If the custom is to be friendly with clients, invite them to restaurants, and so on, then you must do that. You will not be successful in your job if you don't adapt to the work habits. You might also have some useful customs from your own culture. Maybe you have more efficient methods of organizing work. Share your ideas with your coworkers. They might appreciate it.

If you want to be successful in a new country, you have to adapt to its customs. You also need to maintain some of your own customs because they are part of who you are. The important thing is to find a good balance between the two.

131

> Some people think that children should begin their formal education at a very early age and should spend most of their time on their school studies. Others believe that young children should spend most of their time playing. Compare these two views. Which view do you agree with? Why?

Should young children spend more time on school studies or more time playing? The answer to this question depends on several things. It depends on the quality of the school, on the quality of the play, and, most of all, on whether the children are active participants or passive observers in whichever situation they find themselves.

Not all schools are the same. In some schools children must sit still all day and memorize information. Quiet behavior and correct repetition of facts are encouraged. There is a limit to the types of skills a child can develop in such a setting. In other schools, children are encouraged to participate in a variety of activities. They are encouraged to ask questions, interact with other children, and experience things. The range of skills they can develop in this type of setting is very broad.

Not all play is the same. Sometimes it involves little more than sitting quietly in front of the TV doing nothing but watching. Other times it involves lively and imaginative activities and interaction with other children. This type of play facilitates the development of a variety of physical and intellectual skills.

Not all children are the same, but all children have the same requirements for learning. They learn when their minds and bodies are active. They learn when they socialize with other children. They can do these things during school time or play time. It doesn't matter when or where they do these things. It only matters that they do them.

Both formal education and unstructured play can be valuable learning experiences for children. What matters is that the time they spend in either of these settings is quality time, that both their minds and their bodies are actively engaged. Whenever that is the case, then children are sure to have the experiences that they need to learn and grow.

132

> The government has announced that it plans to build a new university. Some people think that your community would be a good place to locate the university. Compare the advantages and disadvantages of establishing a new university in your community. Use specific details in your discussion.

A university can contribute a lot of good things to a city, but it also brings some disadvantages. If we built a university here, it would bring jobs, culture, and interesting new people to our town. On the other hand, it would also destroy land, cause traffic problems, and be a burden on city services. There are two sides to every story.

A university would bring jobs, but it would also destroy land. During construction, the university would have to hire carpenters, electricians, plumbers, etc. After the building is finished, they would hire people to help run and maintain the campus. We need jobs in our community, so this is a big advantage. On the other hand, the university needs land to build on. Would they take over one of our city parks, or tear down some of our houses? Either way, they would destroy things that we use and enjoy now.

The university would bring culture to our community, but it would also bring crowds. The community could take advantage of events at the university such as concerts, lectures, and art exhibits. But a lot of people from all over would also attend these events. They would fill our streets with traffic and cause parking problems. Our community would no longer be a quiet place.

The university would bring interesting people, but it would also cause a burden on our city services. People such as professors, researchers, and visiting lecturers would work at the university. They are sure to contribute a lot to our community life. However, they are also sure to have families. They will need houses, schools, and transportation. How can our city suddenly provide services for a lot of new residents?

A university would bring many advantages to our city, but it would also have some big disadvantages. The fact is, we already have two universities here and I don't think we need any more.

133

> Some people prefer to plan activities for their free time very carefully. Others choose not to make any plans at all for their free time. Compare the benefits of planning free-time activities with the benefits of not making plans. Which do you prefer—planning or not planning for your leisure time? Use specific reasons and examples to explain your choice.

My free time is very valuable. I don't have a lot of free time, so I want to be sure to spend every minute of it well. Therefore, I always try to make plans ahead of time. In this way I don't waste any of my free time, I have a chance to make any necessary preparations, and I can invite my friends to join me.

If I make a plan for the weekend ahead of time, I don't waste any of my free time trying to decide what to do. If I don't have a plan, I might spend all morning thinking about the different things I could do. Before I knew it, half the day would be gone. I would lose half my free time making decisions and it would be too late to start a lot of activities.

If I make a plan for the weekend ahead of time, I can also make my preparations ahead of time. Then I can spend the whole weekend just enjoying myself. For example, if I want to go on a picnic, I can have my food all prepared beforehand. If I want to go to a concert, I can get my tickets ahead of time. By making plans ahead of time, I am sure I will be ready to do just what I want to do.

If I make a plan for the weekend ahead of time, it's easier to invite friends to join me. If I wait until the last minute, my friends might already have plans to do something else. If I make plans ahead of time, I can invite any friends I want to. And even if those particular friends are already busy, I still have time to invite somebody else.

It's always best to plan anything ahead of time. I think it is especially important to plan free time, because my free time is my best time. I want to enjoy every minute of it.

134

> People learn in different ways. Some people learn by doing things; other people learn by reading about things; others learn by listening to people talk about things. Which of these methods of learning is best for you? Use specific examples to support your choice.

I have never been able to learn well from reading or from listening to someone talk. My mind wanders and I can't grasp the situation. The best way for me to learn is by doing things. It helps me understand and remember information better, and it is much more interesting for me than reading and listening.

Doing things helps me understand. Someone may explain to me how a musical instrument works, for example. I don't really understand this, however, until I try to play the instrument myself. Then I can hear and see and feel how the sound is made. I can feel how hard I have to push a key or pluck a string to make the sound I want. Or I could read a recipe in a cookbook. But I don't really understand how to prepare the food until I try to make it myself.

Doing things helps me remember. A teacher could explain some grammar rules to me, but it's hard for me to remember them. However, when I practice using the grammar rules by speaking the language, then I will remember them better. The more I speak the language, the better I remember the rules. I could also read about math formulas in a book. But I can't remember them unless I use them to try to solve some math problems.

Doing things holds my attention. When I listen to a lecture, my thoughts wander to other things and I don't hear the information at all. When I read something, it is hard for me to follow the ideas unless I concentrate really hard. When I do something, on the other hand, I am always interested in it. I have to pay attention because I am the one who is doing it.

We all have our own learning styles. For me, it is clear that I learn best by doing things. It is the only way I can really focus my attention on information, understand it, and remember it.

135

> Some people enjoy change and they look forward to new experiences. Others like their lives to stay the same, and they do not change their usual habits. Compare these two approaches to life. Which approach do you prefer? Why?

Some people seem to thrive on the uncertainty of change while others prefer things to always stay the same. Change is exciting and interesting, but there is a certain security that comes when things stay the same. The approach I prefer has changed with the circumstances of my life.

People who like change are people who look for excitement. Moving to a new place, for example, or starting a new job can be risky, but these things can also be fun. There is a certain sort of thrill that comes when entering a new situation. What will it be like? Who will I meet? It is interesting to wonder and guess about what will happen next, while it can be boring to always know what tomorrow will bring.

People who prefer things to stay the same, on the other hand, tend to feel more comfortable when they know they can count on certain things to always happen. Maybe they like to know what time they will leave the office every day, for instance, and what they will have for dinner when they get home. Then they don't have to worry about making plans or solving problems. They can just relax and enjoy their quiet routines.

My preferences about these two approaches have changed as I've grown older. When I was younger, I frequently sought change. I liked to travel a lot and usually made my plans at the last minute. I liked going to new places and meeting new people and even trying out different kinds of jobs. It was fun and exciting, and I learned a lot. Now I have two small children, so routine is important. Doing things the same way everyday makes it easier for me to care for my children. It also helps my children feel more secure. I don't miss the excitement of my youth because my life is different now.

Change brings excitement and routine brings security. Whichever choice you prefer may depend somewhat on your personality, but I believe it depends even more on the circumstances of your life.

136

> Decisions can be made quickly, or they can be made after careful thought. Do you agree or disagree with the following statement? The decisions that people make quickly are always wrong. Use specific reasons and examples to support your opinion.

I don't agree that quick decisions are always wrong. Sometimes they can be the best decisions we make. A quick decision made about a familiar situation is usually correct. Quick decisions based on a gut feeling, or instinct, can usually be relied on. It's the decisions made out of fear or desperation that we need to watch.

In familiar circumstances you can usually trust yourself to make a good decision quickly. For example, your boss might offer you the opportunity to do a certain job. She doesn't have time to explain the details right away but needs an immediate decision from you. It is probably safe for you to accept the assignment. You know your boss and your boss knows you. You can trust that if your boss thinks this is a good assignment for you, she is probably right.

We can also usually rely on our instinct. You might be looking for a new apartment, for example. You look and look, but none of the apartments you see are right. Then you walk into one and right away you know it is the place for you. You don't know anything about the neighborhood or the landlord and you aren't sure about the rent, but you immediately sign the lease. Some people might think this is crazy. I think you will probably be very happy in that apartment because you listened to your instinct. Your instinct doesn't need a lot of information to make good decisions.

On the other hand, we can get into trouble when we make decisions out of desperation. Let's say you are on a lonely road late at night and your car breaks down. Another driver arrives and offers you a ride. There is something strange about this person. You accept the ride, however, because you are tired and cold. This is not a good decision; in fact, it is a very dangerous decision. It would be better to wait in your own car, all night if necessary, for the police to arrive. You would realize this if you made the decision more carefully.

Not all decisions need to be made carefully. We can usually rely on familiar situations and instinct to guide us in making quick decisions. We need to stop and think more carefully, however, when we make decisions in more difficult circumstances.

137

> **Do you agree or disagree with the following statement? People are never satisfied with what they have; they always want something more or something different. Use specific reasons to support your answer.**

I believe that it is part of human nature to never be completely satisfied with what we have. This is true throughout our entire lives, from the time we are small children, through adolescence, and on into adulthood. We are always trying to have something more or better or different than what we already have.

The desire for something different begins in early childhood. Give a small child a toy to play with, and she's happy—until she sees another toy. Then she wants to play with the other toy. Give her a cookie and give another cookie to her brother. She'll probably think that her brother's cookie is bigger than hers, or somehow different, and cry for it.

The dissatisfaction with what we already have continues into adolescence. A teenager may buy some new clothes. Then he sees his friend has shoes in a different style or pants of a different color. All of a sudden his new clothes are no good; he wants what his friend has. Being like their friends is very important to teens and they constantly change their desires in order to match their friends.

Even in adulthood, we are not free from dissatisfaction. A young adult may be excited to get her first job, but right away she starts thinking about moving up and getting a better job. A young couple is finally able to buy a new house after saving for several years. But soon they start thinking about buying another, bigger house. A man may finally reach a high position in his company after years of hard work. Not long after that, he starts thinking about retirement. We are never satisfied.

It is part of the cycle of life to never be entirely satisfied with what we have. This is actually a good human quality because it pushes us on to each new stage of life. Without dissatisfactions, we would probably always stay in the same place.

138

> **Do you agree or disagree with the following statement? People should read only those books that are about real events, real people, and established facts. Use specific reasons and details to support your opinion.**

Some people read only nonfiction because they say they only want to read about real things. I think this is a big mistake. There is a lot to be gained from reading fiction. In the first place, it actually can teach us about real things. In addition, it allows us develop our creativity, and it helps us express our emotions, as well. These things are just as important as learning about facts.

Even though fiction is about made-up stories, it can teach us about real things and give us a deeper understanding of them. Nonfiction tells us only facts. Novels, on the other hand, can present facts in a way that helps us understand what those facts mean or meant to real people. The novels by Charles Dickens, for example, help us really understand the consequences of poverty in Victorian England.

Fiction also encourages us to develop our creativity. When we read stories, we try to imagine what the places and characters look like. We try to imagine what it would feel like to live the characters' lives. Well-developed creativity is something that is important to have in all areas of our lives, including learning to understand real facts.

Fiction helps us understand and express our emotions. Whether we read romances, tragedies, comedies, or some of each, we read about feelings that we ourselves have. The stories may be invented, but the feelings they express are real. Reading helps us explore these feelings and gives us a mirror for our emotional lives.

It is important to learn facts, but it is also important to develop creativity and explore feelings. Reading fiction as well as nonfiction helps us do this. We should all read a wide range of things to deepen our understanding of ourselves and the world around us.

139

> **Do you agree or disagree with the following statement? All students should be required to study art and music in secondary school. Use specific reasons to support your answer.**

I agree that all students should be required to study art and music in high school. These things are just as important as any other subject a student may learn. Art and music can teach young people many important things. They help students learn about themselves, their society, and the world they live in.

By studying art and music, students can learn a great deal about themselves. Both are natural forms of self expression. Just as our ancestors drew on walls in caves and made music with drums, people today use art and music to explore emotions. Students also explore their likes and dislikes when they choose the music they want to learn to play or when they decide which subjects they want to draw. The process of making music or art is a process of self exploration.

Studying art and music means more than drawing or playing an instrument, however. Students go to museums and concerts, too, in order to have the chance to experience works produced by others. By studying pictures in museums or listening to selections in a musical program, students learn about their own culture. They learn about what their society values. They also learn about the history of their society and how lifestyles and values have changed over time.

The study of art and music from other cultures gives students the opportunity to learn about other people around the world. They learn about what is important in other societies. They learn about similarities and differences between cultures and about the history and lifestyles of other places. New worlds are opened up to them.

By studying art and music in high school, students begin to understand themselves, their own culture, and other cultures, as well. What could have more value than that?

140

> Do you agree or disagree with the following statement? There is nothing young people can teach older people. Use specific reasons and examples to support your position.

Many of us believe that young people have nothing valuable to teach older people. However, that is not always the case. Young people can teach older people about technology, popular culture, and current social issues.

Young people are usually better than older people at using new forms of technology. For example, children these days become familiar with computers at an early age. Older people can learn to use computers from young people. Many older people have difficulty learning to use a DVD player, while for young people this is usually easy. I taught my grandparents how to use a DVD player when I was thirteen, and now they use it regularly.

Older people are usually not familiar with popular culture, and younger people can help here too. For example, most older people don't know much about popular music. When young people teach them about it, however, they may come to enjoy it. I introduced my grandmother to some of my favorite music, and now she and I listen to it together often. I plan to teach her about a popular sport—rollerblading—very soon!

There are also more serious things that younger people can teach older people about. Today's children have grown up knowing about AIDS and school violence. These are serious social issues, but older people don't always understand them. Talking about them with younger people can help the older people learn more.

I know there are people who say, "You can't teach an old dog new tricks." However, it is plain to me that the young have plenty to teach the old if they take the time to try. When they do, I think both gain a new appreciation for each other.

141

> Do you agree or disagree with the following statement? Reading fiction (such as novels and short stories) is more enjoyable than watching movies. Use specific reasons and examples to explain your position.

I strongly agree that reading fiction is more enjoyable than watching movies. In the first place, novels and short stories have more depth than movies. In addition, reading requires you to be more actively involved in the stories. Furthermore, reading is very convenient because you can pick up a book at any time and place you choose. I often choose books over movies.

Most novels and stories have more depth than movies. Of course there are bad books and excellent movies, but usually books contain more than movies. They explain more about the characters and show more details about the action. Part of the reason for this is that most movies have to be close to two hours long. Books, on the other hand, can be as long as the author wants.

Readers are more actively involved in a story than movie watchers are. A movie watcher just has to sit and watch. A reader, on the other hand, has to think and imagine. The reader can't see the scenes like a movie watcher can. He has to picture them in his mind and understand what they are about.

The most enjoyable thing about books is that you can read them at any time and place. You don't have to go to the movie theater or rent a video or wait for a movie to appear on TV. If you want to enjoy a story for a few minutes before dinner or while riding the bus, you can. If you want to relax for a while before going to sleep, there is always a book ready for your enjoyment. Books are the most convenient form of entertainment there is.

Movies are fun, but books are better. Books keep the reader involved and entertained. Books can be read at any time or place. I never go anywhere without a book.

142

> A university plans to develop a new research center in your country. Some people want a center for business research. Other people want a center for research in agriculture (farming). Which of these two kinds of research centers do you recommend for your country? Use specific reasons in your recommendation.

Business research and education is already well developed in my country, so I recommend an agricultural research center. Farmers in my country still follow old-fashioned methods. We need to do research to learn how to grow more crops, grow disease-resistant crops, and educate farmers in modern methods so they can raise their standard of living.

We need to increase agricultural production for several reasons. One is that the population of my country is growing so we need to produce more food. In addition, if we could export more crops, it would be good for our economy. An agricultural research center could develop methods for growing more crops.

We also need to develop disease-resistant crops. Farmers spend a lot of time trying to protect their crops from disease. Often, they lose their crops anyway, so a lot of money and effort are lost. Some farmers end up losing their entire farms because disease kills their crops. An agricultural research center could develop methods to save crops from disease.

Farmers need to learn modern farming methods. They need to learn how to grow more and better crops and they need to learn more efficient work methods. This would benefit the country as a whole and it would also make things better for farmers. Their work would be easier and they would earn more money. An agricultural research center could develop better farming methods and teach them to farmers.

An agricultural research center would benefit everybody. We would all have more food to eat, agricultural exports would help our economy, and the farmers' standard of living would improve.

143

Some young children spend a great amount of their time practicing sports. Discuss the advantages and disadvantages of this. Use specific reasons and examples to support your answer.

Participating in sports is good for children. It helps them stay in good physical shape, it helps them learn teamwork, and helps them learn to develop excellence. However, too much of a good thing is never good, and children need to balance sports with other types of activities.

It is important to stay in shape, and participating in sports is a good way to do this. In sports, children get a chance to run and jump, to develop their muscles and lungs. This is especially important after spending most of the day sitting at a desk doing school-work. However, if children focus too much on sports, they might neglect their homework. They might also be too tired to pay attention in school.

Participating in sports helps children learn to work on a team. They have to pay attention and cooperate and do what is best for the team. This is an important skill that will help them throughout their lives. If children always play on a team, however, they don't have the chance to learn to do things alone. They don't learn to enjoy solitary activities such as reading or drawing, and they don't learn how to play with just one or two other children and no adult supervision. These activities also help develop important skills.

Learning to play sports helps children learn to develop excellence. They want to be really good in the sports they choose. Each one wants to be the best ball player or gymnast possible. While it is good to learn to work toward goals, it is also good to participate in other types of activities. Children need activities that are just for relaxation and enjoyment. They need activities that don't involve competition. If they focus too much on sports, they might not get a chance to do these other activities.

Playing sports is an important part of a child's development. Other activities, however, are equally important. Adults should encourage children to find a balance between different types of activities in their lives.

> Do you agree or disagree with the following statement? *Only* people who earn a lot of money are successful. Use specific reasons and examples to support your answer.

Many people believe that a large income equals success. I believe, however, that success is more than how much money you make. Some of those measures of success include fame, respect, and knowledge.

Most people assume that famous people are rich people, but that isn't always true. For example, some day I would like to be a famous researcher. Few scientists are rich by today's standards. Still, I will feel myself successful if I am well known. Additionally, there are many famous humanitarians who are not rich. Mother Theresa was one. Certainly no one would say she was not successful.

I also believe that being respected by coworkers indicates success. Without that respect, money means very little. For example, I once did some work for a top attorney in a law firm. He made a very good salary, but he wasn't a nice man. No one ever did work for him willingly. He ordered everyone around, and we didn't respect him. In contrast, however, I had a wonderful band director in high school. He had to take extra jobs just to make enough money to support his family. However, his students had great respect for him and always listened to what he said. As a result, we were a very good band. In my opinion, my band director was more successful than the attorney was.

Finally, I think one of the most important indicators of success is knowledge. Wealthy people don't know all the answers. For example, in the movie *Good Will Hunting*, the only person who could solve complex problems was the janitor. He knew a lot and decided what he wanted to do with that knowledge rather than just think about money. In my opinion, he was extremely successful.

When we think of history, there are few people we remember simply because they were rich. Overall, we remember people who did something with their lives—they were influential in politics, or contributed to science or art or religion. If history is the ultimate judge of success, then money surely isn't everything.

For more sample essays visit

barronsbooks.com/TP/TOEFL/Writing

Answer Key

INTEGRATED TASKS
Step 1: Plan

PRACTICE 1 (PAGE 35)

Possible answers:

Reading 1

Main idea | Invasive plants harm native plants.
Supporting details | (1) They are introduced to an area through gardening.
| (2) They escape from the garden and grow wild.
| (3) They push out native species, causing devastating effects on the local ecology.

Lecture 1

Main idea | Garlic mustard is an invasive species that causes problems.
Supporting details | (1) It competes with other spring-blooming species.
| (2) The West Virginia white butterfly is threatened by this plant.
| (3) Garlic mustard was introduced to the United States as a food source.

Reading 2

Main idea | TV viewing has negative effects on children's school performance.
Supporting details | (1) Children who watch a lot of TV get lower grades and test scores.
| (2) Few TV programs teach academic or thinking skills.
| (3) When children spend time watching TV, they spend less time on homework, with other people, and being active.

Lecture 2

Main idea | TV watching can actually improve school performance.
Supporting details | (1) TV exposes children to new ideas and information.
| (2) Children should watch some TV, but not too much.

Reading 3

Main idea   A particular smoking prevention campaign aimed at young people has been successful.

Supporting details
(1) Many teens participated in antismoking events, and many saw antismoking ads.
(2) Teens who saw the ads were less likely to start smoking.
(3) The public health department will continue and expand the campaign.

Lecture 3

Main idea   The initial results of public health campaigns can be misleading.

Supporting details
(1) Over half of the teens had seen the ads and participated in workshops and meetings.
(2) Surveys taken near the end of an antismoking campaign showed 40% unlikely to try smoking.
(3) Surveys taken three months later showed 58% very likely to try smoking.

Reading 4

Main idea   A good mood makes shoppers buy more.

Supporting details
(1) Mood can be affected by weather, personal life, and store environment.
(2) Retailers create a store environment to have a positive impact on mood and therefore on sales.

Lecture 4

Main idea   Studies show that mood can affect customers' behaviors and attitudes.

Supporting details
(1) When listening to slow music, restaurant patrons remained longer and purchased more food.
(2) When listening to familiar music, shoppers stayed in a store longer and expressed more positive opinions about the products.

PRACTICE 2 (PAGE 38)

Possible answers:

Reading 5

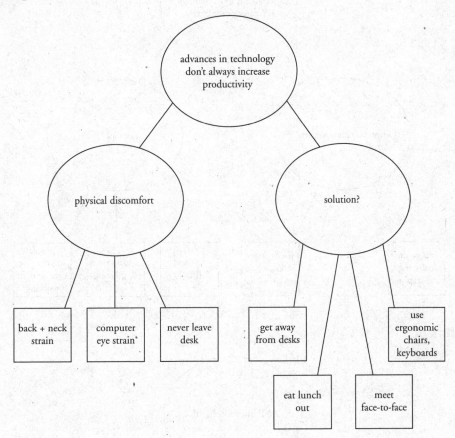

Lecture 5

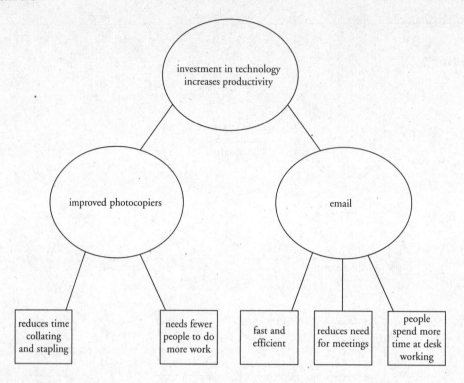

investment in technology increases productivity

- **improved photocopiers**
  - reduces time collating and stapling
  - needs fewer people to do more work
- **email**
  - fast and efficient
  - reduces need for meetings
  - people spend more time at desk working

Reading 6

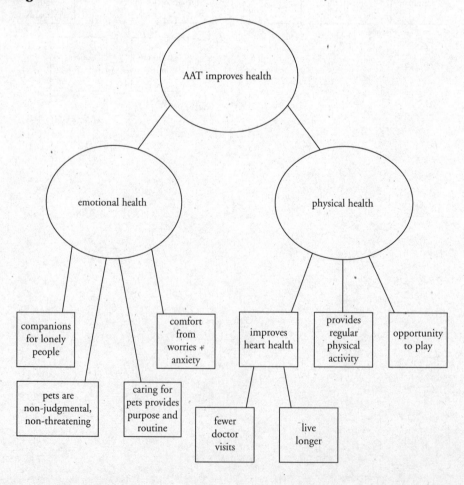

AAT improves health

- **emotional health**
  - companions for lonely people
  - pets are non-judgmental, non-threatening
  - caring for pets provides purpose and routine
  - comfort from worries + anxiety
- **physical health**
  - improves heart health
    - fewer doctor visits
    - live longer
  - provides regular physical activity
  - opportunity to play

Lecture 6

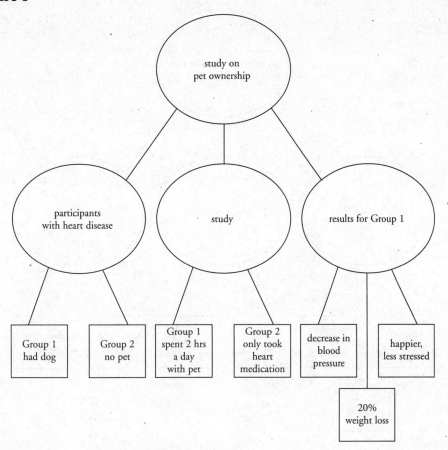

study on pet ownership

- **participants with heart disease**
  - Group 1 had dog
  - Group 2 no pet
- **study**
  - Group 1 spent 2 hrs a day with pet
  - Group 2 only took heart medication
- **results for Group 1**
  - decrease in blood pressure
  - 20% weight loss
  - happier, less stressed

Reading 7

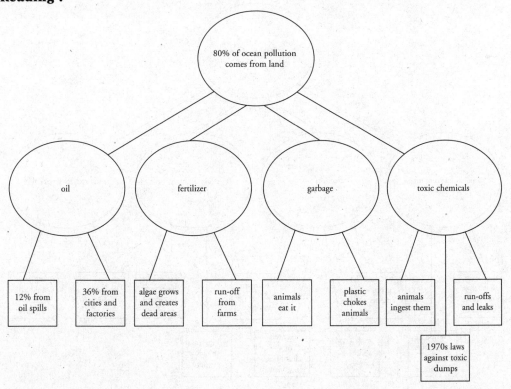

80% of ocean pollution comes from land

- **oil**
  - 12% from oil spills
  - 36% from cities and factories
- **fertilizer**
  - algae grows and creates dead areas
  - run-off from farms
- **garbage**
  - animals eat it
  - plastic chokes animals
- **toxic chemicals**
  - animals ingest them
  - 1970s laws against toxic dumps
  - run-offs and leaks

Lecture 7

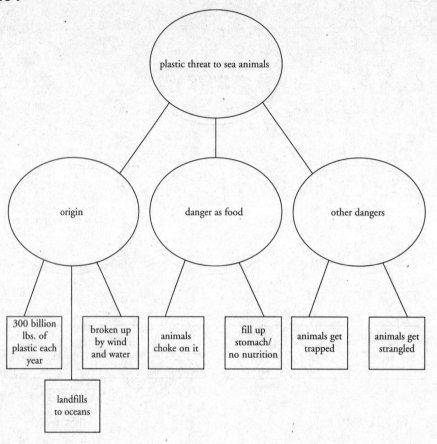

- plastic threat to sea animals
  - origin
    - 300 billion lbs. of plastic each year
    - broken up by wind and water
    - landfills to oceans
  - danger as food
    - animals choke on it
    - fill up stomach/ no nutrition
  - other dangers
    - animals get trapped
    - animals get strangled

Reading 8

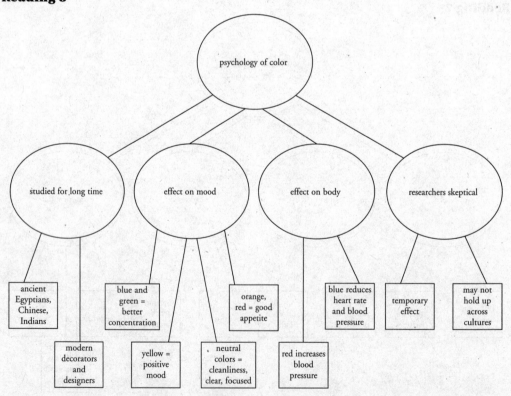

- psychology of color
  - studied for long time
    - ancient Egyptians, Chinese, Indians
    - modern decorators and designers
  - effect on mood
    - blue and green = better concentration
    - yellow = positive mood
    - neutral colors = cleanliness, clear, focused
    - orange, red = good appetite
  - effect on body
    - blue reduces heart rate and blood pressure
    - red increases blood pressure
  - researchers skeptical
    - temporary effect
    - may not hold up across cultures

Lecture 8

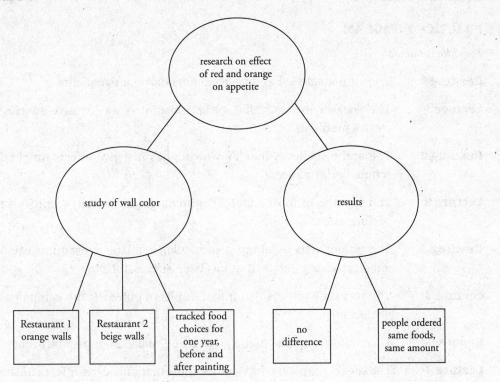

Step 2: Write

PRACTICE 1 (PAGE 43)

Possible answers:

Reading 1   The author states that invasive plants harm native plants.

Lecture 1   The speaker explains that garlic mustard is an invasive species that causes problems.

Reading 2   The author believes that TV viewing has negative effects on children's school performance.

Lecture 2   The speaker proposes that TV watching can actually improve school performance.

Reading 3   The author tells us about a particular smoking prevention campaign aimed at young people that has been successful.

Lecture 3   The speaker warns us that initial results of public health campaigns can be deceptive.

Reading 4   The author proposes that a good mood makes shoppers buy more.

Lecture 4   The speaker explains that studies show that music can affect consumers' behavior and attitude.

Reading 5   The author asserts that advances in technology don't always lead to increased productivity.

Lecture 5   The speaker suggests that investment in technology is paid back in increased productivity.

Reading 6   The author explains that animal-assisted therapy is used to improve emotional and physical health.

Lecture 6   The speaker tells us about a study that showed positive effects of pet ownership on health.

Reading 7   The author warns that ocean pollution is a serious problem.

Lecture 7   The speaker explains how plastic garbage threatens sea animals.

Reading 8   The author describes psychological effects of color.

Lecture 8   The speaker tells us about a study that showed no effect of color on appetite.

PRACTICE 2 (PAGE 45)

Possible answers:

1. The author states that invasive plants harm native plants, and the speaker explains that garlic mustard is an invasive species that causes problems.

2. The author believes that TV viewing has negative effects on children's school performance. The speaker, on the other hand, proposes that TV watching can actually improve school performance.

3. The author tells us about a particular smoking prevention campaign aimed at young people that has been successful. In contrast, the speaker warns us that initial results of public health campaigns can be misleading.

4. The author proposes that a good mood makes shoppers buy more. Similarly, the speaker explains that studies show that music can make consumers spend more time shopping.

5. The author asserts that advances in technology don't always lead to increased productivity. The speaker, in contrast, suggests that investment in technology is paid back in increased productivity.

6. The author explains that animal-assisted therapy is used to improve emotional and physical health, and the speaker tells us about a study that showed positive effects of pet ownership on health.

7. The author warns that ocean pollution is a serious problem. In the same way, the speaker explains how plastic garbage threatens sea animals.

8. The author describes psychological effects of color. In contrast, the speaker tells us about a study that showed no effect of color on appetite.

PRACTICE 3 (PAGE 47)

1. C	4. B	7. A	10. C	13. B
2. A	5. A	8. B	11. C	
3. B	6. C	9. A	12. A	

PRACTICE 4 (PAGE 50)

Possible answers:

1. Garlic mustard is a problem in the U.S. because it threatens other spring-blooming plants by taking up light, nutrients, and space.

2. Garlic mustard also threatens the West Virginia white butterfly. It competes with other types of mustard which are the butterfly's food source.

3. Garlic mustard was first grown on Long Island for food and has since spread to other areas of the country.

4. Children can learn new things from TV.

5. The amount of time spent watching TV is important.

6. More than three hours a day of TV watching results in lower reading and math test scores.

7. Surveys made at the end of an antismoking campaign showed that 50% knew about the campaign and 40% would probably not smoke.

8. Three months later, the numbers had changed.

9. More than half said they would probably smoke, and fewer than one-third said they knew about the campaign.

10. Research showed that slow music caused customers to stay at the restaurant longer and order more food.

11. Some of the study subjects, college students, heard popular music in the store, and others heard older music.

12. Those who heard familiar music shopped longer and said better things about the store's products.

PRACTICE 5 (PAGE 53)

Possible verbs; the quotes are shown where needed.

1. The author explains that invasive plants may have "devastating" results.
2. The author asserts that most children's TV programs don't have "valuable content."
3. The author reports that antismoking campaigns for teens have had "significant success."
4. The speaker claims that offices save money because office workers "can now devote themselves to other tasks."
5. The speaker states that when children watch TV, they "actually do better in school."
6. The author points out that play helps people "live longer, healthier lives."
7. The author remarks that neutral colors are used in health care centers to "convey a sense of cleanliness."

PRACTICE 6 (PAGE 56)

Possible summaries:

Summary 1

The author states that invasive plants harm native plants. Likewise, the speaker explains that garlic mustard is an invasive species that causes problems.

Gardeners have introduced nonnative plants for food and medicine. They have also planted them because they are hardy, drought resistant, or beautiful. However, these plants escape from the garden and cause problems. Invasive plants harm native species by shading them out, strangling them, or using up all the nutrients in the soil. The local ecology suffers because there are fewer native plants and animals lose their homes and food.

The speaker mentions garlic mustard as an example of an invasive plant that harms the local ecology. It threatens other spring-blooming plants by taking up light, nutrients, and space. It also threatens the West Virginia white butterfly by competing with other types of mustard which are the butterfly's food source. Garlic mustard was first grown on Long Island for food and has since spread to other areas of the country.

Summary 2

The author believes that TV viewing has negative effects on children's school performance. The speaker, on the other hand, proposes that TV watching can actually improve school performance.

According to the author, children who have TV sets in their bedrooms don't do as well in school as their classmates. Some people think of TV as educational, but the author asserts that most children's TV programs don't have "valuable content." In addition, TV takes time away from important activities like doing homework or being with other people. Parents can help their children by turning off the television.

The lecturer does not agree with this point of view. It is his opinion that children actually can learn new things from watching TV. The lecturer points out, however, that the amount of time spent watching TV is important. The speaker says that more than three hours a day of TV watching can result in lower reading and math scores.

Summary 3

The author tells us about a particular smoking prevention campaign aimed at young people that has been successful. In contrast, the speaker warns us that initial results of public health campaigns can be misleading.

The antismoking campaign described in the passage included advertising, no-smoking policies, and antismoking events. Many teens participated in the events and many more saw the ads. The public health department plans to continue with this successful campaign to improve public health among young people in the state.

The speaker warns us that we can be deceived by the initial results of public health campaigns. She mentioned a recent antismoking campaign as an example. Surveys made at the end of the campaign showed that more than 50% knew about the campaign and 40% would probably not smoke. Three months later, however, the numbers had changed. Many more said they would probably smoke and many fewer said they knew about the campaign. So, a public health campaign that looks successful at first can look less successful a few months later.

Summary 4

The author proposes that a good mood makes shoppers buy more. Similarly, the speaker explains that studies show that music can affect customers' behavior and attitude.

The reading passage explains that a shopper's mood may be influenced by things that retailers cannot control, such as the weather or personal or work problems. Retailers can, however, influence shoppers' moods by controlling the store environment. Shoppers buy more when retailers use lighting, color, and music to improve shopper mood.

The speaker describes research about the effect of music on consumers. Research showed that slow music caused customers to stay at a restaurant longer and order more food. In another study, some of the subjects, college students, heard popular music in a store, and others heard older music. Those who heard familiar music shopped longer and said better things about the store's products. These two studies show that restaurant and store owners can influence shoppers' moods and encourage shoppers to buy more.

Step 3: Revise

PRACTICE 1 (PAGE 65)

Model Task 2

1–5

   The author explains that (1) animal-assisted therapy is used to improve emotional and physical health, and the speaker tells us about a (2) study that showed positive effects of pet ownership on health.

   The author explains how pets improve both emotional health and physical health. (A) Pets are good companions for lonely people. (B) They <u>also</u> give their owners things to do, like hobbies or club activities. (C) <u>In addition</u>, pets are a comfort to anxious or worried people. Pets are good for physical health, <u>as well</u>. (D) They help people with high blood pressure and heart problems. (E) They help people stay physically active. (F) They give people a chance to play. (G) <u>Finally</u>, pet therapy is used with elderly people.

The speaker supports pet therapy. He describes a study where pets had a positive effect on the health of heart patients. (A) Half the patients had a dog to take care of. The other half only got traditional treatment. (B) After six months, the patients with pets had lower blood pressure, and (C) they had lost more weight than the other patients. (D) They felt happier, <u>too</u>. (E) These are all things that can effect heart disease. This is a case that shows how pet therapy works to improve physical health.

6. There are no grammar or spelling errors.

7. (possible answers)

simple sentence:	Pets are good companions for lonely people. (para. 2)
compound sentence:	After six months, the patients with pets had lower blood pressure, and they had lost more weight than the other patients. (para. 3)
adjective clause:	He describes a study where pets had a positive effect on the health of heart patients.

Model Task 3

1–5

<u>The author warns that (1) ocean pollution is a serious problem. In the same way, the speaker explains how (2) plastic garbage threatens sea animals.</u>

The author explains that different things cause ocean pollution. (A) Oil from factories and cities enters the ocean through rivers and drains. (B) <u>Similarly</u>, fertilizers wash into the ocean, and they cause large growths of algae. (C) Toxic chemicals continue to pollute the ocean, <u>as well</u>. There are laws against dumping these chemicals, but they still leak into the ocean. Animals eat them, and when we eat seafood, we eat these chemicals, <u>too</u>. (C) There is <u>also</u> a lot of garbage in the ocean. Plastic is the worst kind because it doesn't break down quickly. Animals think it is food. They eat it and choke on it.

While the author gives an overview of ocean pollution, the speaker specifically describes the problem of plastic garbage. (A) People produce more than 300 billion pounds of plastic a year, and a lot of this ends up in the ocean. The water and wind break large pieces of plastic into smaller pieces. (B) <u>Then</u> animals try to eat these pieces. An animal may choke on plastic. It may starve because it doesn't feel hungry after eating plastic. (C) Animals are often caught in floating plastic. (D) They are also strangled by it. There are many types of pollution in the ocean. Plastic garbage is one of the worst examples.

6. There are no grammar or spelling errors.

7. (possible answers)

compound sentence:	Similarly, fertilizers wash into the ocean, and they cause large growths of algae. (para. 2)
complex sentence:	Plastic is the worst kind because it does not break down quickly. (para. 2)
simple sentence:	An animal may choke on plastic. (para. 3)

Model Task 4

1–5

<u>The author explains that (1) color has psychological effects. In contrast, the speaker tells us about (2) a study that showed no effect of color on appetite.</u>

The author describes different ways people have used the psychological effects of color. (A) Ancient people used color for healing, and modern designers use color to create mood. (B) They might use yellow to create a positive mood in an office. (C) <u>Likewise</u>, they might use neutral colors to create a clean, clear, and focused mood in health care centers. (D) Restaurants often use orange and red to stimulate the appetite. (E) Some scientists say that blue lowers the heart rate and blood pressure. Red, <u>on the other hand</u>, raises blood pressure. Other scientists don't believe that color affects mood. They say the effect is temporary and also that it is different in every culture.

The speaker describes a study that showed no relationship between color and mood. (A) A fast food restaurant chain had orange walls in half its restaurants and beige walls in the rest of its restaurants. (B) It recorded all the food ordered for two years. (C) There was no difference between the restaurants with orange walls and the restaurants with beige walls. People ordered the same food in both types of places. <u>In other words</u>, according to the company president, there is no effect of color on appetite. He said that he proved it. In this case, at least, there was no psychological effect of color.

6. There are no grammar or spelling errors.

7. (possible answers)

compound sentence:	Ancient people used color for healing and modern designers use color to create mood. (para. 2)
noun clause:	Other scientists do not believe that color affects mood. (para. 2)
simple sentence:	People ordered the same food in both types of places. (para. 3)

PRACTICE 2 (PAGE 68)

1. C	5. C	9. B	13. B	17. C
2. A	6. B	10. A	14. A	18. A
3. B	7. A	11. A	15. B	19. A
4. B	8. C	12. C	16. A	20. B

PRACTICE 3 (PAGE 73)

Missing items:

Paragraph 1: Incomplete thesis statement
Paragraph 2: Main idea
Paragraph 3: none

Grammar and vocabulary errors:

Paragraph 1: none
Paragraph 2: <u>Consequently</u>, the harsh climate...; ...<u>can to</u> be very high...
Paragraph 3: <u>Although</u>, because of the losses...; ...many people in this northern province <u>is</u>...

Rewritten essay.

Possible added and corrected parts are underlined.

The reading passage explains why farming is difficult in far northern regions in general. In a similar way, the lecture describes difficulties faced by farmers in a particular northern province.

According to the author, the cold climate of far northern regions makes it very difficult for farmers to make a living. In the first place, the growing season is very short. It might last three months or less, which is not enough time for most crops to mature. Additionally, few people live in northern regions because the cold weather is not attractive. Therefore, farmers have to pay to transport their crops long distances to cities where they can sell them to a larger market. Finally, the harsh climate causes farm machinery to break down frequently. The cost to repair or replace specialized farm equipment can be very high.

The speaker discusses farmers working in a particular northern province. He explains that many people have stopped farming in that area because they are no longer able to make a living that way. One reason is the disease affecting the rye crop, one of the few crops that can be grown so far north. Another reason is the rising cost of transportation. Fewer and fewer farmers can afford to ship their crops to cities. Furthermore, because of the losses due to the rye disease, many farmers have difficulty paying the cost of maintaining their buildings and equipment. For reasons similar to those outlined in the reading passage, many people in this northern province are leaving their farms to look for jobs in towns and cities.

PRACTICE 4 (PAGE 76)

Corrected words are underlined.

1. Garlic mustard is a problem in the U.S. because it threatens other spring-blooming plants by taking up light, nutrients, and space.
2. Garlic mustard also threatens the West Virginia white butterfly. It competes with another type of mustard which is the butterfly's food source.
3. *correct*
4. Children can learn new things from TV.
5. The amount of time spent watching TV is important.
6. More than three hours a day of TV watching results in lower reading and math test scores.
7. Surveys made at the end of an antismoking campaign showed that more than 50% knew about the campaign and 40% would probably not smoke.
8. *correct*
9. More than half said they would probably smoke, and fewer than one-third said they knew about the campaign.
10. Research showed that slow music caused customers to stay at the restaurant longer and order more food.
11. Some of the study subjects, college students, heard popular music in the store, and others heard older music.
12. Those who heard familiar music shopped longer and said better things about the store's products.

PRACTICE 5, INTEGRATED TASK (PAGE 78)

See Step 2, Practice 6 answers for correctly punctuated versions of these essays.

PRACTICE INTEGRATED TASK (PAGE 80)

Possible response:

The author discusses the dangers of cell phone use while driving. The speaker, however, believes that cell phones are not any more dangerous to drivers than other distractions.

The author explains that talking on the phone while driving is dangerous because it distracts the driver. Because of this, drivers in accidents involving cell phones have been held responsible for the accidents. The author also discusses laws that prohibit the use of cell phones while driving.

The speaker disagrees that using cell phones while driving is so dangerous. She points out that drivers can be distracted by things other than talking on the phone, such as eating, talking to passengers, taking care of children, putting on makeup, and other things. She cites a study that found that cell phone use actually causes fewer accidents than other distractions. She mentions another study that used video. The video showed that drivers were less distracted by their phones than by other activities. Finally, the speaker emphasizes that cell phones contribute to our safety. People use cell phones to report accidents and dangerous drivers on the road.

INDEPENDENT TASKS

Step 1: Plan

PRACTICE 1 (PAGE 82)

1. B
2. F
3. C
4. E
5. A
6. E
7. D
8. F

PRACTICE 2 (PAGE 85)

1. B It mentions a specific decision.
2. A It answers the question *Do you agree or disagree?*
3. C It states one specific thing the writer would change.
4. A It states a preference.
5. B It explains that the writer supports the plan.

PRACTICE 3 (PAGE 89)

Possible answers:

1. I would be healthy.
2. Beach, soccer, bicycle
3. No need to heat the house
4. Bake a cake
5. Machines are neat.
6. Power saw

PRACTICE 4 (PAGE 91)

Answers will vary.

PRACTICE 5 (PAGE 95)

Possible answers:

1. people to teach me about life
2. laugh and joke with me
3. problems
4. history
5. restaurants
6. tourist and craft shops

PRACTICE 6 (PAGE 98)

Answers will vary.

Step 2: Write

PRACTICE 1 (PAGE 101)

1. In my opinion, people's lives are (or are not) easier today.
2. It seems to me that most people prefer (or do not prefer) to spend their leisure time outdoors.
3. To my mind, an apartment building is (or is not) better than a house.
4. From my point of view, it is (or is not) good that English is becoming the world language.

PRACTICE 2 (PAGE 102)

1. I believe that high schools should (or should not) allow students to study what they want.
2. I guess that it is better to be a leader (or member) of a group.
3. I agree that people should (or should not) do things they do not enjoy doing.
4. I suppose that I would rather have the university assign (or not assign) me a roommate.

PRACTICE 3 (PAGE 103)

1. I am sure that children should (or should not) spend a great amount of time practicing sports.
2. I am positive that a shopping center in my neighborhood will (or will not) be a benefit to our community.

PRACTICE 4 (PAGE 104)

1. Maybe a zoo has (or does not have) a useful purpose.
2. Probably, the city (or countryside) is a better place to grow up.
3. Certainly, our generation is (or is not) different from that of our parents.
4. Surely, a sense of humor can sometimes be helpful (or detrimental) in a difficult situation.

PRACTICE 5 (PAGE 105)

1. All things considered, the family is (or is not) the most important influence on young adults.
2. In general, parents are (or are not) the best teachers.
3. By and large, people are never (or are sometimes) too old to attend college.

PRACTICE 6 (PAGE 106)

1. In a way, it is better to make a wrong decision than to make no decision. **Or,** In a way, it is better to make no decision than to make a wrong decision.
2. To some extent, watching movies is (or is not) more enjoyable than reading.
3. In a sense, you can (or cannot) learn as much by losing as by winning.

PRACTICE 7 (PAGE 109)

Possible answers:

1. **Opinion:** I think the more friends we have, the better.
   Paragraph focus: learn how to trust others
   Paragraph focus: learn what to expect from others
   Paragraph focus: help us profit from experiences

2. **Opinion:** I believe that playing games is both fun and useful.
   Paragraph focus: teaches cause-effect relationship
   Paragraph focus: teaches us about teamwork
   Paragraph focus: teaches us to follow rules

3. **Opinion:** Nothing is as important to me as my family.
   Paragraph focus: learned about trust
   Paragraph focus: learned about ambition
   Paragraph focus: learned about love

4. **Opinion:** I prefer to spend time with friends.
   Paragraph focus: keep me company
   Paragraph focus: are enjoyable to talk with
   Paragraph focus: teach me things

5. **Opinion:** Traveling alone is the only way to travel.
   Paragraph focus: meet new people
   Paragraph focus: have new experiences
   Paragraph focus: learn more about yourself

PRACTICE 8 (PAGE 112)

Answers will vary.

PRACTICE 9 (PAGE 115)

1. E—gives advice (*look for another opportunity; don't give up*)
2. E—gives advice (*make sure to dress appropriately for every situation*)
3. C—explains what could happen (*it would bring more variety…, give us the opportunity to amuse ourselves…, bring more jobs…*)
4. D—ends with questions (*Isn't it important…? Don't you want…?*)
5. D—ends with questions (*…wouldn't I? Could you call me…?*)

Step 3: Revise

PRACTICE 1 (PAGE 121)

Essay Topic 9

1. I prefer to prepare food at home.
2. Main ideas: (1) cheaper
                    (2) healthier
                    (3) more convenient
3. Main idea: While eating in restaurants is fast, the money you spend can add up.
   Supporting   (A) When I have dinner in a restaurant, the bill is usually $25
   details: or more.
                   (B) Even lunch at a food stand can easily cost seven or eight
                       dollars.
4. Main idea: Eating at home is better for you, too.
   Supporting   (A) When you cook at home, however, you can control what
   details: you eat.
                   (B) …at home you can control your portion size.
5. Main idea: Cooking at home, however, can actually be more convenient.
   Supporting   (A) There are a lot of simple meals that don't take long to
   details: prepare.
                   (B) In addition, when you eat at home, you don't have to drive
                       to the restaurant, look for a parking space, wait for a table,
                       and wait for service.
6. Para. 3   too
   Para. 3, 4, 5   however
   Para. 4   In addition
7. There are no grammar or spelling errors.

8. (possible answers)

    ss: Eating at home is better for you, too. (para. 3)

    cx/s: When I have dinner in a restaurant, the bill is usually $25 or more. (para. 2)

    adj.c: There are a lot of simple meals that don't take long to prepare. (para. 4)

Essay Topic 10

1. I believe, however, that the disadvantages outweigh the advantages.

2. Main ideas: (1) ...bring more traffic problems to the area.

                     (2) ...attract undesirable people.

                     (3) ...other types of businesses...would be more beneficial to the neighborhood.

3. Main idea: Traffic congestion is already a problem in our neighborhood and a new restaurant would just add to the problem.

   Supporting   (A) Most restaurant customers would arrive by car and crowd

   details: our streets even more.

                     (B) In addition, they would occupy parking spaces and make it even harder for residents to find places to park near their homes.

4. Main idea: I'm also concerned about the type of patrons a new restaurant would bring into our neighborhood.

   Supporting   (A) The restaurant would stay open late and people leaving the

   details: restaurant might be drunk.

                     (B) They could be noisy, too.

5. Main idea: Finally, there are other types of businesses that we need in our neighborhood more.

   Supporting   (A) We already have a restaurant and a couple of coffee shops.

   details: (B) We don't have a bookstore or a pharmacy, however, and we have only one small grocery store.

6. Para. 2   in addition

   Para. 3   also

   Para. 4   Finally, however

   Para. 5   but, Moreover

7. There are no grammar or spelling errors.

8. (possible answers)

    cx/s: If the restaurant serves drinks and has dancing, there could be problems. (para. 3)

    ss: We already have a restaurant and a couple of coffee shops. (para. 4)

    cm/s: It might bring jobs, but it would also bring traffic and noise. (para. 5)

Essay Topic 11

1. In short, teachers provide you with a lot more support and knowledge than you can usually get by yourself.

2. Main ideas: (1) ...help you find the way that you learn best.

                     (2) ...help you stay focused...

                     (3) ...provide you with a wider range of information...

3. Main idea: Teachers can help students learn in the way that is best for each student because teachers understand that different people have different learning styles.

Supporting details:
(A) For example, some students learn better by discussing a topic.
(B) Others learn more by writing about it.
(C) A teacher can help you follow your learning style, while a book can give you only one way of learning something.

4. Main idea: Teachers help you focus on what you are learning.

Supporting details:
(A) They can help you keep from becoming distracted.
(B) They can show you which are the most important points in a lesson to understand.
(C) If you have to study on your own, on the other hand, it might be difficult to keep your attention on the material or know which points are most important.

5. Main idea: Teachers bring their own knowledge and understanding of the topic to the lesson.

Supporting details:
(A) A book presents you with certain information, and the teacher can add more.
(B) The teacher might also have a different point of view from the book and can provide other sources of information and ideas, as well.

6. Para. 2   For example
   Para. 3   on the other hand
   Para. 4   also
   Para. 5   though

7. There are no grammar or spelling errors.

8. (possible answers)

cx/s: Teachers can help students learn in the way that is best for each student because teachers understand that different people have different learning styles. (para. 2)

ss: Others learn more by writing about it. (para. 2)

cm/s: A book presents you with certain information, and the teacher can add more. (para. 4)

Essay Topic 24

1. … there are certain characteristics that all good co-workers have in common.

2. Main ideas:
   (1) cooperative
   (2) adapt well to changes
   (3) helpful

3. Main idea: A good co-worker is very cooperative.

Supporting details:
(A) She does her best to get along with others.
(B) She tries to do her work well because she knows that if one person doesn't get her work done, it affects everyone else.
(C) She also has a positive attitude that creates a pleasant working environment.

4. Main idea: A good co-worker is adaptable.
   Supporting details:
   (A) She is not stubborn about changes in schedules or routines.
   (B) She doesn't object to having her job description revised.
   (C) She has no problem with new procedures.
   (D) In fact, she welcomes changes when they come.

5. Main idea: A good co-worker is helpful.
   Supporting details:
   (A) For instance, she lends a hand when someone falls behind in his or her work.
   (B) She is willing to change her schedule to accommodate another worker's emergency.
   (C) She doesn't keep track of how often she has to take on extra work.

6. Para. 2   also
   Para. 3   In fact
   Para. 4   For instance
   Para. 5   Thus

7. There are no grammar or spelling errors.

8. (possible answers)
   cx/s: She tries to do her work well because she knows that if one person doesn't get her work done, it affects everyone else. (para. 2)
   ss: A good co-worker is adaptable. (para. 3)
   nc: She doesn't keep track of how often she has to take on extra work. (para. 4)

PRACTICE 2 (PAGE 126)

1. B	5. C	9. A	13. A	17. A
2. A	6. C	10. C	14. B	18. C
3. C	7. B	11. A	15. C	19. A
4. A	8. B	12. C	16. B	20. B

PRACTICE 3 (PAGE 131)

Missing items:

Paragraph 1: thesis statement
Paragraph 2: supporting ideas
Paragraph 3: main idea
Paragraph 4: none
Paragraph 5: none

Grammar and vocabulary errors:

Paragraph 1: none
Paragraph 2: …the drinking water <u>are</u>…
Paragraph 3: none
Paragraph 4: Life in the countryside <u>help</u>…; In the countryside, <u>for instance</u>…;…they know where <u>there</u> food comes from.
Paragraph 5: …I plan to let <u>they</u> grow up…

Revised Essay

Added and corrected parts are underlined.

<u>I agree that it is better for children to grow up in the countryside.</u> When children grow up in the countryside, they have a healthier life. They also have a safer life. Children also learn to appreciate nature when they grow up in the countryside.

Life in the countryside is healthier for children than life in the city. Drinking water in the city is usually dirty. In the countryside, on the other hand, the drinking water is clean and pure. <u>Also, the air in the countryside is much cleaner and fresher than city air. In addition, in the countryside children can play outside often, but in the city they have to spend most of their time indoors.</u>

<u>Life in the countryside is safer for children than city life.</u> They don't have to worry about crime because there are fewer criminals in the countryside than in the city. They don't have to worry about traffic accidents, either, because there are fewer cars in the countryside. Furthermore, they don't have to worry about strangers who might hurt them because in the countryside almost everybody knows everybody else.

Life in the countryside <u>helps</u> children appreciate nature. There are few plants in the city. In the countryside, <u>on the other hand</u>, children see trees and flowers around them all the time. They also have opportunities to see wild animals, while in the city they can only see animals in zoos. In addition, they know where <u>their</u> food comes from. In the countryside children are surrounded by farms, but in the city they only see fruits and vegetables in the grocery stores.

Life in the countryside is definitely much better for children than life in the city. It is cleaner, safer, and closer to nature. When I have children, I plan to let <u>them</u> grow up far away from any city.

PRACTICE 4 (PAGE 135)

Why People Are Living Longer

People are living to be much older these days than ever before. The main reasons for this are greater access to health care, improved health care, and better nutrition.

Basic health care is available to many more people now than it was in the past. When someone is ill nowadays, he or she can go to a public hospital instead of having to pay for private care. There are also more clinics and more trained doctors and nurses than there used to be. Years ago, health care was not available to everyone. People who didn't live in big cities often did not have easy access to doctors or hospitals, and many people couldn't afford to pay for the medical care they needed.

In addition to increased access to health care, the quality of that health care has greatly improved over the years. Doctors know now much more about diseases and how to cure them. In the past, people died young because of simple things such as an infection or a virus. Now we have antibiotics and other medicines to cure these diseases. Furthermore, advances in medical science have made it possible to cure certain types of cancer and to treat heart disease. This has prolonged the lives of many, many people.

The quality of nutrition has also improved over time. Because of this, people tend to be healthier than they used to be. Now we know how to eat more healthfully. We know that eating low fat food can prevent heart disease. We know that eating certain fruits and vegetables can prevent cancer. We have information about nutrition that can help us live longer, healthier lives.

Improved health care and healthy eating habits are allowing us to live longer. Now we need to make sure that everyone in the world has these benefits.

BOTH TASKS

PRACTICE 1 (PAGE 140)

1. B
2. A
3. B
4. C
5. C
6. A
7. B

PRACTICE 2 (PAGE 141)

Paragraph 1:

1. first	3. such as	5. As a result of
2. Next	4. In addition	

Paragraph 2:

1. Consequently	3. After	5. In other words
2. such as	4. Moreover	

Paragraph 3:

1. In the first place	3. on the other hand	5. As a result
2. Moreover	4. for example	

Paragraph 4:

1. For example	3. Because of this	5. Although
2. Similarly	4. as well	

Paragraph 5:

1. On the contrary	3. By the same token	5. In fact
2. for instance	4. So	

PRACTICE 3 (PAGE 144)

1. attractive, pretty
2. start
3. opinion
4. enormous, huge, spacious
5. peaceful
6. automobile, private vehicle
7. alternative, option
8. decide on, pick, select
9. count on, rely on
10. costly
11. well-known
12. quick, rapid, speedy

13. aid, assist
14. fresh, recent
15. well-liked
16. buses and trains, mass transit
17. correct
18. go, make a trip

PRACTICE 4 (PAGE 145)

See Essay 35 on page 203 in the Model Essays section of the Appendix for a model response.

PRACTICE 5 (PAGE 147)

1. attractively
2. attract
3. attractive
4. attraction
5. differ
6. differences
7. different
8. differently
9. popularity
10. popular
11. popularize
12. profession
13. professionally
14. professional
15. rest
16. restful
17. rest
18. restfully

PRACTICE 6 (PAGE 149)

Different colors may create different moods. Colors can make people feel excited and energetic. <u>They</u> can also help people feel relaxed. In hospital waiting rooms, for example, people often feel nervous. <u>They</u> may feel better if the room is painted with a soothing color such as blue or gray. Some people like to paint <u>their</u> bedrooms green. <u>They</u> feel that <u>it</u> helps <u>them</u> sleep better because <u>it</u> is a relaxing color. Yellow is an energizing color. <u>It</u> is a good color for a kitchen because it helps people feel awake in the morning. My brother, however, didn't paint <u>his</u> kitchen yellow. <u>He</u> painted <u>it</u> orange. <u>He</u> says that this color makes <u>him</u> feel hungry.

PRACTICE 7 (PAGE 152)

1. maintain
2. think
3. advancing
4. in
5. improve
6. interesting
7. You
8. engineers
9. where my cousins still live
10. to

PRACTICE 8 (PAGE 154)

1. A   2. C   3. C   4. A   5. B   6. A

PRACTICE 9 (PAGE 155)

1. A   2. B   3. B   4. C   5. A   6. C

PRACTICE 10 (PAGE 157)

Paragraph 1:
1. S   2. Cx   3. S   4. Cx   5. S

Paragraph 2:
6. Cx   7. Cx   8. S   9. S   10. Cx   11. Cx

Paragraph 3:
12. S   13. Cx   14. S   15. Cx

Paragraph 4:
16. S   17. S   18. C   19. Cx

Paragraph 5:
20. S   21. S   22. C-Cx

PRACTICE 11 (PAGE 158)

1. City streets are crowded and noisy, and city people are always in a hurry.
2. Most children like to watch TV, but they don't usually watch educational programs.
3. People don't like to go shopping when the weather is bad.
4. Many native plants die after invasive species take over.
5. You will feel more energized if you walk around the room for five minutes.
6. I prefer living in the countryside even though I grew up in a city and most of my relatives still live there.

PRACTICE 12 (PAGE 160)

1. Doing, helps
2. children, do, they, develop
3. tasks, are
4. children, learn
5. They, learn, they, grow up
6. Completing, takes
7. Effort, has
8. Children, feel, they, see
9. Nothing, is
10. Everybody, wants

PRACTICE 13 (PAGE 162)

Paragraph 1:
1. like (active), bring (active)
2. are outweighed (passive)
3. cause (active), bring (active)
4. destroy (active)
5. is (active), oppose (active)

Paragraph 2:
6. cause (active)
7. build (active), breathe (active), will become (active)
8. will be covered (passive)

Paragraph 3:
12. will say (active), will be created (passive)
13. can have (active)
14. will grow (active)

Paragraph 4:
18. will change (active)
19. is (active)
20. is (active)

Paragraph 5:
24. would be helpful (active), outweigh (active)

9. pollute (active)
10. will be (active)
11. will be hurt (passive), will be affected (passive)

15. will be built (passive)
16. will be (active)
17. can cause (active)

21. knows (active)
22. brings (active), will change (active)
23. will be lost (active)

25. would be changed (passive)
26. cannot support (active)

PRACTICE 14 (PAGE 163)

1. A   2. C   3. A   4. B

Audioscripts

INTEGRATED TASK

 Self-Test (Page 24)

Track 1

(male speaker)

After years of warnings from scientists, it has finally become widely accepted that average temperatures on our planet are rising, with many potentially serious consequences. And just in case anyone still has doubts about the actuality of global warming, a recent report on changing conditions in the northeastern United States should help dispel them. Data collected by weather stations throughout the Northeast shows that there has been a definite warming trend in that region over the past half century. The greatest warming has occurred in the winter season. Average temperatures in the December to March period increased between 1965 and 2005. In addition, yearly snowfall totals dropped, while the number of days with at least an inch of snow on the ground fell by an average of nine days. This is a significant change in a region that is traditionally known for its cold and snowy winters.

One sector of the economy that has taken a direct hit from this warming trend is the ski industry. The local economy in many rural areas is dependent on recreational ski centers. Less snowfall means fewer days that ski centers can be open for business. There are also increased expenses from making artificial snow to compensate for the lack of natural snow. The economic impact reaches far beyond the owners of ski resorts. Local hotels, restaurants, ski rental centers, and gift shops all suffer from the decrease in tourism that results from a poor ski season. Warm autumns also have a negative impact on local economies. Brilliant fall foliage brings tourists, and their dollars, to many remote rural areas in the Northeast. A hot summer and warm autumn mean that the fall foliage season is less colorful and less attractive to tourists.

Leading scientists have predicted that average temperatures in the Northeast will increase by several degrees Fahrenheit before the end of this century. In addition, the number of days with snow on the ground will be reduced by 25 to 50 percent. With much of the economy of the Northeast dependent on the tourism that skiing and autumn foliage bring, changes in weather patterns can have a serious effect on the economy of that region.

Practice 1 (Page 35)

 **LECTURE 1 (Page 35)**
Track 2

(female speaker)

Let's take a look at some invasive species that are causing problems locally. Garlic mustard, a European native, has become a problem in several areas in the United States. It's a cool season plant, blooming in midspring. It prefers moist, shady areas at the edge of woods or along roadsides. It thrives in the same habitat as a number of native mid-spring bloomers, such as spring beauty, wild ginger, and trillium. Garlic mustard threatens these native species because it aggressively competes with them for light, nutrients, and space. The presence of garlic mustard also threatens many local animals that depend on the leaves, roots, flowers, and pollen of the threatened native plants as a food source.

The West Virginia white butterfly is particularly vulnerable to invasion by garlic mustard. The plant pushes out certain native species of mustard which constitute the major food source for the caterpillar stage of this rare butterfly. In addition, garlic mustard may contain chemicals which are toxic to the butterfly's eggs. It has been observed that eggs laid on garlic mustard leaves do not hatch. Garlic mustard was introduced to the United States in the nineteenth century as a food source and may have had medicinal uses as well. It was first recorded on Long Island but now thrives throughout the eastern and midwestern United States.

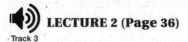 **LECTURE 2 (Page 36)**
Track 3

(male speaker)

TV has been blamed for a lot of things, most particularly for poor school performance. However, we can't blame the mere fact of TV-watching for low achievement in school. For one thing, not all TV watchers are low achievers. Japanese children, who as a whole have higher test scores than American children, watch more hours of TV than their American counterparts. For another thing, in the past two decades, the amount of time American children spend watching TV has declined, but overall test scores have not risen. The fact is, research shows that children who watch an hour or so of TV daily, but not more, actually do better in school than children who don't watch TV at all.

Why is this? TV can expose children to new ideas and information that they might otherwise not have access to. Children who watch TV occasionally are probably discriminating in the programs they choose to view. Research suggests that an important point is the amount of time spent in front of the TV. Children who spend three hours a day or more in front of the TV do poorly in school, scoring lower on both math and reading tests than children who watch some, but less, TV. Guidelines for parents include: limiting children's TV-watching time to no more than two hours a day; guiding children in their choice of programs to watch; discouraging eating while watching TV; and encouraging children to participate in other sorts of activities such as reading, playing outside, or visiting zoos and museums.

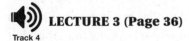

LECTURE 3 (Page 36)

Track 4

(female speaker)

How effective are public health campaigns? They must be evaluated with care because initial results can be deceptive. Evaluations of the effectiveness of a public health campaign too often take place close to the end of the campaign only. To truly understand the impact a public health campaign may—or may not—have had, we have to look at where we stand several months after the campaign has ended. Unfortunately, this piece is often neglected.

To illustrate the point, let's take a look at a recent campaign to reduce smoking among teens in the Midwestern region. Teens in this area were inundated with antismoking information for the better part of a year. There were ads all over the local communities, representatives went into high schools to offer workshops, literature was distributed, antismoking clubs were formed, in short, all the usual activities of a campaign of this sort were instigated. Surveys taken near the end of this campaign, in March of last year, showed that well over half of those surveyed were aware of the campaign. This means they reported that they had seen the ads, participated in workshops, attended a meeting, and so on. At the same time, forty percent of those surveyed reported that they were unlikely to try smoking in the next year. It sounds like a great success, doesn't it? Just three months after the campaign ended, however, this last figure changed dramatically. At the end of June, fifty-eight percent of survey participants reported that they were "very likely" to smoke in the next year. At the same time, less than thirty percent reported awareness of the antismoking campaign, so it seems a number of them had already forgotten the ads they had seen just a few months earlier.

This information puts the whole effort in a completely different light. Naturally, no public health official likes to see such poor numbers resulting from such a huge effort. If we truly aim for effectiveness in our public health work, however, we need to take an honest look at all the figures.

LECTURE 4 (Page 37)

Track 5

(male speaker)

Retailers may find that investment in a good music system for their retail space will bring them a worthwhile return on the money. Several very interesting studies have been published recently which show positive—for the retailer, anyhow—effects of music on shopping behavior.

One study was actually done in a restaurant and compared the effects of fast and slow music on restaurant patrons. The researchers found that patrons who heard music with a slow tempo tended to remain at the restaurant longer than patrons who heard fast music. As they lingered over their meals, they purchased more food and beverages, which of course is the effect desired by the restaurant owner. When restaurant patrons heard fast music, they ate more quickly and tended not to order extras such as appetizers, desserts, and beverages. The average length of time spent in the restaurant when fast music was playing was fifteen minutes less than it was when slow music was playing. In addition, each patron spent on average four dollars less for the meal when fast music was playing.

Another study looked at the effects of familiar and unfamiliar music on shoppers in a clothing store. The study subjects were mostly college students shopping in a store that catered to their age group. Some of them heard currently popular hit songs while shopping—the "familiar" music—while others heard music normally aimed at an older age group. The students who heard familiar music stayed in the store longer than those listening to unfamiliar music. They also expressed more positive opinions of the products offered for sale. This study did not report on how many products study subjects purchased nor on how much money they spent. Retailers reading about such a study would, of course, want to know this type of information. Nevertheless, this study does give us some interesting general information on the effects of music on shopping behavior. Clearly, music has an impact, and retailers need to take this into account.

Practice 2 (Page 38)

 **LECTURE 5 (Page 39)**
Track 6

(female speaker)

Purchasing new office technology and getting office staff trained to use it involves a significant investment of time and money. Quite understandably, companies are often reluctant to keep spending money in this way. Study after study, however, has shown that the investment is almost always paid back many times over in increased worker productivity. For example, in the past, an office assistant could spend a large percentage of the day photocopying documents, then collating and stapling them. It wasn't unusual for busy offices to hire assistants whose main duties involved photocopying. Now, the newest photocopiers not only copy much faster than the old ones, they also fold, collate, and staple. The work is done quickly and accurately, and office assistants can devote themselves to other tasks. Offices can operate with fewer assistants, thus spending a great deal less on salaries and benefits.

Email is another example of how technology has improved office procedures. Communication by email is fast and convenient. It's also cheap. It costs no more to send an email to a colleague in an overseas office than it does to send one to someone sitting at the next desk. Email can help projects run more smoothly. Many times, a matter can be resolved quickly through email, thus eliminating the need for frequent meetings. Important updates can be communicated to staff members in a timely manner, allowing everyone to work more efficiently. All of this means workers can spend more time at their desks producing. Hiring trained staff to keep email, websites, and Internet access running smoothly does require some investment of company resources, but the payback more than makes up for it. No doubt about it—investment in office technology is a sound business choice.

(male speaker)

University Hospital, a leader in the field of cardiac disease research, recently conducted a study of the effects of pet ownership on health, more specifically, on heart health. The results showed overwhelmingly that pets can contribute to improving the health of heart patients. Participants in the study were being treated for heart disease at the hospital's Powell Memorial Heart Clinic. Most were in recovery from cardiac bypass surgery. Half the participants were given a dog to care for at home during the course of the study. They were asked to spend one to two hours a day caring for the pet, including walking it twice a day, playing with it, feeding and bathing it, and petting it. The dogs chosen for the study came from a local animal shelter and were all considered to be mild-tempered, well trained, friendly, and easy to care for. The remaining study participants continued with traditional heart disease treatments only, which included both drug and physical therapy and dietary recommendations, but did not involve any specific exercise program to follow at home.

At the end of six months, it was found that those who had been caring for dogs had a decrease in blood pressure as compared to the patients who had received traditional treatment only. They also had an average weight loss 20 percent greater than the traditional patients. Many also reported feeling much happier and less stressed. High blood pressure, weight gain, and stress are factors contributing to heart disease. If you're wondering what happened to the dogs, put your mind at rest. The majority of dog caretakers in the study elected to keep their pets after the study was over. Several of the study participants who had been on traditional treatment only also expressed interest in the dogs. Other research hospitals in the country are looking to carry out similar studies with hopes of replicating the results. It looks like dogs may truly turn out to be man's best friend.

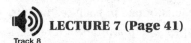

(female speaker)

Plastic garbage poses a serious threat to ocean animals. Every year, billions of pounds of plastic are produced. Much of this plastic is in the form of bags, bottles, and other sorts of packaging, which is used once, then thrown away. Where does all this plastic garbage go? Some of it ends up in landfills, but significant amounts make their way into our oceans. Rainstorms wash all sorts of garbage into storm drains and rivers, and from there, sooner or later it reaches the ocean.

Plastic decomposes very slowly. In the ocean, large pieces eventually get broken up into smaller pieces by the movement of the water and wind. Those smaller pieces can end up floating around in the ocean's waters for decades or even centuries. Sea animals often mistake these pieces of plastic for food. A floating plastic bag could look like a tasty jellyfish to a sea turtle. Sea birds can confuse small bits of plastic with the fish eggs they usually dine on. An animal that tries to swallow plastic may choke on it. Other animals starve to death after filling their stomachs with plastic. Plastic has no nutrition, but the animal doesn't look for more food since it feels full.

Plastic bags, balloons, bottle tops, and other sorts of plastic trash have been found blocking the breathing passages and stomachs of many sea animals, but plastic can be dangerous even if an animal doesn't try to eat it. Animals frequently get caught in the middle of large accumulations of plastic garbage that float around our oceans. Others get strangled by plastic straps or plastic rings. The death toll from plastic in the oceans is high. It has been estimated that tens of thousands of sea turtles and other marine animals are killed each year by plastic garbage in the ocean. For birds the figures are much higher. As many as one million sea birds a year may fall victim to plastic garbage.

 LECTURE 8 (Page 41)

Track 9

(male speaker)

Have you ever noticed that many restaurants have red or orange walls? This fashion comes from the widely held belief that these two colors stimulate the appetite. Restaurateurs hope that by stimulating the appetites of their customers in this way, they can encourage them to order more food.

A large fast-food chain recently decided to test the notion that the color of the decor affects how much food their customers order. This company has restaurants in major cities across the country and caters to customers of all ages, including small children. The traditional décor of this restaurant chain includes beige paint on the walls. Several years ago, the company painted the walls in half of its restaurants orange, leaving the other half of its restaurants with their original beige walls. In order to compensate for the possible influence of cultural differences between cities, the company made sure that in every city where its restaurants are located, there were both restaurants with orange walls and restaurants with beige walls.

The restaurant chain kept track of exactly what foods were ordered in each restaurant for one year before the walls were painted, and then again for one year after the walls had been painted. They found no difference. On average, customers in each restaurant, whether it had beige or orange walls, ordered the same types and quantities of food. "It's a myth that the color of walls has an effect on appetite, a complete myth," the president of the company said. "We have proven it." The walls of all the restaurants in the chain have been restored to their original beige color. The company president explained that this color is part of the company's image. Now that the study is over, people might be confused if they walked into a restaurant expecting beige walls and got orange instead, so the company president explained.

 Practice Integrated Task (Page 80)

Track 10

(female speaker)

Cell phones have been accused by many of making the highways dangerous, but it's time to take a hard look at the facts. What's really behind the majority of traffic accidents? A recent study found that close to eighty percent of automobile crashes were caused by driver inattention. Of course, talking on the phone is a common cause of driver inattention, but it's certainly not the only one. Other causes found in the study were drowsiness, talking with passengers, eating or drinking, and reaching for a falling object. In fact, the study found that while drivers talking on a cell phone increased their risk of an accident, those other distractions increased the risk even more. Another study looked at driver behavior, using video cameras installed in the cars of 70 drivers. The videos showed that drivers were much less distracted by their cell phones than they were by other activities such as reaching for items or talking to passengers. The Department of Transportation lists a number of common causes of inattentive driving in addition to cell phone use. These include eating, talking, putting on make-up, changing the radio, and attending to children. It even includes things like watching videos or reading while driving! The latest distraction is, of course, using GPS.

Discussions about the dangers of cell phone use while driving tend to overlook an important fact about cell phones, which is that they actually contribute to our safety on the road. Drivers place over 100,000 emergency calls on their cell phones every day. They report accidents, road hazards, and problem drivers, thus helping keep the roads safe for everyone. Drivers' use of cell phones to report emergencies has greatly reduced response times and helped save lives. Individual drivers' own security is protected by using cell phones to contact help when they experience mechanical problems while on the road.

We cannot, of course, say that cell phones are completely innocent. Certainly, cell phone use has contributed to traffic accidents, but so have many other things. It is better to be clear-headed about the facts and look at all sides of the issue.

 Model Test 1—Integrated Task (Page 168)

Track 11

(male speaker)

School systems across the country are devoting resources to equipping their classrooms with computers and training teachers to use them. In reality, how well prepared are teachers to use computers with their students? The government recently conducted a survey to find out, gathering information from over one hundred schools across the country. Ninety-six percent of the teachers surveyed reported that their training consisted mainly of developing basic computer skills, which they already had prior to training. Skills and knowledge that would help them incorporate the use of computers more fully into their lessons were not addressed in most training programs. Seventy-eight percent reported that the training they received was too brief, averaging less than five hours in total. Sixty-five percent said they were not comfortable using technology and rarely or never made use of computers in their classrooms. Of those who did use computers, the majority used them for skill and drill exercises and did not feel that the use of computers had changed their approach to teaching in any significant way. School administrators are wondering whether money invested in educational technology might yield better results if used to support other educational needs.

This is a bleak picture indeed. However, there is hope. Let's look at a success story that shows how technology can support education. Five years ago, the Riverdale School District implemented a program to train teachers to integrate technology into their lessons. Teachers who participated in the program received two hundred hours of training on using technology with their students to develop critical-thinking and problem-solving skills. The training occurred over a two-year period. In addition, teachers were assigned mentors who could assist them in implementing computer-based activities in the classroom. As a result of this, computers were fully integrated into the lesson plans of these teachers. Rather than the skill and drill software so commonly used, these teachers had their students working with simulation software to solve problems. When their students took the statewide achievement tests at the end of the first year of the program, they scored significantly higher than students who were not participating in the program.

Clearly, a commitment to filling schools with computers is not enough. An equal, if not greater, commitment must be made to training teachers to use this technology in ways that enrich the learning experience of their students.

 Model Test 2—Integrated Task (Page 170)

Track 12

(female speaker)

The subject of animal intelligence has long been of interest to scientists. One issue is how do we define or describe intelligence? The ability to feel empathy for fellow creatures is often considered as one mark of intelligence, and has been the subject of a number of research studies. This brings up the question of how do we measure empathy? Scientists believe that an animal must be able to perceive itself as an individual in order to empathize with another. Therefore, an important step in researching the ability to empathize is to test self-recognition. The most common way to do this is to use mirrors. Elephants, dolphins, and great apes are the only animals in addition to humans that demonstrate recognition of self in a mirror. When presented with a mirror, these animals often react to their image, touching it, displaying their teeth, or preening.

There is another test that scientists commonly use to test self recognition. In this test, a mark is painted on the animal, somewhere on or near its face. The animal is then shown a mirror. If the animal tries to wipe the mark off its face while looking at its image in the mirror, this shows, scientists say, that the animal recognizes the mirror image as a reflection of itself. In a study done with dolphins, some dolphins received marks on their bodies, others were touched with a marker but no mark was made, and still other dolphins were left completely alone. A mirror was placed in the dolphins' tank. All those that had felt the marker on their body rushed to the mirror to look. Those that actually had marks used the mirror to look at them closely. In similar experiments, elephants, chimpanzees, and orangutans have responded to marks in a like way. Not all scientists agree that such a test proves self recognition. Showing interest in the painted mark does not necessarily mean that the animal makes a connection between the mirror image and the self, they say. There are still many controversies surrounding research on animal intelligence.

 Model Test 3—Integrated Task (Page 172)

Track 13

(male speaker)

There is a popular idea going around that William Shakespeare did not actually write his own plays. Although attempts have been made to cast doubt on the authorship of these plays, no one has yet produced any real evidence that they were not written by William Shakespeare, humble resident of Stratford-on-Avon, himself. Proponents of the theory that Shakespeare did not write the plays claim that he was too poor, too obscure, and too uneducated to have written them himself. Poor and obscure though he may have been, it is not certain that he was uneducated. There was a school in Stratford-on-Avon, and the young Shakespeare may well have attended it along with other boys of his social class. As a student at the local school, he would have gained the knowledge of literature and the classics that the author of the plays certainly had. And although he was not an aristocrat himself, through his work at the theater he had plenty of opportunity to come into contact with the aristocratic classes that he often wrote about. He could easily have observed in this way the aristocratic manners and customs that he gave characters in his plays.

The lack of records about Shakespeare's life is also not evidence that he did not write the plays. As a commoner, there would not have been many records kept about him, and any records that may have existed could easily have been lost over the course of time. Neither has there been convincing evidence that another person actually authored the plays. One of the more popular theories is that Francis Bacon was the one who actually wrote the Shakespeare plays, but it does not hold up. Some claim as proof a similarity between Bacon's writings and those attributed to Shakespeare. Even a quick comparison of works by the two authors, however, clearly shows that the writing styles of the two men are completely different.

 ## Model Test 4—Integrated Task (Page 174)

Track 14

(female speaker)

It's widely accepted that the bubonic plague, which devastated the world in the fourteenth century, originated in Asia. There is new evidence, however, that suggests that it may actually have started in North Africa. Outbreaks of the plague still occur in Africa today.

An archeologist discovered evidence of the plague in ancient Egypt accidentally. She was studying insect fossils at the site of an ancient village when she came across human and cat flea remains. According to the archeologist, insect remains can tell us a great deal about how people lived in the past. For example, the remains can give clues about what kinds of animals people kept. In the case of the flea remains, she knew this meant that the plague could have been present in the ancient village. Previous research had turned up evidence of rats living along the Nile River as long ago as the sixteenth and seventeenth centuries B.C. Those rats are known carriers of the type of flea that carries the bubonic plague. Many ancient towns and cities were built along the Nile River. Periodic flooding in the area would have driven rats out of their natural homes and into human settlements— an ideal scenario for spreading plague among human communities. Further research brought up evidence that ancient Egyptians had suffered epidemics of a disease that seemed remarkably similar to the bubonic plague. The archeologist suggests that the plague was transported to Europe by rats that carried plague-ridden fleas onto ships crossing the Mediterranean Sea.

The bubonic plague is not only a disease of the ancient world or the Middle Ages. Contrary to popular belief, it did not disappear in the seventeenth century, but still occurs today. In Madagascar, for example, between 500 and 2,000 new cases of the disease are reported each year. According to the World Health Organization, every year there are as many as 3,000 new cases of the plague worldwide. Scientists continue to study the disease. Research on epidemics both past and present help scientists understand how epidemics spread and may help predict when new outbreaks will occur. There are still many mysteries surrounding the bubonic plague. It can disappear for years, or even centuries, then reappear suddenly, and just as suddenly disappear again. Scientists have a great deal to learn about this disease.

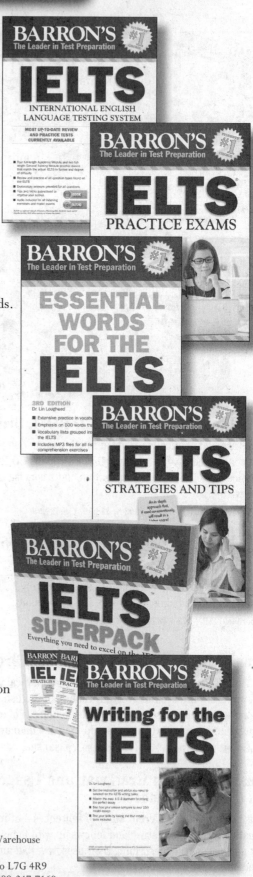

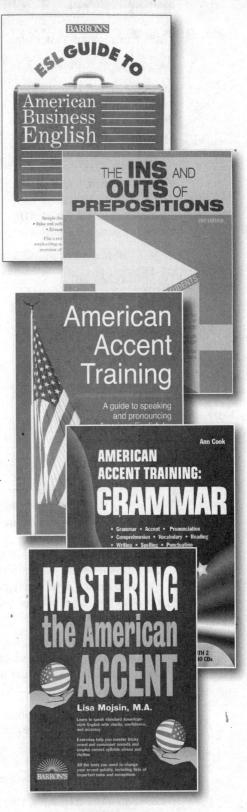

MP3 TRACK LISTING